Violence
AND
Civilization

Violence
AND
Civilization

*An Introduction to the Work of
Norbert Elias*

Jonathan Fletcher

Polity Press

First published in 1997 by Polity Press
in association with Blackwell Publishers Ltd.

2 4 6 8 10 9 7 5 3 1

Editorial office:
Polity Press
65 Bridge Street
Cambridge CB2 1UR, UK

Marketing and production:
Blackwell Publishers Ltd
108 Cowley Road
Oxford OX4 1JF, UK

Published in the USA by
Blackwell Publishers Inc.
Commerce Place
350 Main Street
Malden, MA 02148, USA

ISBN 0-7456-1434-5
ISBN 0-7456-1879-0 (pbk)

A CIP catalogue record for this book is available from the British Library and the Library of Congress.

Typeset in 10½ on 12 pt Palatino
by Ace Filmsetting Ltd, Frome, Somerset
Printed in Great Britain by Hartnolls Ltd, Bodmin, Cornwall

This book is printed on acid-free paper.

For my friends and teachers,
Pete, Eric, Stephen, Helmut, Joop and Cas.

Contents

Acknowledgements

Above all, I would like to thank my mother, Margaret Gwilym, and my father, John Fletcher, from whom I have learnt the most.

Several people read all or parts of this book through its various stages of production. I owe a great debt to John Thompson, who supervised the project as a PhD thesis. His advice, support, criticism and encouragement proved invaluable. I am also particularly grateful to Eric Dunning, Tony Giddens, Joop Goudsblom, Johan Heilbron, Helmut Kuzmics and Stephen Mennell.

Special thanks go to Cas Wouters for his constant encouragement, enduring friendship and detailed commentary on my work. His enthusiasm for civilized conversation over involved and sometimes decivilizing topics is a rare treasure.

In Cambridge I was able to share ideas with many people of exceptional talent, among them, my friends Graeme Gilloch, Adrian Gregory, Montse Guibernau, Roxanne Hakim, Patrick McGinn, Denis McManus, Dominic O'Brien and Nick Pilgrim. My debt to Lisa Driver Davidson is incalculable. I cannot underestimate how important her companionship and support have been for me.

Without my Dutch friends in Amsterdam this book would probably have been completed sooner. Their welcome distraction, as they often made me realize, proved to be a necessity. They helped me feel at home in an unfamiliar country and with a language that deserves its reputation as the 'Chinese of the West'. In particular, I would like to mention Reneé IJbema and Ellen Griffioen for their acceptance, faith and enduring support; Annemarie Waterhout, for her boundless warmth and understanding; Florien Linck, simply because she's wonderful; Louran van Keulen, the tallest person I know, for his support and gentle encouragement with my 'prille' Nederlands; Hank(erchief) Roland Poot, for unforgettable memories of the Zeedijk; Jan Ott, for the gezelligheid of Café de Kletskop; and Peter Mader, for overseeing the neighbourhood. Hartelijk bedankt. Jullie hebben mij enorm geholpen.

I would also like to thank those who have provided the funding which has allowed me to complete this project. In particular, I would like to thank Syl Hughes, trustee to the estate of Thelma George, without whose financial planning and personal generosity I would not have been able to start this book as a PhD in Cambridge.

From King's College, Cambridge I received a two-year Research Studentship, as well as financial assistance for one month's research at the University of Graz, Austria, and funding to attend conferences on Elias in the Netherlands, Austria and Germany. Rob Wallach, financial tutor at King's, extended his generous understanding throughout my period in Cambridge.

The German Academic Exchange Service (DAAD) funded four months' research at the University of Bochum, Germany.

I am also grateful to the Leverhulme Trust, from whom I received a two-year Study Abroad Studentship which enabled me to complete this book in Amsterdam.

Finally, I would like to thank the students and staff at the Amsterdam School for Social Science Research. It was gratifying to work among such a committed and talented group of social scientists.

CHAPTER ONE

Introduction

On 1 September 1939, German troops invaded Poland on the orders of Adolf Hitler. The same year saw the publication in Switzerland of a two-volume work entitled *The Civilizing Process*. Its author, Norbert Elias, was a German of Jewish descent who had already fled his homeland with the ascent of the Nazis in 1933. By 1941, Elias's parents had lost their lives under Nazi rule: his father in Breslau and his mother in the Auschwitz concentration camp, although the true character of the regime was only to emerge clearly with its defeat by Allied forces.[1]

The processes traced in *The Civilizing Process* seemed irrelevant to many, given events which were then overtaking continental Europe. There was simply no market for such a book, especially one written by a German Jew, and indeed, only a small number of copies were sold.[2] It appears that few people were willing to read a work on 'civilization' at the very time when the nations of the Western world were witnessing the eclipse of all that the term was thought to represent. In such a context it does seem surprising that Elias had completed a long-term study of state formation and the development of manners among the European secular upper classes in conjunction with the term 'civilization'. The seeming contradiction between the process identified by the book's title and the violent events of more recent European history form one of the main themes of this book.

Elias studied medicine, philosophy and later sociology at the universities of Breslau and Heidelberg, subsequently becoming Karl Mannheim's assistant at the Department of Sociology at the University of Frankfurt. After fleeing Germany and spending some time in Paris, he moved to England in 1935 and remained there until the mid 1970s, working as a guest lecturer at the London School of Economics and later as Reader in Sociology at the University of Leicester. Elias received the title of professor from the University of Ghana in the late 1960s, and for the last fifteen years of his life he lived and worked in Amsterdam, where he died on 1 August 1990, at the age of 93. With such a biography,[3] it is not surprising to learn that Elias was interested in developing a sociological understanding of violence and violence controls in twentieth-century European societies more generally, and of the National Socialists and the Holocaust in particular. But it was not until some twenty years after having left Germany that he wrote in any detail about events in the Third Reich.

It is no exaggeration to say that, along with other murderous episodes, two world wars and the Holocaust in Germany have shattered many of the connotations which hitherto seemed to enshroud the concept of civilization with an aura of mystique. These connotations were carried over from certain beliefs generated in the eighteenth century and earlier, accompanying the rise of industrialism, technological innovation, colonization and a belief in the inherent 'progress' associated with such developments. The events of the twentieth century have exposed many of these beliefs as delusions. A sense of caution and even despondency has resulted. In turn, this general attitude has brought forth a strong reaction against the very use of the word 'civilization'. Indeed, 'barbarization' would seem to many to be a more appropriate term with which to characterize the twentieth century so far.

As regards the work of Norbert Elias, this general reaction has often taken the form of dismissive and sometimes even tasteless commentaries (see respectively Leach 1986: 13; and Hunt 1988: 30). Others have described his theory of civilizing processes variously in terms of its simplicity (Lasch 1985: 714), evolutionism (Lenhardt 1979: 127; Giddens 1984: 241), its inability to account for the 'barbarism' of the present century (Coser 1978: 6; Buck-Morss 1978: 187–9), or even its ethnocentrism and racism (Blok in Wilterdink 1984: 290).[4] Some of these reactions can only be understood in the context of the pervasive sense of disillusionment which has come to permeate Western culture. But to what extent are they an accurate assessment of Elias's perspective? Or is the strength of these responses an over-reaction?

In criticizing Elias for his use of the terms 'civilization' or 'civilizing process', many writers have overlooked the implications of his ideas for developing an understanding of 'breakdowns in civilization'. The attention to violence and its controls lies at the centre of his theory, and this book seeks to clarify the insights provided by Elias's approach with respect to the notions of 'civilizing' and 'decivilizing' processes. It also includes a critical assessment of some of Elias's main ideas on violence and its controls. A considerable amount of space is given to exposition, particularly with respect to Elias's work in *The Germans*. I attempt to provide clear, accurate summaries of Elias's comments on specific themes to do with violence, civilization and decivilization, themes which are central to an understanding of the broad spectrum of Elias's writing. This book therefore serves as an introduction to his work as a whole. Needless to say, it is not a substitute for reading Elias's books and articles themselves.

Even this focus on violence and civilization, however, is a broad enough task in relation to Elias's work. Whilst seeking answers to several key questions which I pose below, I have therefore restricted the scope of this book to include only some examples Elias draws from England, providing a comparative contrast to his use of examples from Germany up until the end of the Second World War. Apart from lack of space, one important reason for not considering Elias's work on Germany after 1945 was that I wanted to understand how far his approach is relevant to an understanding of Nazism. Certainly, Elias's work on the civilizing process is far from being the product of blind naivety to the world at the time of the book's production in the 1930s. But the extent to which it was in fact *inspired* by a pressing need to develop a more detached understanding of social processes including the rise of Nazism and the 'barbarization' of the twentieth century has remained obscured, particularly in the Anglo-American world, for a variety of reasons. Among others, these reasons include Elias's idiosyncratic pattern with respect to the publication of his work; the intrinsic complexity of the synthesis to which he sought to contribute, a synthesis that is sociological, psychological, historical and equally theoretical and empirical; and the fact that his approach did not fit in with the 'philosophical', 'present-day' orientation which overtook British sociology during the 1960s. This perceived inability to account for 'reversals' of civilizing processes may also result from the fact that Elias tended to focus on civilizing processes rather than their deterioration, leading in part to the widespread misunderstanding of his theory as teleological, evolutionary and overly optimistic.

The central task of this book, then, is to clarify the relationship between violence, civilization and decivilization in Elias's work through seeking answers to the following questions: What does Elias mean by civilization, civilizing and decivilizing processes? What does he mean by violence? What are the characteristics of social processes he specifies which may generate violence? What is the relationship between violence, civilization and decivilization in modern twentieth-century societies? And how do these issues connect with historical examples which feature most significantly in Elias's discussions? Several related questions are also considered. Elias attempts to develop a concept of civilization which he believes to be largely non-normative, but to what extent did he succeed in this? Did he reveal any ambiguity in using this concept when dealing with events in Nazi Germany? And if so, would this be fatal for his overall approach? In addition, although Elias did not develop a theory of decivilizing processes, is it logically implied in his theory of civilizing processes? Lastly, while Elias's work tends to emphasize societal continuities, does this in fact involve teleology and evolutionism in considering problems of violence and its controls, and if so, to what extent?

I do not intend to detail how his work differs from other writers who have dealt with similar topics, for example, Freud, Max and Alfred Weber, Horkheimer and Adorno, Goffman or Foucault. Instead, I critically analyse the themes mentioned in order to highlight their interconnections in relation to the various subjects on which Elias has written. While my critical exposition of Elias's work includes some assessment of commentaries on his approach, I have not attempted to cover all these critics' perspectives; nor do I focus on them in detail unless they are of particular relevance to an issue at hand. From my central questions, it follows that my primary concern is to show how Elias develops his perspective and applies it in the context of historical studies, particularly in his consideration of England and Germany. In order to do this, I focus on Elias's most significant publications so as to gain an appreciation of his approach as a whole.[5]

This book is distinctive in emphasizing the role of violence in civilizing and decivilizing processes in Elias's work, an aspect which few commentators have drawn out so explicitly.[6] Also, in showing how Elias develops and applies his sociological concepts in relation to England and Germany, I emphasize a comparative side to his writings that has received scant attention. In order to address the key questions of this book, I highlight the central role played by the concept of habitus in Elias's work, as well as his ideas on the formation of group identity. However, both themes, while generally neglected in English-language works on Elias, appear to be of central importance for the understanding of civilizing and decivilizing processes.

The book falls into two main parts. Chapters 2, 3 and 4 present a critical exposition of the main themes in Elias's work on violence and habitus in civilizing processes, state formation, his development of sociological process models and how they can account for violent social processes. Chapters 5, 6 and 7 consider how these themes and models are woven into Elias's approach to specific socio-historical situations, concentrating on England and particularly Germany. At the same time, the advantages and shortcomings of his approach are addressed. Chapter 8 summarizes the issues discussed and highlights the key problems surrounding Elias's ideas on violence, civilization and civilizing processes. In addition, I point to the main elements of Elias's approach that are relevant to a sociological understanding of violence, focusing on the example of the former Yugoslavia in terms of a decivilizing process.

Through exposing some of the lacunae in Elias's work on violence and civilization and through suggesting how these may be dealt with, or not, as the case may be, this book forms part of the ongoing assessment of his contribution to social science and, more generally, to the development of an understanding of the way in which people are willing and able to achieve a more adequate perspective on violence and its controls.

CHAPTER TWO

Civilization, Habitus and Civilizing Processes

The concept of civilization developed by Elias shows marked differences in comparison to other writers who have used the term. The main task of this chapter is to show how it is employed by him to refer to a transformation of behaviour in the secular upper classes of the West. The term is also essential to an understanding of aggression and violence in Elias's work. This chapter begins with his account of the emergence of the word civilization before specifying the way in which he connects this to behavioural dispositions, aggression, violence and shame. The concept of habitus is also shown to be highly significant for Elias's project.

The development of civilization as a concept

A useful summary of many important formulations of civilization as a concept and empirical referent among several prominent historians is given by Fernand Braudel (1980: 177–218). However, while he discusses the work of various writers, including Guizot, Burckhardt, Spengler, Toynbee, Bagby and Alfred Weber, there is no mention of the significant contribution of Norbert Elias. The concept of civilization has been used variously either as an ideological, evaluative weapon employed by generations of historians in the service of Western colonialist aspirations, or as a generic term used to refer to the level of economic, political and social development achieved by a particular society in the past or present.[1]

In contrast, Norbert Elias elaborates a different concept of civilization. His formulation was partly inspired by the public debate between Thomas and Heinrich Mann, in which Thomas indirectly denounced his brother as a *Zivilisationsliterat*. By this he meant that Heinrich was a French-influenced, superficial, democracy-smitten, Enlightenment-orientated revolutionary novelist who had no appreciation of 'truly German' poetry and art. Elias's sensitive discussion of the concepts of *Zivilisation* and *Kultur* in the first volume of *The Civilizing Process* in Germany evokes all the nationalist connotations and intentions which these terms generated at the time. He begins his study with a concerted attempt to understand the development of these terms in connection with the development of the societies of which they are a part. *The Civilizing Process* forms the keystone of his theory of civilizing processes.[2]

Inter-group tensions and conceptual developments

Elias argues that the concept of civilization develops through inter-group tensions and rivalries. In Germany, for example, he places the development of *Zivilisation* and *Kultur* in the larger context of the formation of group identities, world-views and personality structures among particular social classes within that country and between Germany and other nations. By tracing the development of the antithetical concepts *Kultur* and *Zivilisation* in Germany and 'civilization' in France and England, he focuses on aspects of a social and psychical transformation. From around 1500 to 1525, the concept of *civilité* developed as a badge of the French courtly circles: *civility* in England, *civiltà* in Italy and *Zivilität* in Germany all fulfilled similar functions. They were all precursors of the later concept of civilization and they emerged in order to demarcate the behaviour of courtly circles from the rest of society.

By the eighteenth century, the ruling classes in Germany spoke French and they tended to imitate the French courts, while German was considered by them to be a coarse and unrefined language. In contrast, the relatively small German bourgeoisie generally spoke German. They were excluded from court society: not only were they denied social access but, more importantly, they had no voice in political decision-making processes. The bourgeoisie were effectively politically impotent – their struggle with the nobility took place largely outside the political realm. As a consequence, the German bourgeoisie developed their own world-view and self-identity. In contrast to what they perceived as the superficiality or *Zivilisation* of court life, they employed another symbol of their own self-image: *Kultur*. This was highly particularistic; great importance was placed on books, scholarship, religion, art, philosophy and inner enrichment leading to the intellectual formation (*Bildung*) of the individual.

The antithesis between the court-aristocracy and these middle classes expressed in the concepts *Kultur* and *Zivilisation* was transformed from a 'social' to a national one. This occurred in conjunction with the slow rise of the German bourgeoisie to a class which bore the 'national consciousness' (Elias 1994a: 25): it was defined first in terms of its relation to the nobility and then in terms of its relation to other nations. Along with this development there occurred a change in the perception of German 'national character'. Honesty and sincerity were held up as typical of the German people, in contrast to superficial courtesy, an attitude which stemmed from the relatively isolated and clearly defined German middle class, which found expression in the German intelligentsia through their artistic and literary products. Thus, with the slow rise of the middle classes, the social characteristics of this class gradually broadened to the national level.

The concept of *civilisation* originated in France, replacing the terms *courtoisie* and *civilité*. There, in contrast to Germany, sections of the bourgeoisie were drawn into courtly life relatively early on, which allowed them to develop a capability of thinking and acting in political categories. Having considerable influence at court gave them access to even the highest government positions; their power in relation to the aristocracy made them indispensable to the king. Consequently, continuous and close social contact emerged between people of different social backgrounds. Sections of the bourgeoisie then formed part of the courtly ruling class and increasingly copied the manners of the nobility. This occurred long before the Revolution, which, although it destroyed the old political structures, did not erase the old courtly forms of manners. Thus, while the bourgeoisie in Germany was confined to the realm of 'ideas' and the 'mind', with the university as their social base, their French counterparts existed more in the 'real world', as they were more politically informed because of their access to courtly circles and their prominence in higher administrative positions.

Elias aligns the development of the concept of *civilisation* in France with the emergence of the reform movement in the late eighteenth century. It was the Physiocrats who articulated for a wider audience sentiments that were more general among those connected with and influenced by the court. These reformers shared several ideas centring on the notion that kings and ministers were not all-powerful in the regulation of affairs and that there were broader social forces with their own laws operating above and beyond the wishes of rulers. They argued that a rational and planned administration was necessary in order to cope more adequately with these social processes. *Civilisation* emerged as a banner proclaiming these reformist goals and also as an indication of the existence of systematic social regularities. Towards the end of the eighteenth century, *civilisation* became infused with two central ideas: first, it stood as a courtly concept in opposition to 'barbarism'; and second, it constituted the notion of a process with a goal. It is the latter which represents an extension of the original courtly concept in the hands of the reformists. Anything from trade to education, within which 'barbaric' practices could be discerned, came under the province of reform in the name of *civilisation*, involving the refinement of manners and the internal pacification of the country by the kings (1994a: 39). This formed part and parcel of what has been described as a 'civilizing offensive' (cf. Kruithof 1980; Mitzman 1987: 663–87; Van Krieken 1989: 193–218).

To an English person, the concept of civilization usually appears relatively clear, referring to political, economic, religious, technical, moral or other social facts (1994a: 4). The concept developed roughly the same meaning in France, where it expressed the social situation, behaviour- and feeling-codes of an upper class which comprised aristocratic and bourgeois elements and which was more unified than in Germany. By the early part of the twentieth century the concept of civilization was used by people in Western societies to refer to a completed process. They increasingly saw themselves as the vanguard of a particular form of personality make-up which they felt compelled to disseminate. But 'of the whole preceding process of civilization', says Elias of those living at that time, 'nothing remains in their consciousness except a vague residue' (1994a: 41). They were mostly unaware of this change as it occurred: it was an unplanned process.

Changes in social and individual habitus

Elias's discussion of the development of 'civilization' is bound up with his use of the term 'habitus'. The significance of this notion in Elias's work is usually lost to his non-German reading audience. While the word is usually associated with the work of Pierre Bourdieu (1990), it is in fact a Latin term which gained currency among academics in the Middle Ages. It was also popular in German social science around the time Elias wrote *The Civilizing Process*, and the term appears in the German edition as 'psychical habitus' or simply 'habitus' (for example, see 1988a: lxxiii, lxxv, lxxvi, lxxviii; 1988b: 315, 316, 319, 320, 333, 387, 388, 484n). But in the English translations, habitus is misleadingly rendered as 'psychological make-up', 'make-up', 'social make-up', 'habits', or even simply 'personality', but never as 'habitus' (for example, 1994a: xii, xiii, xv, xvi, 444, 445, 446, 447, 454, 485, 540n). In a later publication, *The Society of Individuals* (1991a), Elias makes greater use of the term 'habitus' and provides a more differentiated application of the concept.[3] The notion of social habitus as used by Elias is one of the keys which can be used to escape what he calls the either–or approach to considerations of the individual and society. The social habitus of people forms the basis from which the more individual characteristics of a person can emerge:

> This make-up [*Gepräge*], the social habitus of individuals, forms, as it were, the soil from which grow the personal characteristics through which an individual differs from other members of his society . . . The concept of social habitus enables us to bring social phenomena within the field of scientific investigation previously inaccessible to them. (1991a: 182)

For Elias, individuals have little free choice in relation to their own group identity and social habitus: 'these things cannot be simply changed like clothes' (1991a: 224–5). The social habitus is expressed in an individual's codes of feeling and behaviour, the social standards of which change over generations. So Elias uses the term 'habitus' to refer to changes on this 'individual' level of the civilizing process.[4] One can distinguish between individual habitus, which refers to the learned emotional and behavioural dispositions which are specific to a particular person, and social habitus, which denotes the learned dispositions shared by most members of a group or society.

The concept of habitus enables Elias to introduce a way of comprehending broad social and psychical processes which is relatively free of evaluations, a social-scientific understanding.[5] He does this by urging us to suspend all feelings of embarrassment and superiority when considering the social habitus of people in the past or in other societies. This particularly applies to the value judgements associated with the concepts 'civilized' and 'uncivilized':

> Our kind of behaviour has grown out of that which we call uncivilized. But these concepts grasp the actual change too statically and coarsely. In reality, our terms 'civilized' and 'uncivilized' do not constitute an antithesis of the kind that exists between 'good' and 'bad', but represent stages in a development which, moreover, is still continuing. (1994a: 47).

This emphasis on a sequence of changes in an ongoing process of civilization leads Elias to focus on a 'specific transformation of behaviour' (1994a: 42–178) which is connected to other changes which cannot be seen and must be inferred. Elias ties in the conceptual development of words such as 'civilization' to concrete social dynamics and the directional changes of standards in behaviour- and feeling-codes – to changes in social and individual habitus – which are in turn connected with underlying social dynamics and shifts in balances of power between various social groups.

The transformation of words and manners

From the sixteenth century, people in Western European societies tended to perceive their behaviour and that of others with greater differentiation and with more even and stricter controls over their emotions than before. Manners increasingly became a social problem and the precepts contained in books on the subject were derived from the experience of social life, as opposed to traditions passed down through word of mouth. This was a transition period, during which the old feudal knightly nobility was in decline and the new aristocracy of the absolutist courts was still forming, while at the same time bourgeois groups were rising.

In stressing the *socio*genesis of concepts, Elias singles out one individual in the hands of whom *civilité* gained a specific and characteristically novel meaning: Erasmus of Rotterdam. In his popular book, *De civilitate morum puerilium* (*On Civility in Children*, 1530), Erasmus reworked the long-established word *civilitas*. Dedicated to the son of a noble, this book discussed the way people looked, how they carried themselves, their facial expressions, dress and also some gestures which later generations might find strange. Elias seeks to establish that the precepts contained in the work are embodiments of a mental and emotional structure among the secular upper classes of the Middle Ages which differed from that which is predominantly characteristic of ourselves (1994a: 45).[6] Erasmus was writing amid a 'loosening' transformation between the old medieval social formation and the crystallization of social relations around the formation of court societies. This structural transition in the pattern of social relations was not sudden, but it generated an increasing tendency for people to mould their own and others' behaviour more deliberately than before. The whole transformation is neatly summed up in Caxton's phrase from his *Book of Curtesye* in the late fifteenth century: 'Thingis somtyme alowed is now repreuid' (1994a: 66). This suggests that people like Erasmus were able to mention things which at a later stage became imbued with shame and embarrassment. Individuals from different social origins were thrown together as the rising and declining social fortunes of various groups accelerated. From the sixteenth century, an increasingly rigid social hierarchy set in at the same time as a growing need for particular groups to establish a uniform code of behaviour and distinguishing group traits. Increasingly, a 'threat from below' was perceived by the established ruling groups, demanding an increased sensitivity and social pressure to exert greater vigilance over one's own impulses and immediate desires. A compelling form of social control began to establish itself which became more effective 'in inculcating lasting habits, than insults, mockery, or any threat of outward physical violence' (1994a: 65). *External* compulsions were more and more transformed into *internal* compulsions. This is a key aspect of Elias's analysis of social controls, or constraints by others, and the development of particular types of self-restraint.[7]

The precepts for behaviour contained in the manners books studied by Elias were aimed at a specific group of people: the upper class and the knights who lived at court. They were addressed to adults *as well as* to children. Examples include not picking one's nose in public, farting at the table or speaking when one's mouth is full, spitting in public, wiping one's nose on one's clothing, and so on. He chooses examples relating to manners and bodily functions in order to diminish the ambiguity of historical interpretation – the problems surrounding the control of physical functions need to be dealt with in all cultures. All of Elias's examples are drawn from sources written between the Middle Ages and the middle of the nineteenth century, and, where possible, he uses the same, or variations on the same, precept in each quotation in order to establish before the reader's eyes the sequence of development which he is ultimately concerned to demonstrate. Interspersed between these citations, Elias offers his interpretations of the examples he quotes. It is these comments, where his conception of socio-historical interpretation is to be found, which I shall comment on below.

The various aspects of bodily functions are mentioned by the authors of the manners books in a matter of fact way; there appears to be a very low level of embarrassment surrounding the mention of, for example, defecating on tapestries, in a manner which suggests that certain actions, simply the mention of which to a later observer would most likely be regarded with some distaste, were in fact once relatively common. People became more sensitive towards one another, especially as regards bodily fluids and orifices. Many of the quoted examples are excluded from subsequent editions of a particular work because, Elias suggests, the forms of behaviour mentioned no longer need to be considered since they had become part of people's own consciousness and self-steering, and therefore external prompting was no longer required: the topics dealt with are themselves deemed too distasteful to be mentioned. Today, for example, these aspects of bodily behaviour are not covered in etiquette books because they have already been 'imprinted' in early socialization and are taken for granted. As for behaviour at table, Elias suggests that it was not the lack of utensils that forced people to maintain what to us may appear coarse standards of manners, but that, given the characteristic affect-economy of these people, nothing else was deemed necessary. Regulations of conduct while eating provide the modern reader with 'a segment . . . of the totality of socially instilled forms of conduct' (1994a: 54), corresponding to a different social structure: it is not just a curious excursus into seemingly trite or even quaint forms of behaviour which prompts Elias to cite these examples in all their richness. Common features within specific groups in different countries appear, revealing a 'unity of actual behaviour in the medieval upper class, measured against the modern period' (1994a: 53).

While this process of change in people's behaviour had its fluctuations, Elias points to an overall trend. It is this search for the structural dynamics of social relations which provides the driving force behind his project: to perceive lines of development in apparently random forms of human behaviour with special reference to the advancing thresholds of shame and embarrassment bound up with notions of 'refinement' or 'civilization'. 'A particular social dynamism', writes Elias, 'triggers a particular psychological one, which has its own regularities' (1994a: 82). This social dynamism is the growing interdependence of the bourgeois classes and aristocratic groups involving the increasingly felt need on the part of the former to imitate the forms of behaviour prevalent at court. For Elias then, the different sensibilities found in different societies are the result of observable, long-term social processes which in retrospect can be seen to have taken a particular direction. However, he does not conceive of this 'directional' change as smooth, unilinear or even 'necessary', but rather as one which shows fluctuations and short-term changes of direction which follow smaller and larger curves (1994a: 67; this point will be explored further in chapter 3).

In focusing on the secular upper classes, Elias reveals a developmental curve. The change in standards is clear to him: in medieval society, control by others within the small courts characteristic of that stage did impinge upon the emotional life of individuals, but in a relatively relaxed way. Subsequent changes were clearly unplanned and blind social processes. For example, forks were introduced to the courts, not so as to serve some rational purpose such as a need for greater efficiency in moving food from plate to mouth. The advance in the thresholds of shame and embarrassment – the standards of revulsion towards, or moral precepts against, the perpetration of certain forms of behaviour – did not come about through the conscious plan of any single individual, or through consciously rational considerations of large groups of people. Nor are such changes in standards explicable in terms of a growing awareness of personal hygiene. These types of explanation become prevalent only *after* the observable changes have occurred. Rational, calculating consideration, suggests Elias, is not the driving force in the development of civilization. Rather, it is the unplanned dynamics of social competition and social interweaving that foster the development of 'delicate' sensibilities. Feelings and affects are transformed in this way first among the upper classes, and it is only the changing structure of society as a whole which allows the transmission of the new standards to permeate other segments of the population. The medieval social structure was less amenable to the reception of models of social behaviour which developed in a specific social centre, spreading throughout large segments of the populace (Elias 1994a: 95; cf. Chartier 1988: 89–90). There was no single, clearly dominant centre, and chains of interdependence were shorter, which meant that opportunities for local autonomy and differentiation were greater. While in the course of the sixteenth century, a new, relatively more ossified social hierarchy established itself, it was formed by people of much more diverse origins than in, for instance, the Roman Empire. The new upper class of courtiers that emerged throughout Europe did not all share hereditary descendency from the old warrior classes. This led to questions of manners and behaviour becoming highly important to them, and in tandem with an increased social interdependency, they also developed an increase in the level of mutual identification, adding further impetus to the spread of their model of social habitus.

Aggressive knights and the medieval personality

In his discussion of the manners and behaviour of the European secular upper classes, Elias also looks at the life of knights in order to demonstrate changes in sensibilities with respect to aggression and violence. The majority of the adult males in the medieval upper classes were warriors who led armed groups into battle, and so Elias focuses primarily on public violence in wars, but he does not neglect everyday life in towns and cities.

Elias argues that the conscience or super-ego[8] of these people was relatively weak and undifferentiated. This is not to say that people were at one time devoid of conscience or some type of cognitive self-steering processes, but that the types of automatic self-restraint which developed later were largely absent. These later types emerged together with increasing social integration and extended networks of social interdependency. While there were many differences between the standards of behaviour and emotion management found within the various classes of medieval secular society, the emotional expression of medieval people generally can be said to be *relatively* more spontaneous and unrestrained than in the following period (1994a: 176).

Even in the Middle Ages the expression of aggressive affects in battle was, Elias suggests, slightly more tame than in the earlier period of the Great Migrations, although compared to later times it was certainly more free and unfettered. The perpetration of violence was regarded as a pleasure by many of the powerful in the medieval period: mostly men, but also women were able to indulge in such violent pleasures.[9] In the more developed state societies of our day, it is only during times of social unrest or situations of looser controls by others that the release of affects becomes more direct, uninhibited and less impeded by shame and revulsion (Elias 1978b: 230).

Once again, literary sources provide Elias with evidence of the transformation of aggressive behaviour and the more open enjoyment of impulsive violence in former times.[10] He also makes use of the woodcut prints in Das Mittelalterliche Hausbuch (Bossert and Storck 1912), and it is especially these pictorial examples that serve to demonstrate a different standard of affectual expression and control from those forms which developed later. For Elias, the pictures reveal:

a society in which people gave way to drives and feelings incompa-
rably more easily, quickly, spontaneously, and openly than today, in
which the emotions were less restrained and, as a consequence, less
evenly regulated and more liable to oscillate more violently between
extremes. (1994a: 175–6)

We are given an impression of the attitude of the knightly classes
who revelled in the perpetration of what most people in the
industrialized West would tend to see as unusually violent and
atrocious acts against other human beings. The life of knights
was spent training for or being involved in physical combat and
there was no social power which could legitimately restrict the
scope of their affective outbursts. The social structure encouraged this kind of behaviour, although these types of emotional
outburst could also be followed by extreme feelings of pity and
identification with the victims of violence. Social fears were
pervasive, life was lived for the moment, and, as a consequence,
fortunes might change quickly. This was reflected in the ease
with which pleasure could quickly change into fear, or fear into
pleasure or rage.

Within a barter economy, the income of these knightly groups
was secured through raids and wars. But with the rising importance of markets and other social processes, the knightly classes
gradually lost their function. Since they held a precarious,
outsider position in the general process of commercialization,
they were less bound in their conduct by economic ties – their
primary form of livelihood was through their ability to use
weapons. Among other processes, the growth of a money
economy and the division of labour saw a shift in the affective
controls of some of their number. Before this, there was no
necessity for them to develop a more strongly differentiated
super-ego. Rather, a form of self-restraint was required
which was more appropriate to the immediate emotional demands of battle; a self-steering that was 'wild, cruel, prone to
violent outbreaks and abandoned to the joy of the moment'
(1994a: 319).

In the Middle Ages, the early stages of a twin process of the
emergence of the great courts and the towns became evident.
Primarily the larger of these courts, and especially those pre-
sided over by a lady,[11] became centres in which obligatory forms
of conduct developed along the lines of stricter, more even self-
restraint. The warriors who experienced a devaluation of their

own social function were often drawn into court life in order to survive, into a situation demanding restraint, renunciation and the transformation of drives. Knightly feudal forms of conduct combined with courtly forms, generating the sociogenesis of the term *courtoisie*, an expression of particular forms of conduct and sentiment (1994a: 330). Elias refers to the whole process as the 'courtization of warriors' (1994a: 500–1).

In contrast, however, Benjo Maso (1982) has argued that there was in fact an increase, not a decrease, in knightly belligerence during this period. This was because they had to maintain traditions of a knightly calling, rather than fight for the possession of lands, as their predecessors were obliged to do. He argues that this led them to over-exaggerate their supposed virtues of ferocity and honour in an attempt to legitimate their weakened position. However, Elias suggests that only a minority of the warrior knights were actually drawn into life at court, while those remaining petered out. He also points out that the presence of these knights at court was larger and more important at the end of the Middle Ages than at the beginning (1994a: 319).

Several critics have also drawn attention to what they consider to be the exaggerated picture painted by Elias of the level of violence and 'anarchy' in the Middle Ages.[12] But it would seem this criticism is itself somewhat exaggerated as there is a good deal of evidence which supports Elias's interpretation.[13] Elias provides documentary evidence which shows that the readiness to fight was a precondition of social survival, not only for the secular upper classes, but also for the burghers in towns whose lives were often dogged by private feuds and vendettas. This is contrary to one commentator (Seigel 1979: 123), who seems to have missed the section in *The Civilizing Process* which deals at length with the case of Mathieu d'Escouchy, whose 'Chronicle' of his own life demonstrates the readiness and extent to which violence was used in the settling of disputes between townsfolk (see also Elias 1994a: 162–4). Elias writes: 'Family vendettas . . . not only existed among the noble-born; the towns of the fifteenth century were no less filled with private wars between families and cliques. Even the little people – hat makers, tailors, shepherds – they all had the knife quickly to hand' (Elias 1978b: 237).

Elias regards volatility as part of the aggressive behaviour of knights. Compared with ourselves, he suggests, they tended to show relatively little regard for the future and to swing unexpectedly from the expression of joy to violent aggression. Robert van Krieken has questioned the very assumption of this type of medieval personality structure which swings between extremes. He argues that if one assumes medieval personality structures were so radically different from our own, one then becomes blind to the possibility that behaviour can be explained by reference to direct responses to situations (Van Krieken 1989: 207), an argument which seems to suggest that only situations change, and that the personality structures of human beings do not change through history. One answer to this is that one has only to travel outside the richer European societies in order to experience such differences for oneself. In other words, we cannot go back in time, but it is possible to use cultural differences as a justification for the existence of historical differences, provided there is evidence to back up these claims (cf. Elias 1994a: xiv). But this would not be proof of changing personality structures, as the affective expression of those being studied could still depend upon situational stimuli (see Argyle 1976: 145–86). Elias effectively by-passes these issues by arguing that the distinction between 'situational' and 'personality-traits' is a spurious one. But it is simply very difficult to establish the extent to which 'traits' of personality – for example, stability or aggressiveness – are the result of intergenerationally reproduced patterns, the law, the economy, or the product of training in early childhood. It would seem that we – like Elias – are seldom in a position to make use of the necessary empirical information required to draw such conclusions. So Elias's claim that there has been a change in attitudes with regard to the perpetration of violent acts causing harm to other people, animals or even property in Western societies is interesting, but it requires further empirical corroboration. Also, his use of pictorial evidence can be criticized as naive since he is arguably relying on the 'exaggerated imagery' of these drawings and presenting them as evidence of the *actual* behavioural and emotional standards found in European societies of the time. The conclusions Elias draws from these pictures are consistent with his other evidence, and his discussion of their relevance is explicit; his non-critical use of such material effectively smooths over doubts as to their accuracy and reliability as historical sources. But for now, in the absence of further research, these questions of interpretation remain open.

Other critics have pointed to Elias's neglect of the role of religion in tempering conduct (see Buck-Morss 1978: 192; Albrow 1969: 231; Barraclough 1982: 38; Thomas 1978: 30; and Wehowsky 1978: 73–6). However, Elias argues that religion in itself did not dampen this volatility because it is only as 'civilized' as the society or class which upholds it (1994a: 164). Nevertheless, religion as an institutional organization, in which the lives of individuals are patterned through adhering to ritualistic practices and codes which mould behaviour and identities, is certainly absent from his work. Indeed, Elias could have strengthened his arguments if he had made more explicit reference to Max Weber's work on the Protestant Ethic (Weber 1930). The important point remains, however, that if Elias had taken the religious upper classes into account in a more systematic fashion, the structure of his argument would probably have taken a different form (cf. Goudsblom 1995).

Elias's thesis of a civilizing process is woven continuously around theoretical threads of argumentation interspersed with empirical details in an ever-rising spiral. His argument is therefore repetitious, but each time he deviates from a particular segment of the spiral in order to provide examples for a theoretical point, he returns to the issue at hand armed with one more contribution to the development of the theory's explanatory power. Hence the constant reference to the seemingly irrelevant and small scale, such as conversation, the modelling of speech or the use of the fork. This has led some critics to suggest that Elias's approach is idealist and neglects the historical importance of the means of production. For example, Susan Buck-Morss (1978: 189) relies on Marxian categories in her critique of Elias, implying his neglect of the role of the economy generally. Harte (1979: 602) accuses him of interweaving 'speculative-philosophical' interpretations into his evidence. Other critics have accused him of *neglecting* the role of ideas in historical development (cf. Albrow 1969: 232; and Lasch 1985: 719). But what we actually find throughout *The Civilizing Process* is an emphasis on developing an interpretation in conjunction with historical evidence in a manner which does not prioritize either economic, political or social processes, but considers them as inextricably woven together.

This chapter has focused on the way Elias explains the development of civilization as a concept and how this is related to changes of social and individual habitus among the secular upper classes in Western European societies. The manners books provide evidence in condensed form of changes in behaviour through revealing small segments of social life, recorded out of the need to establish particular behaviour-codes. Their function in Elias's work is not simply to reveal details of the standards of past eras, but also to illuminate the very tissue of social interdependencies in which people were enmeshed and how the networks of such interdependencies change over several hundred years. The standards of behaviour in face-to-face interaction, psychological and emotional make-up which he discusses are conditioned by broader social processes which will be considered in more detail in chapter 3.

Socialization, aggression and shame

The course of the civilizing process is characterized by the observation that, increasingly, what is considered to be distasteful is 'removed behind the scenes of social life' (1994a: 99) or removed altogether. The observable changes and ritualization in standards of behaviour represent a broad change in the very structure of human drive-controls and emotions. Drawing on Freud, Elias argues that children are socialized into these forms of behaviour from 'outside' by others. Over generations, this external control becomes increasingly internalized and a particular type of self-restraint develops which constitutes the self-steering of an individual, sometimes even contrary to his or her own wishes. The process by which shame and embarrassment thresholds advance is re-enacted in abbreviated form in the life of each individual; Elias considers this to be a 'fundamental law of sociogenesis and psychogenesis' (1994a: 105).[14] This has been misinterpreted by Lewis Coser who suggests that Elias 'explicitly asserts, in the wake of Auguste Comte, that ontogeny repeats phylogeny, that Western people have gone through a process of development that is similar to the growth of human beings from childhood to maturity' (Coser: 1978: 565). Elias merely suggests that an infant has to be inculcated with the dominant standards of behaviour regarded as more or less

acceptable within the particular social process into which he or
she is born, regardless of class (see Elias 1994a: xiiin) – obviously,
a phase of feudalism or court absolutism cannot be found in
individual civilizing processes.

Anxiety is consistently aroused when the socially acceptable
limits of embarrassment and shame thresholds are transgressed.
Elias uses the term affect-economy to describe the balance of
tensions within the personality; in other words, the drives and
their place in the configuration of human social life. The term
affect-economy is taken over from Freud's notions concerning
the transformations of spontaneous satisfaction into a relatively
more secure and sublimated gratification (Freud 1982). Elias
employs many economic metaphors to describe psychical
processes, which again are derivative (*Libidohaushalt* is an
example in Freud's work). However, a clear difference between
the two is Elias's formulation of the *socialization* of drives.
Contrary to the view of some commentators (for example Garland
1990: 219), Elias does not suggest that there are 'raw' emotions
or drives which are, as it were, tamed 'afterwards' by social life.
Rather, implicit in Elias's conception of drives is the idea that
they are themselves socially malleable and as much a product of
social learning as are I-functions and drive-controls (cf. Kilminster
and Wouters 1995: 109–14).

A stricter regulation of impulses – more even and all-round
self-restraint – emerges within court society as the result of
increasing pressures from 'above' and from 'below'. It is only
later on, with the rise of the middle classes, that the family
becomes the most important social institution for the instilling
of drive-controls, thus increasing the importance and duration
of the child's dependence on its parents, but above all the length
of the period of primary socialization. The particular individual
pattern of self-restraint (individual habitus) corresponds more
or less to the *dominant* pattern of self-regulation or social habitus
of an individual's social position. Changes in the social structure
at large go hand in hand with changes in the psychical make-up
of people as well as vice versa. The psychological distance
between adults and children has increased as a corollary of this
process: previously, the dominant pattern of self-restraint
expected by adults of other adults did not differ greatly from
that expected of children. 'By precisely this increased social
proscription of many impulses', Elias suggests, 'by their

"repression" from the surface both of social life and of consciousness, the distance between the personality structure and
behavior of adults and children necessarily increased' (1994a:
117). Within a Freudian model, Elias sees the more 'anti-social'
drives as increasingly defined with negative labels. These impulses have disappeared from the consciousness of adults
through a particular form of social conditioning: they are buried
in the unconscious or are rarely allowed to reappear. However,
contrary to Freud, Elias sees the mechanisms of repression to be
the product of a particular socio-historical development: the
neuroses of the past are seen as qualitatively distinct from those
produced within the social web of the present.

Drives, instincts and aggression

Elias emphasizes that the affect structure of human beings is a
whole (1978b: 229): human drives may be differentiated concep-
tually, but they are inseparable in reality. He uses the term drive
(*Trieb*) in order to distance himself from the more essentialist
notions of instinct, with their connotations of innate, biologically determined and unchangeable aspects of human behaviour. But while he does sometimes give the impression in *The
Civilizing Process* that he tacitly agrees with this aspect of instinct
theory,[15] it is a formulation he seeks consciously to avoid in
subsequent publications where he is at pains to stress the
inherent malleability of human drives. The term instinct (*Instinkt*)
does not in fact appear in the German edition of *The Civilizing
Process*, but it occurs frequently in the English edition and
scattered references to instincts can be found in several English
pieces. This compounds the impression of his adherence to an
instinct theory of aggression, particularly for the English reader.
But the appearance of the term in Elias's English publications
can be seen simply as a way of avoiding confusion with earlier
translations of the German word *Trieb* (drive) as *instinct*, especially in the work of Freud (see Bettelheim 1982: 103–7). In a later
article by Elias (1988c), a rewritten version of the section 'On
Changes in Aggressiveness' in volume 1 of *The Civilizing Process*
(1978b: 227–53), we find a more explicit formulation of his
thinking on the subject. It is clear from these later comments (e.g.
1988c: 178) that he considers conflict situations and power

relations to be more 'fundamental' to an understanding of human aggressiveness than reference to an innate aggressive instinct. This does not mean that he is unaware of the biological *capacity* for humans to behave aggressively, believing that humans, like other animals, have a nervous system which prepares them for the classic 'fight or flight' reaction in threatening situations. But he suggests that this inbuilt tendency is necessarily developed in different ways via social learning.[16] More usefully, Elias prefers to talk of conflict between groups, which is not the result of an innate aggressive drive (1988d: 188); rather, it is conflicts which tend to activate the human potential for aggression. When people encounter conflict, become angry or hate, he suggests that the *primary* behaviour is for them to 'attack each other or to strike or murder each other' (1988c: 178–9).

In *The Civilizing Process*, Elias conceptualizes human aggression[17] as a drive which is inseparable from the configuration of human drives, and remains subject to changes along with those in the personality structure as a whole; and, in turn, with changes in the division of social functions and the extent and density of social interdependencies. As a form of pleasure, aggression is transformed: dreams are usually the only arena in which aggression and violence are allowed free reign. Otherwise, they (aggression and violence) are interpreted in terms which define them as abnormal (Elias 1978b: 230). But even within those areas of social life in which emotions and affects are allowed freer expression, for example in combat (war) situations, they are relatively tame in the modern West. The restraint called for in the everyday life of more civilized societies cannot be easily reversed; the character of modern warfare rarely allows for this. Among mass populations, Elias suggests that it would require a great deal of effort, social upheaval and urgency, encouraged by co-ordinated propaganda, to legitimize the free expression of the destructive emotions which are more or less withdrawn from social life within many present-day nation-state societies. Sports are one way of allowing the expression of these emotions in a somewhat attenuated and controlled form. The 'living-out' of the affects is also made possible through forms of mass entertainment such as the cinema and television. Active enjoyment becomes transformed to spectator pleasure: sight becomes increasingly important as the mediator of pleasure, while opportunities for the direct satisfaction of desires are increasingly prohibited (Elias 1978b: 240). Most Westerners no longer find it exciting or enjoyable to watch the public burning of live cats suspended in a sack over a large fire, as many did on Midsummer Day in Paris during the sixteenth century (1994a: 167). The fact that even the mention of this institution revolts most people who have grown up in the more industrialized countries of the West is evidence for Elias of a long-term change in personality structures. Someone who today derived pleasure from such forms of 'entertainment' would be considered to have transgressed socially constructed boundaries of acceptable behaviour, and, in extreme cases, might themselves be 'removed behind the scenes of social life' and placed in an institution. The enjoyment of those watching such events, in comparison to the mass spectator events of more recent times, for example, boxing matches or horse races, demonstrates the changes in dominant social standards of affect control. Even those forms of behaviour which are 'at root' pleasurable, for example, sex, defecating and eating, can become associated with fears and anxieties instilled in the individual psyche through the recurrence of prohibiting threats. This psychical process is 'triggered' by changes in the structure of social relations. For Elias then, the question of why behaviour and emotions change is really the same as the question of why forms of life change (1994a: 168).

Various commentators have criticized Elias's use of Freudian categories and his theory of socialization. Christopher Lasch (1985: 712–13) argues that he simplifies the transformation of personality structures since the Middle Ages and points to Elias's ignorance of civilization's discontents, his use of 'ego' and 'super-ego' as synonyms for self-control and his lack of differentiation between repression and sublimation. Wehowsky (1978: 65–80) goes so far as to suggest that Elias has no theory of subjectivity and argues for a reinterpretation of his formulations which adhere more closely to Freud's theory of civilization. Buck-Morss (1978: 186–7) rightly points to a behaviourist aspect in Elias's notion of conditioning in socialization, but argues that he does not have an adequate theory of sublimation.[18]

However, as Alan Sica has noted (1984: 67), Elias's use of Freudian psychology 'does not make or break the book'. While he uses psychoanalytic concepts, his relationship to Freud's work is distanced by his reluctance to state explicitly his theoretical interpretations on this issue (Bogner 1987: 252–3,

261). It is more accurate to see Elias's psychology as a neo-Freudian synthesis involving elements of behaviourism and also Gestalt psychological theory. Where Freud can be described as a 'pan-sexualist', Elias is more accurately categorized as a 'pan-powerist'. In this sense, his work is closer to that of Alfred Adler (1958) than to Freud. In emphasizing power relations in socialization processes (the civilizing process at the individual level), he is able to downplay the role of genital sexuality in personal identity formation, and by historicizing Freud's basic categories Elias thus releases himself from Freud's reductionist and static notions. Tensions within the personality are present throughout life in the form of a balance between self-restraint and constraint by others; it is not enough to focus, as Freud does, on tensions and conflicts within earlier stages of life, particularly with regard to sexuality. While early childhood experiences remain essential to Elias's theory, they are not attributed the importance given to them by more orthodox Freudian formulations which may over-extend their significance, especially when it comes to the understanding of sexual development. Rather, the trajectory of a lifetime within competitive relations or balances of power with others is Elias's unit of analysis (cf. 1994b: xliiff). An individual's interdependencies will take on certain characteristics depending on the time and place in which his or her life process develops. Thus, impulse or drive management may vary intergenerationally. By investigating these changes empirically, using verbatim texts, Elias distances himself from other approaches to civilization. The investigations of Marcuse (1969), Freud (1982) and particularly Horkheimer and Adorno (1979) took a more 'philosophical' direction and were thus less amenable to empirical comparison and assessment. So while Horkheimer and Adorno might speak of 'the master–servant relationship' in the process of production and social domination in general, Elias's discussion centres on specific groups of individuals enmeshed in long-term social processes and the implications this has for personality structure with close reference to historical sources (Bogner 1987: 250–1, 265, 274).

Shame and violence

The psychical changes in the civilizing process move in a direction of growing complexity and stability of conduct controls which are increasingly instilled within the individual from infancy and which become automatic in the self-restraint of the personality. What is 'good' or 'bad' behaviour comes to be maintained in the conscience by an invisible wall of deep-rooted fears (1994a: 446) which may produce tensions and which may be perceived by the individuals bound up in these social processes as having negative psychological consequences. Civilization has its price (see Kuzmics 1989: 79–142; Freud 1982; Wouters 1995).

Elias is aware that the individual civilizing process undergone by all members of society is frequently a painful experience which inevitably leaves its scars. This process, like that at the social level, is still largely blind. Some people may become permanently restless and dissatisfied because the gratification of their impulses can only come about indirectly through fantasy; some may experience a numbing of affects as the inhibition over-extends itself and an all-pervading feeling of boredom results; unwanted compulsive forms of behaviour may predominate; or the transformation of energies may flow in an uncontrolled manner in eccentric attachments and repulsions (1994a: 453–4). However, with respect to aggression and violence, Elias has little to say about the costs of civilizing processes. He seems implicitly to assume that the social and psychical repression of aggression is uniformly positive in its effects and downplays the extent to which growing inhibition leads to neurosis: the generation of shame when neither flight nor aggression is possible. To a certain extent, however, people have of course developed means of dealing with aggression. Elias and Dunning talk of the controlled decontrolling of emotions (1986a: 44, 49, 96)[19] whereby, in more pacified societies, affects are allowed to spill out in a confined setting within which physical injury is minimized, for example through watching or participating in sports and sport-games.[20] Many people now deliberately seek out situations in which they may risk life and limb, and this risk-seeking is not confined to physical activities such as sport, sport-games, dancing, drug use or travel. It has become a necessary part of forms of emotion management in Western welfare-state societies which generate intense processes of status competition (Wouters 1992: 229–52; see also Elias 1988d: 186).

In Elias's view, shame is closely linked to aggression and violence: it is in situations where using violence is impossible that shame becomes expressed as the fear of others' gestures of superiority (1994a: 492). During long-term civilizing processes, problems of lapsing into inferiority become more difficult to resolve by resorting to physical means or aggressive behaviour. Shame feelings appear as a conflict felt within the person whenever he or she transgresses conscience-controls; that is, when there is both conflict with others and within one's own self (cf. Scheff and Retzinger 1991). Fears centre on the potential loss of love or respect of others. People become defenceless against the gestures of superiority of others when they cannot use violence to retaliate. This is because they automatically adopt an attitude towards themselves that is generated by the superior's attitude towards them. This is a function of the general process whereby extreme fluctuations in behaviour are moderated and people become more sensitive to nuances of behaviour. They increasingly experience themselves and their 'inner world' in a more complex fashion as the strong wall of affects which previously barred access to these reflections is brought more gradually under conscious control (1994a: 496). Fears which were once more frequently inspired in people by others are lessened, without disappearing, while inner fears increase; the balance between the two types of fears tips in favour of the latter. The inner fears of adults are inextricably bound up with their childhood fears; in other words, fears of people who are much larger and more powerful: adults. However, Elias over-emphasizes the extent to which shame feelings are a function of status or power conflicts. He does not systematically elaborate upon the idea that this feeling also results, in more modern times, through the fear of the loss of intimacy, although the latter is very closely related to power for Elias. For example, the fear of the loss of intimacy is bound up with the fear of becoming small in the eyes of the loved one. If the other becomes smaller, one loses love in a way that turns feelings of mutual respect (warm feelings of admiration and caring) into superiority feelings.

The concepts of shame and repugnance are central to Elias's

conception of psychodynamics, but in a relational context of changing patterns and density of interdependence networks. Shame links social and individual pacification or control of violence as a means to solve social and personal conflicts. The psychical shame dynamic can be observed with reference to symbols of violence, such as the knife and its use at table, which, over many generations, has become imbued with various shades of anxiety-producing precepts and restrictions. As actual physical attack has become increasingly rare in present-day nation states compared with their feudal predecessors, the sensitivity towards any form of behaviour reminiscent of attack has become more highly developed. This type of sensitivity, first developed and refined within courtly circles, attained a high social prestige value and was gradually disseminated throughout society. In this way, anxiety is aroused through both status tensions and aggressive associations (1994a: 498).

For Elias, the sensibilities exhibited by particular individuals are conditioned by the specific socio-historical configuration including the extent to which violence is monopolized by a central authority, the accompanying pacification of social spaces and the compulsion of those living within these spaces to develop particular forms of self-restraint (these issues will be discussed in the next chapter). Of course, within these pacified social spaces, the behaviour of people will not take on a uniformity. Rather, forms of life and emotion management multiply within the confines of increased security; contrasts diminish and varieties increase (1994a: 460–5). The relatively more differentiated personality structure and the more all-round ability to refrain from the immediate gratification of impulsive desires is a precondition for participating in the 'normal' day-to-day existence within these more 'developed' societies. But it is evident that not all people within generally pacified societies have undergone an equally successful individual civilizing process. Their capacity and willingness to exhibit self-restraint with respect to acts of physical violence vary: some do not meet the dominant standard of self-restraint. Civilization is not a homogeneous entity. There are groups of people who are not members of the armed services or the police force for whom aggression and violence are not removed behind the scenes of social life. The football hooligans of modern Britain are clear evidence of this (see Dunning et al. 1988; Williams et al. 1984;

and Murphy et al. 1990). Similarly, parts of urban areas in many industrialized societies are relatively violent places and the physical safety of people within them can often be described as anything but secure.

To summarize then, the first volume of *The Civilizing Process* documents the advancing thresholds of shame and embarrassment with regard to bodily functions and behaviour, which are themselves representative of changes in social and individual habitus – or civilizing processes. The second volume connects this development to structural transformations of society and clarifies how aggression and violence are dealt with and experienced by people living in relatively more developed societies. Together with particular socio-structural changes, people within modern societies became relatively more physically secure and the whole affectual make-up of people was transformed, leading to a general advance in the thresholds of shame and repugnance with regard to the perpetration or witnessing of acts of physical violence, except within highly regulated and 'safe' situations where the actual threat of injury to oneself or others is minimal and is recognized as such. In the next chapter, Elias's insights into changing manners and habitus are placed in a wider context. I focus on how his work connects the way in which controls emerge over the perpetration and witnessing of violence to the structure of broader social dynamics and the monopoly of power resources.

CHAPTER THREE

Violence, Habitus and State Formation

In discussing the connections between psychological developments and wider social processes in the second volume of *The
Civilizing Process*, Elias focuses on the development of French
society and absolutist rule. He considers long-term social processes involving the lengthening and increasing density of
interdependency chains, particularly the process of state
formation and the formation of violence monopolies, and the
consequences these have for more general shifts in the structure
of social relations and the use and control of violence. I outline
his argument in more detail below before considering the
concepts of civilization, civilizing and decivilizing processes
and violence in more detail. This chapter not only highlights
those aspects of social processes which generate what Elias calls
more civilized personalities, but also clarifies the central concepts
of this book.

Violence monopolies and pacification

In answering the question why the patterns of emotion management of Western medieval people were more extreme than
those found in modern industrialized societies, Elias suggests
that it was largely to do with the lack of a strong central power
within a particular region which was able to *force* people to

restrain themselves. If such an authority develops, the results are quite specific:

> the moulding of affects and the standards of the drive economy are very gradually changed as well ... [T]he reserve and 'mutual consideration' of people increase, first in normal everyday life. And the discharge of affects in physical attack is limited to certain temporal and spatial enclaves. Once the monopoly of physical power has passed to central authorities, not every strong man can afford the pleasure of physical attack. This is now reserved to those few legitimized by the central authority (e.g., the police against the criminal), and to larger numbers only in exceptional times of war or revolution, in the socially legitimated struggle against internal or external enemies. (1994a: 165)[1]

When Elias refers to the monopoly of violence, he seems to use the phrase to denote the *means* and *use* of physical force: the former being weapons, modes of transport and communication, and structural chains of command and obedience institutionalized in bureaucratic organizational forms; the latter constituting the employment or execution of physical force. This is clearly the meaning of the phrase 'monopoly of violence' in Elias's work because of his frequent use of the phrase 'monopoly of the means of physical force' or 'monopoly of the means of violence' in similar contexts. Elsewhere, he describes this monopoly as a 'socio-technical' invention of the human species which develops without planning in the course of many generations (Elias 1988c: 189). He also points out that the status of this monopoly is highly equivocal because it is both protective and repressive: it has a Janus-head.

The formation of monopolies

Max Weber's ideas on the state were influential in Elias's conception of the monopoly of violence (Elias 1994a: xv, 533n). Weber defines the state as a political organization whose 'administrative staff successfully upholds the claim to the *monopoly* of the *legitimate* use of physical force in the enforcement of its order' (Weber 1978: 54, original emphasis).[2]

But while Weber tends to focus on the 'state', Elias traces the process of state formation: the development of the monopoly over the means of violence by a centralized state authority which was only possible with a concurrent monopoly of taxation, neither being more 'fundamental' than the other (1994a: 346). Throughout the Middle Ages, an elimination contest ensued between the continental territorial lords – the number of competitors was reduced while the size of the territories increased, and violence between them was the inevitable result. Violence and elimination contests between feudal magnates had important implications for the levels of violence within the areas controlled by them. It resulted in internal pacification, the slow, relatively incomplete process of the restriction of the use of violence between people under the ruling of a central authority. Without these violent actions and the forces of free competition the monopoly of violence and the attendant suppression and control of violence over large areas could not occur (1994a: 388).

Elias argues that this process had a compelling character for those bound up within it. Individual lords *had* to engage in warfare to save themselves and their families. If they did not, then sooner or later they would be overtaken by another lord and have to submit to his rule or be killed. The general pattern in Germany took the form of the fragmentary consolidation of many centralized monopolies from the former imperial territory. This was markedly different from the state-formation process in England, where the opposite was the case (more on this in chapter 5). The advancing 'division of social functions', or division of labour, and the increasing density of interdependence networks, meant that fewer warrior families controlled larger areas, forming centralized, stable and relatively high levels of monopolization over the means of violence and taxation within them. Eventually, the function of the central ruler was taken over by the central institutions and the operation of these central institutions became imbued with norms of conduct and control.[3]

Elias broadens the concept of 'competition' as it is commonly used to refer to forms of struggle within the economic sphere and identifies it as a much more pervasive fact of social life (1994a: 381). Through a process of free competition for the means of social power, there is a high probability that, eventually, fewer people will control increasing opportunities as larger numbers of units are eliminated from the competition (1994a: 347). The mechanism[4] of monopoly formation remains the same.

Because of the particular competitive tensions within a social formation, an immanent regularity emerges whereby territorial rulers are set against one another in a frequently violent struggle for social survival. Eventually, it is probable that one victor will emerge and gain exclusive access to, or create, key power monopolies. Elias is careful to say that the actual detail in the operations of the process itself will vary a great deal, but as it emerges the density and lengthening of human interdependency chains increase, precipitating a reorganization of affectual moulding. The means of struggle for key monopolies of power eventually become more refined so that restraint of the affects is increasingly imposed on individuals by their dependence on the monopoly ruler. Without a highly centralized co-ordination of the instruments of force, social tensions would usually lead to warlike actions (1994a: 500).

Two phases in the formation of these monopolies are specified by Elias: first, free competition and an elimination contest; and second, control over the monopolies moving from the individual to increasing numbers of people – from *private* to *public*. The central administrative apparatus grows, and as it does, it comes under the control of broader sections of the population. Thus, the warrior nobility of the medieval period was gradually transformed into a court nobility as the monarchs were able increasingly to bring the warrior lords and nobles into their service within the courts as courtiers. The pacification of warriors, their transformation into courtiers – which Elias calls courtization[5] – between the eleventh and eighteenth centuries, represented a civilizing transformation which formed the precondition for subsequent 'spurts' and 'counter-spurts' in the civilizing process (1994a: 466).

Within states, Elias points to the crucial role played by the king under the concept of the 'royal mechanism', again with special reference to France. This concept refers to the slow consolidation of power by the king, resulting in the absolutist monarchies of the later seventeenth and eighteenth centuries. Growing royal power, however, increased the monarch's dependence on increasing numbers of other people who were necessary, above all, for their administrative ability. More people became dependent for their social existence on increasing numbers of others. With this increasing length and density of interdependencies there developed a growing ambivalence of interest between the various interdependent groups (1994a: 394). Social advancement became less dependent upon one's ability to wield arms, and more dependent upon one's ability to compete with words and planned strategies with which to win the favour of social superiors. Inconclusive struggles between social groups favoured the tipping of the scales of power in the direction of the ruler, in this case, the king. In this situation of 'multi-polar', but essentially 'bi-polar' tensions, the skillful manipulation of group differences shifts power chances in favour of the king and enables him effectively to deflect challenges to his power (1994a: 397).[6] At the same time his power is consolidated because his own interests do not coincide directly with any one of the competing groups below him. In fact, it serves his cause to lend support to the second strongest social group over which he rules, thereby increasing the tensions between the ruled and further bolstering his own power chances. The king first sided with the bourgeoisie and then later with the aristocracy as the balance of power between them changed in favour of the former. Conflicts within societies were thereby transformed within the civilizing process, not removed. This configuration of the 'royal mechanism' was most successful in France, especially in the case of Louis XIV. However, the different paths of development within England and Germany (to be discussed later in chapters 5, 6 and 7) do not fit in so neatly with this general model.

Any particular monopoly of the means of violence is never absolute: it is usually only more or less successful according to the practical concerns of surveillance and enforcement. Clearly, many people do use weapons and perpetrate violence without a central ruler's permission. However, the point is that it becomes an offence to perpetrate acts of physical force within the confines of a particular central authority's jurisdiction, unless the violent actions are ratified in some way, for example, through membership of an army or police force. Once a stable monopoly of the means of violence is established, competition between groups focuses on the right to control this power resource, although sometimes attempts are made to undermine its existence. Tensions within a shifting balance of power always exist between the 'state', its representatives and those who have little or no access to control of state power monopolies.

Internal pacification is bound up with the process of the

monopolization of physical force. But pacification is not necessarily uniform. Artur Bogner (1992b: 4) suggests that it can be
differentiated into three aspects: pacification of observable *behaviour*, of behavioural *norms* held to be valid, and of *emotions*
(the extent of mutual identification and levels of repugnance
thresholds with respect to witnessing or perpetrating violence).
All these aspects of pacification – behaviour, norms and emotions – may not operate at the same time or with equal significance. Norms against violence, for example, may be highly
developed and operative within a society which is characterized
by frequently observable acts of violence. Generally, however,
these three aspects are a measure of internal pacification and can
be seen as stages in the pacification process (Bogner 1992b: 5). In
other words, they are a measure of the extent to which pacification of behaviour has generated normative sanctions against the
use of violence, and the extent to which this in turn has generated a relative increase in mutual identification and a rise in
repugnance thresholds with respect to witnessing or perpetrating violence.

   According to Elias, economic relations in more developed
Western state societies are now largely devoid of violence:[7]
physical force in these societies is largely 'confined to barracks'
(1994a: 450). Competition is transformed into a socially legitimate form in the marketplace. Economic competition within
states gained in social importance by the nineteenth century,
parting somewhat from the military aspect of economic relations. Indeed, the market was only able to flourish in conditions
where there was a monopoly of the means of physical force in a
particular area, that is, within pacified social spaces. Thus, in
contrast to Marx, Elias stresses that monopolization is not
confined to the economic sphere and points out that a relatively
successful monopoly of the means of production is only one
type of monopolization: this in fact becomes more evident once
the exercise of violence has been restricted and has become
largely impersonal. The monopolies of the means of violence
and the means of production and consumption are interconnected, but one does not determine the other.

Violence and civilization in 'simpler' or pre-state societies

Hans Peter Duerr (1988: 1–4) argues that the civilizing process outlined by Elias is in fact a 'myth'. He has amassed vast amounts of empirical data from many different societies, both 'simpler' societies and industrialized 'complex' societies of the past and present, to show that a sense of propriety and strict rules surrounding nakedness and sexual behaviour are ubiquitous. Duerr argues that a civilizing process has not taken place in Europe: that sexual shame has been a human universal over the last 40,000 years. In doing this, however, he seems to attribute to Elias the notion that, in medieval societies, people lacked self-restraint totally in this respect, and that it is only from this time on that we witness a rise in the levels of shame and embarrassment surrounding sex and nakedness (see for example 1994a: 39, 176 and 1992a: 148, 151). But this interpretation does not take into account Elias's repeated comments in relation to the nature of civilizing processes in which he reiterates that while the patterning of drive- and impulse-controls varies in different societies, there is no society in which they are absent (1988d: 183; 1992a: 146; 1994a: 131). Also, in answer to Duerr's thesis, Elias replies in a newspaper article that Duerr remained blind to the evidence because he assumed from the start that self-steering mechanisms have not really changed from the Middle Ages to the present (1988e: 38; cf. Schröter 1990; Wouters 1994).

More specifically, anthropologists have challenged Elias's views on the relationships between personality structures and the institutionalized state control of the means of violence. They point to societies where people exhibit 'civilized' personality traits in the absence of such macro-social formations and lengthened chains of interdependence. Van Velzen (1982: 85–97)[8] uses the example of the Maroons of Surinam (the Djuka), Rasing (1982: 225–42) refers to the nomadic Inuit Eskimos, and Jagers (1987: 210–24) makes use of a variety of evidence from several tribal societies. They argue that in the absence of a state apparatus of control over the means of physical force, examples can still be found of societies in which self-restraint is highly valued and practised, where etiquette is highly developed and where violence is often or usually highly controlled and employed in a very instrumental fashion, rather than involving displays of affectual release.

Stephen Mennell suggests that these studies are ahistorical and do not pay enough attention to the broader relational dynamics in which these tribal people live (see also Goudsblom 1984b; Kilminster and Wouters 1995: 114–15). In particular, he argues, the degree of influence of colonial administrations on the respective societies is not emphasized. With regard to the environmental conditions in which these people live, Mennell argues,

> it is entirely plausible . . . that the physical context in which Eskimos (or Bushmen) exist will produce very strong interdependencies, and an awareness of how violent conflict would jeopardize survival. Conceptually, the strength of external constraints may vary from one society to another . . . [and the] shift in the balance of controls may be produced by functional alternatives to state formation and division of functions. (1992: 240–1)

The obvious objection to this line of argument is that it seeks to immunize Elias's theory of civilizing processes from any attempt at falsification. At present, however, it is enough to say that his theory of pacification processes may simply be shown to have its limits within the boundaries of European societies, which do not provide the same kind of evidence as that presented by the anthropologists so far. But it should also be pointed out that none of these anthropologists look at the civilizing or pacification *processes* of the societies they are considering.

What is clear from these anthropological studies is that more research into these issues is needed. A crucial aspect of pacification processes emphasized by Elias but frequently missed by such criticisms mentioned above is the importance of their relative *stability*. It is only when state formation and lengthening chains of interdependence are relatively continuous over several generations that such civilized traits – *relatively* stable and more even self-restraint – can emerge. Elias wanted to develop a developmental theory and from his material he drew conclusions relating to the importance of centralized power in the form of government (the state), and lengthening chains of interdependencies in pacification processes. It is an open question as to what extent his developmental theory should be adapted or changed to fit the examples of relatively small groups, living in relative isolation, giving more emphasis to kinship networks in the control of violence, and 'customs and common law and the authority of priests and legal specialists' (Kuzmics 1987: 524) in pre-state societies.⁹ All of these could also have a taming influence on personalities in face-to-face interactive situations. The European development from the Middle Ages onwards was a specific example of human entanglement in feuds and inter-group conflict, which in fact enabled Elias to draw his 'curve of civilization' with such clarity, despite claims that he exaggerated the levels of violence in these contexts. Hence it may be that once a certain phase is reached in the development of societies, particularly in terms of numbers and social complexity, then civilizing and decivilizing processes generate an endogenous dynamic of their own. In which case, Elias's theory would be more relevant to societies which have developed beyond specified levels of complexity and length of interdependency chains.

Linearity, development and evolution

Behind the historical narrative of *The Civilizing Process* Elias works through a consistent theory of social transformation. The theory of civilizing processes is part of a larger model of social processes which Elias was continuously elaborating throughout his long sociological career (see Elias 1974, 1978a, 1983: 221). In this view, social processes are long term (at least three generations), directional and structured (cf. Elias 1992c: 234–40). Yet they are also 'blind', with no inherent purpose and are characterized by emergent properties which are *sui generis*, relatively autonomous from the plans and intentions of any single individual bound up within them and with their own discoverable immanent dynamics and structural regularities. On the more general level of societal development, Elias specifies criteria with which to draw comparisons between different stages of social processes and to determine what he refers to as their 'directions'.[10] These criteria do not stand alone and should not be considered in isolation, nor should they be conceived in terms of simple increases or decreases; they are interrelated in an overall configuration of shifting balances:

One of the simplest of these criteria is the number of routine contacts which people of different classes, ages and sex have at one stage of social development as compared to another. Others are the number, length, density and strength of the chains of interdependence which individual people form with others within a time–space continuum at a certain stage as compared to earlier or later stages. A standard criterion that could be better calibrated than is the case at present is the central balance of tensions in a society: the number of power centers increases with a growing differentiation of functions; inequality in the distribution of power – without disappearing – is reduced. Lastly, these criteria include the level of the three fundamental controls of people in society – the control of extra-human Nature, the control of people over each other, and the control of each individual over himself. (1983: 221)[11]

Thus, Elias's problematic centres around the calibration of the relationship between face-to-face interactions and systemic relationships. But this emphasis on unplanned, relatively autonomous dynamics can be read as playing down the role of individual agency and scope for action (Van Krieken 1989: 199) whereby the civilizing process is seen as a historically usurping roller-coaster and a catch-all phrase to cover over problems of historical interpretation rather than to reveal social processes. However, Elias's conception of social dynamics is actually a call to locate individual agency in its proper socio-historical context. He seeks to develop a means with which to investigate the social level of the universe and argues that this *is* characterized, in particular processes, by a relative impotence of particular individuals. He does not necessarily imply that individuals themselves are naive or stupid in some inherent sense, nor that they are wholly 'determined' by social structures beyond their control. These social 'structures' are, after all, nothing other than the patterns formed by interdependent individuals. Rather, he seeks to demonstrate that the interweaving of aggregates of individual actions (perhaps planned more or less intelligently and rationally) generates an order of social processes *sui generis*.[12] For Elias, changes in affect-economies and particular ways of behaving and feeling came about as a result of social processes that are not planned by any single individual and yet with a force more compelling than any individual's wishes or intentions, a conception derived from a social science tradition stemming from the work of Smith, Ferguson and Mandeville, and, more importantly for him, Hegel.[13] But while these processes do not have a necessary direction, their directional changes are characterized by greater or lesser degrees of probability. His conception of social processes differs from the earlier 'invisible-hand'-type theories in that he applied his model to a different area: the study of military and political configurations.

But one might still maintain that in *The Civilizing Process* Elias does seem to underestimate the role of intentional actions in the inculcation of 'civilized' traits, and in this sense he does not pay enough attention to social and urban reform, including the established church and its representatives, within the context of blind social processes of state formation and lengthening chains of interdependency. But Elias's primary focus in his book is on changes in the behaviour of the secular upper classes. Van Krieken suggests that the intended consequences of actions should be placed *alongside* the unintended consequences of other actions identified by Elias (Van Krieken 1989: 199). But this is also inadequate because it fails to appreciate fully the fact that 'intended actions' always take place in the context of unplanned interdependencies. Moreover, it misses the point that people only formulate some forms of intended consequences of their actions (for example, the idea of a 'civilizing mission') at a particular stage in a civilizing process. I would argue that social processes can be seen in terms of a *balance* between intended actions and their intended/unintended results within the context of a number of generations. It is important to note that Elias later defined a social process as being at least three generations in length (1992c: 234), which implies that his work is concerned primarily with unplanned processes.

Susan Buck-Morss (1978: 190) argues that Elias's general approach neglects the discontinuities between courtly and bourgeois culture and sees this as a result of his blindness to the dynamic importance of the mode of production in historical processes. She suggests that Elias fails to develop a realistic theory of social change and that his approach is gradualist. However, Kuzmics (1988: 159) rightly points out that all Elias seeks to do is demonstrate how the monopoly of the means of violence develops and provides the *conditions* for the further development of the means of production. Furthermore, the bourgeois character retained remnants of the courtly character and was conditioned in its development by social and psychological processes which were not restricted only to those involving the development of the Protestant Ethic. *Pace* Buck-Morss, it seems that Elias was aware of the discontinuities (see Elias 1994a: 394–5) between courtly and bourgeois society and of the oppressive nature of capitalist social relations in which the workers struggle to improve their power potential in industrial societies (cf. Elias 1978b: 156–8).

Several critics have accused Elias of putting forward a 'unilinear evolutionary' model of history (cf. Buck-Morss 1978: 188; Coser 1978: 565; MacRae 1978: 884; Seigel 1979: 126; Robinson 1987; and Giddens 1984: 241). While lack of space precludes a more detailed consideration of all the issues involved with 'linearity' and 'evolutionism', I shall briefly comment on both themes in relation to Elias's work (cf. Mennell 1992: 234–6). It is more appropriate to see his theory as multilinear, because he traces many different strands of social development, including commercialization, population growth, migration, urbanization, developing communications networks, the division of labour, industrialization (development of the means of production) and, of course, state formation, all woven together in a complex conceptual web. Furthermore, and contrary to the 'unilinearity' interpretation, Elias talks of 'waves of expansion of the standards of civilized conduct' (1994a: 506) – the spread of such conduct to other sections of society – which have two phases: first, a process of colonization or assimilation in which larger, socially inferior outsider groups take on board the dominant behavioural codes of the established groups; and second, repulsion, differentiation or emancipation 'in which the rising group gains perceptibly in social power and self-confidence and in which the upper group is forced into increased restraint and isolation, and the contrasts and tensions in society are increased' (1994a: 507).[14] Such a description is not part of a unilinear conception of social development, nor does it appear to be a long-term theory of 'progress' in the sense of a movement towards a 'better' future, as some have suggested (for example Leach 1986: 13; and Lasch 1985: 713).

The question of evolutionism in Elias's work can be clarified with reference to some points made by one of his critics, Anthony Giddens, who highlights the following claims made by evolutionary theorists: historical mechanisms result in the emergence of Western societies; there are some dominant continuities which are shared cross-culturally; and these continuities reveal a movement from the simple to the more complex (Giddens 1985: 32). With respect to human history, Giddens highlights two broad streams of evolutionism: the first sees social change as governed mainly by incremental processes of development in which there are no fundamental discontinuities; the second stream claims that history is driven by the process of struggle which involves the occurrence of discontinuities between developmental stages. Durkheim and Comte are cited as examples of the former, while historical materialism or social Darwinism fit into the latter category.[15] More generally, Giddens argues that evolutionary theory assumes a link with biological evolution and searches for a 'mechanism' of change which goes beyond speaking of increasing complexity or 'progression', which Giddens seems to agree is an acceptable term to use in its descriptive sense. However, while evolutionary theory also seeks to specify a series of 'stages', Giddens rightly argues against the normative notion of 'progress' with all its attendant colonialist and ethnocentric associations. Lastly, according to Giddens, most evolutionary theory tends to see the notion of adaptation as the dominant mechanism of social change (Giddens 1984: 233).

Elias's notion of social development parts company with the evolutionary theorists of the nineteenth century. He clearly specifies a distinction between biological evolution and social processes of development. If, on the one hand, evolutionism is taken to mean the long-term process of social development during which a predetermined plan is unfurled, or an irreversible movement is assumed, that is, something akin to biological evolution (Lasch 1985: 712; Coser 1978: 565), then Elias's theory cannot be categorized as evolutionary. He uses the concept of development to refer specifically to social processes, as distinct from biological processes. For Elias, 'development' is a neutral symbol for a sequential order of changes in the flux of social life (1978b: 160). Social processes are made possible but are not determined by the biological evolution of the human species.[16] Furthermore, in contrast to biological processes of evolution, social processes of development are reversible (see Elias 1978b: 158–74; 1987e: 351; 1986b: 143; and 1996: 299–402). Human beings are not civilized by nature, but they have a biological *potential* to undergo civilizing processes. They have to undergo this process, at least as individuals, but they do not possess an

inborn drive and affect regulation. Rather, this ability is acti-
vated in specific relationships with other human beings: self-
restraint is largely learned from other humans, but their learned
knowledge can be forgotten (Elias 1992d: 382–3).

If, on the other hand, evolutionism is taken to mean a gradual
change which may be seen retrospectively to tend towards a
particular direction, but without the imputation of teleology,
then Elias's theory of civilizing processes would fit this description. In this sense, Elias's ideas coincide broadly with the first
stream specified by Giddens: Elias does emphasize the long-
term continuities in social processes and movements from more
simple to more complex forms of social organization. But as the
discussion of state formation above has shown, Elias did not
think of social development as devoid of struggle: indeed,
struggle is integral to such processes. Also, he does not put
forward a teleological notion of historical transformation in the
sense of proposing a predetermined future existence, or some
kind of 'need' required by social structures (as suggested by
Horne and Jary 1987: 100).

From the preceding remarks I hope to have made clear that
Elias's theory may be seen as 'evolutionary', but not in the way
the term is more usually employed in social theory. He explicitly
distances himself from biological notions and from teleological
assumptions. Nevertheless, Elias's theory can be seen as evolutionary in the simple sense of long-term continuities and processes of differentiation and integration. I think that his ideas
offer a way out of conceiving of social change in terms of the
more traditional evolutionary ideas and the inherent problems
with 'progress' and ethnocentrism outlined by Giddens. While
employing the term 'progressions', Elias does not refer to
'progress'. Conversely, 'regression' simply refers to changes in
social processes which tend to move in a direction *away* from
standards or circumstances which previously existed, and is
also without pejorative connotations. Many concepts used by
Elias can have more controversial meanings in other contexts –
in particular his notion of civilization which will be discussed in
more detail below – and his use of the concept of progression is
no exception.

On the concepts of violence and civilization

'Civilization' is frequently used by historians and archaeologists to describe a specified social organization with certain 'levels' of achievement in its social, political, economic, religious and/or artistic features; for example, the past 'civilizations' of Sumer, the Inca, Greece, India, Egypt, and so on. This use of the term is quite uncontroversial. As we have already seen, Elias traces the antithetical development of the terms *Zivilisation* and *Kultur* in Germany, and *civilisation* in France and England in *The Civilizing Process* (1994a: 3–28) and shows how 'civilization' is derivative of courtesy and civility, a sequence of terms for socially desirable upper-class behaviour. He discusses the way in which the term developed as a conceptual badge with which established Western elites described themselves in a particular historical era: it was (and to a large extent still is) the expression of their we-image. 'Civilization' was first widely popularized and understood in process terms by the Physiocrats. The development of this use of the word is closely associated with its normative connotation referring to a 'higher' state, frequently seen as a 'progression' in the sense of 'better' than that which had previously existed, associations from which Elias sought consciously to distance himself. This meaning of 'civilization' is often contrasted with a 'barbaric' or 'primitive' state of human existence and is used as a substantive in polar opposition to these two terms: it has obvious ethnocentric connotations.

Yet there is some residual ambiguity surrounding the concept of civilization used by Elias.[17] It is not completely clear whether the normative aspect of the term features in his work – he does not consistently place 'civilization' in inverted commas to indicate a normative valuation (cf. Mennell 1992: 30). While it is Elias's *intention* to develop a more detached, social-scientific or descriptive concept of civilization, normative connotations in his use of the term are implied simply because of his failure to be more explicit on the matter (cf. Schröter 1990: 43ff; Mennell 1992: 30; Blok in Wilterdink 1984: 287–91).

One of the main aims of *The Civilizing Process* is to demonstrate the process character of civilization, in contrast to a static use of the term in opposition to 'barbarism' (1994a: 39, 41). Elias clearly restates and differentiates his intentions in the 1968 introduction to *The Civilizing Process* where he again emphasizes the process character of his notion of civilization (1994a: 183). In several places in the book the term civilization appears without quotation marks but it is quite obvious in these contexts that the word has a processual meaning. But it is used without qualification in a number of places throughout the book (see 1994a: 165–7, 461, 485, 491, 493, 507, 511, 523, 524). This is less true of *The Court Society*, where the term appears without quotation marks in relatively few places (cf. 1983: 257, 259, 261, 263, 264, 265). But despite Elias's ambiguity on this issue, I would maintain that the *dominant* meaning he seeks to develop is a descriptive one.

When Elias wrote *The Civilizing Process*, the use of the word civilization permeated popular culture and academic discourse and was not as controversial as it is today. Elias points out much later on in an article for a German magazine (1988e: 37) that while he was writing the book he searched for a different concept to use, one with less ideological connotations, but when he could not find one, he decided instead to carry out detailed empirical research in close association with the term. If we take him at his word, we can conclude that, in this respect, he exhibited a high degree of detachment for his time.[18] As he writes in the introduction to the 1968 German edition of *The Civilizing Process*:[19]

> Here, the attempt is made to isolate the factual core to which the current prescientific notion of the civilizing process refers. This core consists primarily of the structural change in people toward an increased consolidation and differentiation of their affect controls, and therefore both of their experience (e.g., in the form of an advance in the threshold of shame and revulsion) and of their behaviour (e.g., in the differentiation of the implements used at table). (1994a: 183)

Furthermore, I do not see any reason to draw a distinction between Elias's use of the terms civilization and civilizing process, so long as it is clear that both terms can be used in a technical sense to refer to processes rather than to static conditions. This process character of civilization in his work is succinctly encapsulated in the following quotation which is taken from an essay first published in German: 'The civilization *of which I speak* is never completed and constantly endangered' (1980: 98, my emphasis).[20] So, both 'civilization' and the concept of 'civilizing processes' have specific meanings in Elias's work which differ from the more everyday use of these terms. As Eric Dunning points out, 'just as other sociologists employ terms such as 'class' and 'bureaucracy' in a sense that is more detached than their everyday usage, so Elias used the concept of civilizing processes in a more detached sense' (1992: 262). Having said all this, however, a residual question still stands, the answer to which remains open: is it in fact possible at this stage in the development of Western societies, and despite Elias's disclaimers, to remove the rhetorical content of the term civilization in sociological discourse?

The concept of violence

What Elias actually means when he uses the term violence is still unclear. Violence is difficult to define without creating either a restrictively specific or a uselessly abstract general category (see Williams 1989: 329–31; and Peuckert 1992: 114–17). In my view, violence can only be defined in context. An inclusive definition is impossible because of the cultural or situational variability in the perception of certain forms of behaviour. But it should be possible to develop a working conception, one which is not intended to be universal and which would avoid an unproductive relativism.

Elias clearly refers to physical force when employing the term violence. He uses the word *Gewalt* in his German publications, which generally indicates force, but its meaning in German is somewhat more differentiated. It may refer simply to power or coercion, or it may have state (*staatsrechtliche*) connotations (as in *Gewaltenteilung* or *Gewaltentrennung*) where an implied separation of legislative, executive and juridical powers is intended (cf. Weber 1978: 54; and Peuckert 1992: 114). In everyday speech, violence tends to refer to the (usually sudden) exercise of physical force so as to inflict injury or damage on humans, animals or things. More precisely, violence with respect to humans would include actions which infringe *physical* integrity, such as torture, wounding, killing and rape, or destruction by impact or arson (cf. Van Benthem van den Bergh 1980a: 15). I would suggest that this is identical to the way in which Elias uses the term violence throughout his work. This conception refers to the direct violation of physical integrity, and for the sake of clarity I shall use the term only in this way.[21] In order to differentiate the changing forms of violence and the meanings associated with them, the following comments are based on a typology of violence developed by Eric Dunning, which I have revised and expanded elsewhere (1986: 226; cf. Fletcher 1993: 75).

(1)   The extent to which violence takes a play or serious form is a prominent feature of Elias's writing, particularly his later work on sport (see chapter 5). As we have seen above, Elias argues that in modern societies sports and sport-games offer a means of entering into a combat situation in relative safety. People may 'play' at being violent, but they do not usually intend to harm each other (although frequently, of course, harm is intended and produced). A good example is the American television game *Gladiators* in which the competitors wear a great deal of protective clothing. This is not only for their benefit, of course, but also for the benefit of their opponents. The fights between the combatants are a far cry from the gladiatorial contests of the Ancient Roman world.

(2)   Ritual and non-ritual violence, and violence perpetrated against inanimate matter do not feature significantly in Elias's earlier work. However, ritualized violence takes a prominent position in his discussions of duelling in the imperial German establishment (see chapter 6 below).

(3)   The number of people involved in violence is crucial for Elias. Violence is often the infringement of a group norm and is bound up with we-images, although Elias does not always make this explicit. Different kinds of violence affect different we-images of groups: kin and family identity tend to be more closely associated with criminal violence; identification with a particular ruling or opposition establishment or social class is more bound up with political violence; and larger scale inter-group violence (war and the threat of war) is more intertwined with identities centred on a particular state or nation (Van Benthem van den Bergh 1980a: 7–8). Problems of I-identification emerge when a person struggles with his or her own conscience. Elias traces the development of this I-aspect in *The Civilizing Process*.

Elias shows how some forms of violence in Western European societies have receded as the we-identifications of family and village have become less intense. In this process, face-to-face combat in the form of duelling, or the use of violence in the

settlement of disputes in family feuds as forms of *private* violence, have receded. Also, in dynastic states, war was a private
affair, whereas in the present day, the we-identity bound up
with the nation has become far more important in the perpetration of *public* forms of violence, such as wars, revolutions and
terrorism, and increasingly involves the civilian population in
the wielding of state power. While Elias recognizes violence
behind closed doors in the form of torture as an *instrumental*
form of rule, particularly in the context of Nazi Germany, he
simply neglects the issue of domestic violence.

The issue of whether violence exacts a cost on its perpetrators,
and if so, in what way, is bound up, once again, with the identity-
levels of individuals. One obvious example is the conflict within
the individual at the level of I-identification mentioned above.
According to Elias, the problems at the I-level surrounding the
execution of violence are more accentuated for people living in
the more developed, modern societies, with their relatively
stable monopolies over the means of violence, than they were
for their pre-modern ancestors. A higher level of self-restraint
emerges which is expressed in terms of deeply rooted cultural
and psychological taboos surrounding violence in the more
developed Western societies. Many people who perpetrate,
witness or even think about violence in such societies are
sometimes left with severe guilt feelings or feelings of revulsion.
The psychological problems faced by the Nazi *Einsatzgruppen* as
the result of shooting hundreds of people in cold blood are well
known (see Manvell 1969; and Dicks 1972). So too are the
personal torments of some Nazi officers running death camps
(Lifton 1986). The guilt feelings associated with violence can
also permeate the national we-image level of the personality, as
was the case, and to a large extent still is, in Germany after the
Second World War (see Mitscherlich and Mitscherlich 1975).
However, Elias has little to say about the physical and economic
or material costs on the perpetrators of violence.

As regards gender, in both volumes of *The Civilizing Process*
Elias focuses on violence perpetrated by men, usually against
other males, in processes of state formation. He has relatively
little to say about violence between the sexes or genders, apart
from one passage in the first volume where he talks of the wife
of a knight joining her husband in perpetrating vicious mutila-
tions (1994a: 159). With reference to the more modern states, he

tends to examine the processes by which it has become possible
for people to live together (including gender relations) with a
relative lack of violence, a state of affairs which he finds curious.[22]
Veronika Bennholdt-Thomsen (1985: 23–35) correctly argues
that Elias neglects to consider both violence against women and
against other peoples in processes of colonization in the state
formation of Western societies. Jennifer Hargreaves (1992: 176–
7) also criticizes Elias for not taking issues of violence against
women sufficiently into account in his discussion of civilizing
processes. However, she mistakenly suggests that Elias assumes modern states are characteristic in their absence of violence towards women in everyday life, although this is an
understandable assumption, given that Elias has relatively little
to say about women throughout his published work,[23] let alone
their experience of violence, except in a short passage in *The
Civilizing Process* where he refers to knights physically attacking
them (1994a: 324–5). Elias also does not mention sexual violence
specifically. It is arguable that all forms of violence may involve
a sexual aspect in terms of the pleasurable feelings which may
be aroused in its perpetration. But while the neglect of violence
involving women is a significant oversight in Elias's work, I do
not intend to dwell on this further in this book.

Whether violence involves the use of animals, machines, or
other implements, and whether it occurs face to face, or is the
result of longer action chains, are issues which cover the changing means by which violence is perpetrated, as well as the bodily
and emotional control this involves. Obviously, with the development of more sophisticated technology, the weapons of war
and of policing have become more efficient and more effective
in their aims. In his discussion of the Nazi perpetration of mass
murder, Elias talks of this increase in capacity as one of the
characteristic features of modern societies. Mass killing at the
push of a button (or the dropping of gas pellets) is indicative of
the potential embodied in modern forms of social organization.
The intended victims need not even be seen, at least not by many
people. They may be so far down the chain of actions linking
human beings that they become completely dehumanized in the
form of numbers, as they were for bureaucrats such as Adolf
Eichmann and hundreds like him in the Third Reich. This
'killing at a distance' also occurs whenever long-range weapons
of war are used; from machine-guns at a distance through to

fighter aircraft and inter-continental ballistic missiles.

Whether violence is intentional or the accidental consequence of an action sequence that was not intended to result in violence at the outset; and whether it is initiated without provocation, or is a retaliatory response to an intentionally or unintentionally violent act, are significant themes in Elias's work. As I have outlined above in the first section of this chapter, he explains some aspects of state formation in which feudal lords were drawn into an elimination contest against their will. Elias refers to these unplanned, reciprocally augmenting social processes which may engender violence as 'double-bind processes' (more on this in chapter 4). Examples in Elias's work of violence perpetrated without provocation are medieval knights' indulgence in violent pleasures and the Nazi mass murder of the Jews and others which is also bound up with processes of we- and they-image formation, especially with group fantasies (see chapter 4).

As I have already said above, Elias avoids the notion of legitimacy in the context of the formation of monopolies of violence. Legitimacy claimed by governments has to be vindicated. Of course, the standards of legitimacy can vary from group to group, stratum to stratum. Legitimate forms of violence among football hooligans may differ from those legitimized by terrorists. In the process of state formation the forms of violence change as well as the meaning that violence has for individuals. Therefore, standards of what is considered 'legitimate' violence will vary over time within and between societies. Dunning et al. elaborate upon how this can lead to positive sanctions in the perpetration of violence:

> For people with a particular type of conscience and/or when there is a legitimating ideology, (connected, for example, with a notion of occupational or national 'duty' or 'loyalty' to a community), certain forms of violence and aggressive behaviour can be positively sanctioned and enjoyable. There is no need to postulate an 'aggressive instinct' in order to account for such satisfactions. People are sometimes trained to behave aggressively and rewarded on that account: soldiers, policemen and professionals in certain sports are examples. (Some people are attracted to occupations of this kind because of the opportunities they allow for aggressiveness.) In such cases, apart from the prestige and financial rewards that can accrue, the pleasure and enjoyment derived from acting aggressively are, in part, a form of self-reward for a 'job well done'. (Dunning et al. 1988: 192)

For Elias, violence is seen as an inherent feature of human social life with which humans must learn to cope. But its total elimination is doubtful and possibly even undesirable. Violence takes various forms and degrees, but it can at best only be mitigated rather than eradicated: every form of control of violence implies the threat of violence and a certain degree of the use of violence (Van Benthem van den Bergh 1980a: 10, 11).

One of the most important issues in Elias's work concerns whether violence is rationally chosen as a means of securing the achievement of a given goal (instrumental), or engaged in as an emotionally satisfying end in itself (expressive), a distinction which itself changes through time. He traces the taming of *Angriffslust* and the rise in the rational application of violence both within and between states: the growing sophistication in the technologies of violence. There has been a shift in the balance between the generation of violence through expressive forms towards more instrumental forms. The standards of expression vary both within and between societies. Within the European civilizing process, there have been four notable transformations associated with the taming of expressive aggression (*Angriffslust*): a rise in the repugnance threshold with respect to witnessing or perpetrating violence expressively; an increase in the strict taboos surrounding violence in the form of the super-ego or conscience within the person, accompanied by a sense of guilt associated with violent actions; a dominant trend of placing violence 'behind the scenes of social life'; and an increase in the *planned* use of violence as the result of a general increase in planning and calculation (Dunning 1986: 228). But the role of instrumental violence within colonization processes seems to have been neglected by Elias.[24] This is important because it means that Elias underestimates the extent to which the internal pacification of European states was necessarily accompanied by the use of instrumental violence against 'outsider' populations, for example, in the slave trade or through imperial expansion.

To summarize the themes of this and the previous chapter, Elias points out that civilizing processes depend upon the control of violence. In Elias's explanatory model of state formation, larger landowners were drawn into a violent competitive elimination contest, without which the attendant suppression and control of violence over large areas and the development of lengthening chains of interdependence could not occur. Within the European civilizing process the propensity of most people to abstain from aggressiveness increased, in conjunction with state formation and pacification processes. Violence was increasingly 'confined to barracks', legitimately practised only by members of the armed forces and the police, or within specific, controlled contexts such as sporting competitions. People became more sensitive with respect to witnessing or perpetrating impulsive violence, while at the same time an increase in the planned use of physical force occurred. This disposition became incorporated within the personality structure in the form of a specific kind of conscience formation, generating heightened guilt and repugnance feelings surrounding violent actions.

The patterning of drive and impulse controls varies in different societies, although there is no society in which they are absent (Elias 1994a: 481; 1992a: 146; 1988d: 183).[25] Civilizing processes are not confined to the development of Western European societies.[26] They can be found wherever a stable and durable control of the means of physical force takes place, and in the European case this was related to the competitive pressures increasing the division of social functions and the numbers of people dependent upon one another. This condition allows and requires co-operation on a level which is more determined by controls over vehement emotions, and demands longer-term hindsight and foresight, together with the need for more differentiated interpretations of the actions and intentions of others (Elias 1994a: 456; cf. 1992a). The long-term changes in habitus of people in the secular upper classes of the West involved the patterning of self-restraint becoming stricter, more even, more all round, more stable and more differentiated, and these dispositions spread and interwove with those characteristic of other social classes lower down on the social ladder of these societies. These changes in social and individual habitus – civilizing processes – were interconnected with the dynamics of power and dependency relations. In particular, Elias specifies the increasing division of social functions and state-formation processes to be crucial for the sociogenesis of European civilizing processes.[27]

Chapters 2 and 3 have provided an exposition, critique and summary of Elias's theory of civilizing processes; how these processes are connected to state formation and pacification; and the meaning of the concepts of civilization and violence in

Elias's work. Elias clearly uses the concept of civilization in a relatively more detached way and, for him, violence refers to the infringement of physical integrity. What now stands out in greater relief is that violence and civilization in the work of Elias are not antithetical concepts, but are intertwined with each other. They are also bound up with his conception of sociological process models, which are considered in the following chapter.

CHAPTER FOUR

Identity, Violence and Process Models

Elias develops 'figurational' process models which he uses to understand violence in conjunction with concepts such as interdependence and power, social bonds, habitus and the we–I balance, established-outsider relations and global processes of social integration. These models form the subject of the present chapter. While they are more implicit in Elias's earlier work, the models in fact inform the structure of his arguments in *The Civilizing Process*. It is therefore important to detail their contours in order to clarify Elias's treatment of various historical examples of violence, civilizing and decivilizing processes, especially in relation to England and Germany, which are covered in subsequent chapters. I present the main concepts Elias uses in his models and show how they are relevant to an understanding of the sociogenesis of violence and its controls. I then isolate criteria of civilizing processes mentioned by Elias, before suggesting three main criteria of decivilizing processes which follow logically from Elias's criteria of civilizing. I also highlight the conditions under which decivilizing processes would be likely to occur and sketch their various dimensions.

Interdependence, social bonds and the we–I balance

Clearly, 'social' and 'psychical' processes are seen by Elias to be intertwined. He rejects the notion that the 'individual' can be conceived separately from 'society'. Analytically, this is possible and necessary, but as a representation of reality, argues Elias, this is demonstrably false. He refers to the model of the independently existing individual as a *Homo clausus* (closed person), which he contrasts with a more realistic model of individuals as *Homines aperti* (open people) who form *figurations* with one another (1978a: 119, 125, 135; see also Elias 1969). As will become clear, the concept of figuration is designed to place human interdependencies at the centre of the sociological agenda and allows for the conceptual possibility of resisting what Elias perceives to be a socially conditioned and historical pressure preventing humans from perceiving themselves as individuals at the same time as societies (1978a: 129).[1]

For Elias, power is a central feature of human figurations. Apart from *The Civilizing Process*, the development of his notion of power can be found in publications such as *The Court Society* (1983) and most succinctly in *What Is Sociology?* (1978a). Elias argues that balances of power are constitutive of all human relationships, be they bi-polar or multi-polar. His concept of power is closely tied up with that of 'function', to which he assigns a different meaning from those associations found in 'structural-functionalism'. To say something or someone has a 'function' for something or someone else is not to introduce some abstract notion of fulfilling the 'needs' of a social system in maintaining some kind of harmonious 'whole'. Rather, the concept of function is relational; social functions refer to more or less constraining interdependencies. In other words, writes Elias,

> when one person (or a group of persons) lacks something which another person or group has the power to withhold, the latter has a function for the former. Thus men have a function for women and women for men, parents for children and children for parents. Enemies have a function for each other, because once they have become interdependent they have the power to withhold from each other such elementary requirements as that of preserving their physical and social integrity, and ultimately of survival. (1978a: 78)

Wherever there is a functional interdependence between people, however great the inequality, a balance of power always exists. Power is therefore not considered in a substantive way by

Elias, as a thing which some possess while others do not. This would constitute a reification of the concept of power, or even a personification. He sees power as a structural characteristic of all human relationships in which people have become dependent on one another (1978a: 74); that is, they have a function for one another:

> We depend on others; others depend on us. In so far as we are more dependent on others than they are on us, more directed by others than they are by us, they have power over us, whether we have become dependent on them by their use of naked force or by our need to be loved, our need for money, healing, status, a career, or simply for excitement. (1978a: 93)

Elias develops the heuristic device of 'game models' in order to demonstrate the 'relational character of power in simplified form' (1978a: 75). To show that the interdependence between human groups can be structured while at the same time proceed without shared rules and norms, Elias introduces a model of the Primal Contest. In this model, two small tribes become dependent on each other through the lack of food resources in a particular area. They become involved in a long, drawn-out conflict, raiding each other's camps and killing each other. Nonetheless, this antagonistic relationship is a form of functional interdependence. The 'moves' (actions, plans and aims) of one group are not comprehensible without reference to those of the other. Thus, interdependence of this type is no less a functional relationship than those between friends, allies or those bonded to each other through the division of labour (1978a: 77).

The Primal Contest represents a processual, bi-polar relationship in which both groups seek violently to deprive the other of their social and physical existence. This 'last resort' relationship illuminates the problems surrounding the ability of people to come to terms with and regulate their interdependencies without resorting to violence as a means of resolving tensions and conflicts. The model reveals the immanent dynamics of conflict relationships. Since both sides do not share any common norms and means of orientation, the plans and actions of both groups are determined primarily by one group's perhaps fanciful ideas about the power resources of the other group in relation to its own resources: 'on its idea of their respective strength, cunning, weapons, food supply and food reserves' (1978a: 79). Despite this interweaving of group actions and plans, their interdependence reveals a processual structure. As we shall see, particularly in the case of his analysis of war and battle situations, this model of conflict underlies all of Elias's comments on violence and antagonistic group relations. The model provides a picture of the dynamics of human relations within which either shared norms are absent from the beginning, or where these norms have broken down.[2] An example of this process is that of human identification in a civilizing process which takes many generations to emerge and can very quickly vanish in times of social conflict and war or processes of social disintegration (1978a: 98).

In short, this model of a conflict situation in which two groups are locked together in shared mutual hatred and suspicion describes Elias's concept of a 'double-bind' process in which violence becomes highly likely (see 1978a: 22, 166; 1986a: 26; 1987a: 49ff, 72–4). Such circular processes result from a lack of control over natural or social processes, the dynamics of which are relatively or completely autonomous from the wishes and intentions of those involved with them. A lessening or lack of human control over any set of events will increase the tendency for people's thinking about such events to involve a higher emotional and fantasy content; and the more emotional their thinking becomes, the less able they are to formulate more realistic or adequate models of these events (1978a: 156). Elias introduces the notion of the triad of basic controls of human beings: the extent of their control chances over non-human complexes of events (nature), over interpersonal relationships (society) and over themselves. He later elaborates upon this (1996: 32) and talks of four types of constraint to which people are exposed: those imposed on people because of their animal nature (the hunger and thirst drive, for example); those arising from dependence on non-human, natural events; those people exercise over each other; and those arising from self-control. In their knowledge of the natural world, humans have removed a great deal of fantasy which had previously dominated their thinking in this area and have developed relatively more adequate models with which to represent physical processes. With respect to social relations, however, fantasy and emotion-laden explanations of events frequently gain the upper hand, or are even mixed together with explanations imbued with respectability by laying claim to the status of 'science', such as the explanations of social problems offered by National Socialists in terms derived from biology (1978a: 27).

With more general reference to modern Western societies, Elias gives examples of how the structure of power ratios has changed, together with counter-trends, over the last two centuries (1978a: 65–8). First, there has been a reduction of power differentials between governments and the governed, along with the extension of the franchise to broader sections of the population. Second, a reduction of power differentials between strata within these societies has taken place. Third, there has arisen a transformation of all social relationships towards an increase in the degree of reciprocal, multi-polar dependence and control. Elias refers to the overall process as 'functional democratization'. However, he is careful to distinguish between democratization in the sociological and political senses. The former refers to the relative equalizing of power balances between specific social positions within and between generations, while the latter refers to transformations in specifically governmental offices, especially in the way representatives on all levels are elected. When human relations change, the distribution of power chances change (1978a: 80). This applies to intra- and inter-state relations, the tensions within which make up part of an interdependent whole of humanity which forms the broadest scope of sociological investigations.

In *The Court Society*, Elias makes a distinction between social rank and social power (1983: 269–70); the former refers to status positioning within a society, the latter to the actual ability to utilize resources and position in order to influence the conduct of others (1983: 96–7, 269–71). This is similar to Max Weber's famous definition of power, but Elias distances himself from Weber's formulations which, he argues, were extensive, rather then intensive (1983: 21. Cf. Weber 1978: 212–301). Weber sought to develop 'ideal-types', which are built out of many examples, but which then take on a problematic relationship to the social phenomenon they are intended to explore: Elias gives the example of Weber's discussion of 'patrimonialism' (1983: 21–2). Where Weber favours the development of 'ideal-types', Elias argues for the intensive and detailed investigation of single examples, or 'real-types' (1994a: 526n). The term 'real-type' does not actually appear in *The Court Society*, but the best example of what Elias means by the concept is to be found there in his investigation of power in the court society of Louis XIV. There are, however, more similarities between Elias and Weber than Elias himself would allow. For example, what is for Weber an 'ideal-type' is rendered easily in Eliasian language as a 'model'. The major difference can be found, not in the use of terms, but in the methods of reasoning: Weber was more analytical, whilst Elias sought to develop empirically synthesizing concepts, rather than inclusive conceptual systems.

Problems with the term figuration

Before moving on to discuss social bonds and transformations of violence, I should like to present my reservations regarding the use of the *word* figuration, but not the concept to which it refers. Although Elias claims a particular significance for the term, and although it was introduced as a central concept (1978a: 128–33), I would suggest that it has been assigned a place within Elias-orientated sociology which it arguably does not deserve. It undoubtedly performed a valuable rhetorical function in Elias's attempts to popularize the reorientation of sociology towards his own point of view. As Elias and Scotson wrote with reference to the concept of configuration, 'there is nothing new in perceiving and presenting social phenomena as configurations. Familiar terms like 'pattern' or 'situation' point very much in the same direction' (1994b: 167). The same point, however, can be made regarding the term figuration. In reply to my objection to the use of the *word*, one may claim that Elias seeks to develop means of conceptualization which are more appropriate to the human social universe and which are not derivative of other, and in particular the physical, sciences (see especially 1978a: 113ff). Indeed, along these lines he later clarified the *concept* of figuration in relation to the study of human societies when he writes: 'There are configurations of stars and also of plants and animals. Humans alone form figurations with each other' (Elias 1992b: 89). However, I would suggest the word figuration is simply unnecessary. While it is certainly less cumbersome than the phrase 'networks of interdependent human beings, with shifting asymmetrical power balances' (Van Benthem van den Bergh 1971: 19), which neatly encapsulates the *concept,* I see no reason why the term interdependency networks, or even simply 'configuration', will not suffice as conceptual tools with which to avoid the determinist connotations of 'structure' and the voluntaristic associations of 'agency'. One reason why Elias drops the prefix from configuration in favour of the word figuration may be that the 'con-', stemming from the Latin meaning 'with', is itself redundant. It is therefore unnecessary to say that human beings form configurations 'with' one another. Nevertheless, the word configuration is in common usage and its meaning is intuitively quite clear.

Eric Dunning (1992: 241) has argued that the linguistic properties of the term figuration make it particularly appropriate to the study of human societies. One may speak of a pattern *formed by* human beings or a 'situation' *in which* they find themselves. Moreover, one can refer to a figuration *of* human beings without separating the structures formed by them from the humans themselves. This, argues Dunning, allows us to avoid reifying structures, that is, giving the impression that they exist independently of the people who constitute them. However, these properties are not only expressed in the term itself, but more importantly in the manner and context of theorizing. This Dunning concedes in describing the term, after Herbert Blumer (1969: 149, in Goudsblom 1977a: 100–1), as a 'sensitizing concept', and he goes on to suggest that 'it is intended to direct the attention of researchers to the interdependency chains and networks formed by acting human beings' (Dunning 1992: 242).

Social bonds and the we–I balance

Types of social bonding to broader social units form a major focus for Elias and are instrumental in the sociogenesis of intergroup conflict. He differentiates affectual bonds from economic or political bonds, and introduces a sociological notion of social bonding which is partly rooted in that developed by Durkheim (1984), referring to socially produced relationships which can be observed and which are not the product of a hypothetical gene pattern (Dunning 1986: 225). The latter concept is characteristic of the way in which the notion is employed by sociobiologists and ethologists (for example, see Tiger 1969). Instead of reducing human bonding, as did Freud, to the level of libidinal attachments, Elias talks of the network of valencies (Elias 1969; 1978a: 135–6, 175n) which push individuals into or out of relationships with others. Some valencies may be operative, while others remain open, seeking attachment with other people. On the level of smaller-scale social groupings, all of the valencies operate within the social web of the group, while symbols as a medium of social bonding gain in importance as the scale of social organizations increases. Different valencies tend to bond to different symbols of larger social units, such as coats of arms, flags or emotionally charged ideas like 'socialism', 'capitalism', 'freedom' or 'democracy'. Levels of bonding, from face-to-face relations to those mediated through symbolic representations, can be blended with other more impersonal forms of bonding such as economic bonding, or the division of labour involving increasing reciprocal dependence.

The emotional bonds or valencies underlie the extent to which people say of themselves 'we' or 'I' in relation to other members of their own group (1978a: 137; cf. 1991a: 155–237). Within smaller social units, the I-function is relatively diminished in comparison with, for example, that found in nation-state societies. Feelings of individual solidarity and cohesion in collectivities like villages, towns, principalities or kingdoms represent earlier phases in social development. In societies which have a noble line of inheritance, or dynastic states which exhibit relatively uneven power ratios between princes and social inferiors, a different character of bonding exists in comparison with that found in nation states, particularly in conjunction with processes of democratization. In nation states, millions of people are bonded to one another and develop a picture of an entity of which they are members and with which they can identify through the medium of national symbols, and for which in turn they may develop strong emotions of attachment, or even love (1978a: 137). But this love is never simply the love of other humans of whom one may say 'they', it is also the love of a collective of which one can say 'we', and is thus also a form of self-love (1996: 151). Therefore, the image which members of a society have of this collectivity is also a form of self-image. The value people hold in the sense of a nation is also an expression of the value people hold of themselves and of their relative superiority or inferiority *vis-à-vis* other nations.

The potential threat of losing this meaning and value can be one of the most painful experiences in an individual's life and is bound up with the fate of the nation of which he or she is a part.

One of the reasons why emotional valencies in nation states can take priority over bonds to other forms of social grouping (such as towns, tribes and villages) is that in nation states there exists a relatively strict control over the use of violence in relationships between their own members (1978a: 138). At the same time, however, these members are allowed and are sometimes actively encouraged to use violence against people who are not members of their own nation state: these states are characterized by a 'duality of norm canons' (1996: 154ff). For those involved, there are three main functions of this type of social bonding: the common defence of their own lives; the survival of their own group in the face of attack; and the readiness to launch a united attack on other groups. Elias therefore refers to social formations as attack and defence units, or survival units, which at the current phase in the development of humanity are predominantly nation states, rather than dynastic states, city states or tribes. He is also at pains to point out that the survival function of these units cannot be reduced to or separated from economics (1978a: 139).

With respect to economic and political bonds, Elias sees them as part of an overall social process of development, as inseparable from the 'whole functional nexus of society' (1978a: 141). For Elias, aspects of social processes such as 'culture', 'society' or the 'state' are themselves complex interwoven processes:

> As aspects of a social process most of them have both active and passive functions. They form and are formed, drive and are driven or are active through the sheer resistance with which they are able to influence each other and the development of society as a whole varies. On account of their peculiar properties some of the many part-processes which we tend to represent as 'spheres' in the development of a country – the 'economic', 'cultural', 'political spheres', etc. – are more powerful agent of change than others. But their power in relation to each other is by no means always the same in all types of society, at all stages of social development. And they are, moreover, not always so sharply separated as our present-day terminology makes it appear. This terminology has become more differentiated as society itself has become more differentiated and complex. (1996: 336)

This complexity can determine the extent to which people can gain insight and control the various 'part-processes'. State institutions, for example, have become somewhat more amenable to conscious intervention than other part-processes represented by symbols like 'culture' or 'national characteristics'. In a similar vein, the 'political sphere' was more consciously the focus of intervention for the progenitors of the Russian Revolution than those of the American and French Revolutions, and more so for these than was the case for Cromwell and his supporters. Sometimes, however, there is a 'lag' between the level of development of the functional differentiation within a society and the development of integrating and co-ordinating institutions. Elias gives the example of England from around 1800. One could also point to the rapid process of differentiation in Germany which occurred in the second half of the nineteenth-century and outstripped attempts to develop corresponding political (organizational, integrating) institutions. But in general, the political or the economic sphere cannot be seen as somehow more 'fundamental', since the development of one without the other is unimaginable: 'both are part of developing webs of interdependence' (1978a: 141).

It seems that Elias's concept of *differentiation* processes corresponds roughly to events in what is usually referred to as the economic sphere and his notion of *integration* processes refers to the political sphere, while in both spheres differentiation and integration coincide. A new division of labour, a new department or a new political party require new policies aimed at co-ordination or integration. So, for example, in the development outlined by Elias in Western European societies, the growing division of labour and the expansion of markets was connected with the development of the monopoly of violence, including protection of goods and persons in transit (among other things), and the growth of these political institutions was bound up with expanding networks of trade and industrial development. In this way Elias moves beyond Max Weber's famous definition of the state[3] through emphasizing that the monopoly of violence function was one aspect of an overall social process which was inextricably bound up with fiscal and commercial activities.

Social habitus and national we-identity

We have already seen that the individual habitus refers to the learned emotional and behavioural dispositions which are unique to a particular individual, while the concept of social habitus refers to those learned characteristics of personality which individuals share with other members of the same group. National and traditional habitus are both aspects of social habitus, but they refer to the durability of the intergenerational transmission of learned collective feeling- and behaviour-codes with respect to a particular form of identification. Habitus has many intersecting layers within individuals or groups, depending on the level of differentiation of the society or group to which they belong. In less differentiated societies the social habitus may have only a few layers. In societies of greater social complexity, it is likely to have many layers (1991a: 183). Elias's notion of social habitus bears similarities to the concept of 'national character',[4] but the concept of social habitus can be more differentiated and refers to processes, rather than static entities which the notion of national character frequently brings to mind (1991a: 209–32). The notion of national character also has the added disadvantage of stressing individual aspects to the exclusion of those arising from patterns in networks of interdependencies (social structure). One could argue that the idea of a 'national' or 'social habitus' is a myth; but once the processual dimension is highlighted, it becomes clear that institutionalized patterns of dominant behaviour- and feeling-codes do indeed change.

The we–I balance expresses dimensions of the social habitus: the balance between one's individual and social identity. For Elias 'there is no I-identity without we-identity' (1991a: 184). This implies that he sees the personality as including perceptions and images developed through socialization (the individual level of the civilizing process) and the differing patterns of this process both between societies and between different groups within them. It is a characteristic of democratization processes among various types of societies – whether multi- or single-party states, parliamentary or dictatorial governments – that most of the population directs appropriate emotions towards the society in which they are born and of which they form a part (cf. Armstrong 1982: 4). Symbols of this orientation have, among other things, the function of emotion-laden symbols of a we-group. Within increasingly differentiated industrial societies, social dynamics become relatively unclear, and thus the binding together of individuals through the medium of collective symbols gains a relatively higher value. In comparison to less developed societies, these symbols and symbolwords of group membership have a much more impersonal character, but they can exude a kind of emotional radiation which gives to the collective a sort of 'omniscient' quality, with overtones of holiness and awe: words like 'nation', 'state' or 'country'. 'Nation' becomes highly valued as the expression of all that can be specified to be in the name or interests of the collectivity. Furthermore, these symbol-words usually extend 'to everything which can be said to belong to the nation or to be in the national interest, including the use of force, of fraud, deception or, if it comes to that, of torture and of killing' (1996: 147).

Differing strengths or involvements of we-identity can be observed, for example when comparing family ties to the strength of feelings surrounding super-national integration, such as the newly emerging European identity of today. National group identity is from birth a firmly imprinted layer of the social habitus. But while it is deeply ingrained and durable, this 'national habitus' is also flexible and constantly in flux (1991a: 209). The longer and more continuous the chains of generations within which a particular social habitus has been transmitted from parents to children, the greater will be the hold they command over an individual person within any specified survival unit. The individual develops an I-image and I-ideal, and at the same time a we-image and we-ideal. Therefore, 'nation' forms part of the last two categories and is an example of the correspondence between social and personality structures.

In times of crisis the we–I balance tends to swing in favour of the we, for the group can then appear as the primary means of defence. We-ideals and we-images come to the fore and people tend to acquiesce in the belief which emphasizes the survival of the group over and above the individual. In nation states this belief is maintained and inculcated in times of peace through various organizational and educational institutions within nation states (1996: 334). Both times of crisis and times when

international tensions are not so pronounced result in conflicting desires between individual and group concerns: external
compulsions develop their counterpart as internal compulsions
embodied within individuals in the form of conscience and we-
ideals (1996: 335). Insecurity surrounding the survival of one's
group (and through the group, one's self) generates inherently
dangerous reciprocal hostilities and tensions between and within
national populations. Such hostilities may lead to a situation
where groups get into a 'spin', in which case, says Elias, 'civilization goes into reverse and approaches its breakdown' (1996:
353). Fears and threats on the inter-group level may act as
'releasers' generating actions in the name of group ideals and
norms, thereby fuelling the 'spin' process and the likelihood of
violent armed conflict. These recurrent processes also serve to
maintain group feelings and behaviour traditions which are
used to justify negative feelings towards members of other
groups or towards minority groups within one's own. Thus,
national belief systems serve to increase feelings of superiority
over other nations, but within nations they are also instruments
of power over groups with relatively few power chances: for
example immigrants or others who fall within the general
category of outsiders.

Within modern societies over the nineteenth and twentieth
centuries, interdependence and tensions have increased between classes. However, strong national feelings of loyalty and
togetherness are generated which cut across class differences
and borders within a society, particularly through schools and
the military, and which allow for a convergence of sectional
interests through a society's ruling groups. This emerges clearly
in times of war. The national belief and value systems generated
in the more highly developed countries are generally backward-
looking. The 'virtue' of a national self-image is grounded in its
own interpretation of the past (cf. Kohn 1976: 12; cf. Hobsbawm
1990). Changes in we- and they-feelings, that is, of identifications and exclusions, form the precondition for the development of national sentiments, values and belief-doctrines. The
previous middle classes have achieved the position of the most
powerful intra-state group, not only as leaders of the states and
countries, but also as leaders of nations. The decline in the rule
from kings and ministers as the fulcrums of social power and
changes resulting from democratization processes within

society have been accompanied by a change in peoples' feeling orientation. Most people become 'nationalized' and this is deeply rooted in their feelings, consciousness, I–we image and I–we ideal (1996: 157). But most of the populations of these nation states have little knowledge of inter-state relations and little means of attaining it because of the restricted access to such knowledge made available to public scrutiny. Therefore, people tend to develop a deeply felt belief in their own state as having the highest possible value, and of course social elites manipulate national symbols to mobilize the mass of the population in order to defend the nation if they perceive its integrity to be under threat. The tensions between states can and do generate this orientation within them with frequent ease.

The self-perception or we-image of formerly powerful nations may often be over-exaggerated (1994b: xliii–xliv), a process which is generated by a change in the power balance between nations. Changes in national we-images and patterning of emotions and strategies can take some time, but the 'reality shock' comes eventually and may be traumatic, depending upon the rigidity of the particular we-image involved. During these changes, conflict frequently arises as groups seek to maintain their power position. This applies to nations (national we-images), as it does to classes and smaller groups. In such struggles to maintain power, the issue is often not simply one of maintaining control over 'material' resources, but one resulting from a threat to self-images, of what gives value and meaning to life. In certain situations, those whose monopolies over particular resources are threatened may be defeated not only by the physical and social power of their opponents, but also by the feeling that their own life is no longer worth living. They perceive a threat to their own pride and self-respect. Powerful groups' standards of conduct often function as symbols of their own power and superiority, but the greater the feelings of insecurity and the weaker they become in their decline, Elias suggests, 'the more they develop the sense that they are fighting for their supremacy with their backs against the wall, the more savage for the most part does their behaviour become and the more acute the danger that they will disregard and destroy the civilized standards of conduct on which they pride themselves . . . With their backs against the wall, the champions [of civilization] easily become the greatest destroyers of civilization. They tend easily to become barbarians' (1996: 358–9).[5]

Feelings of insecurity and weakness show similarities in their effects for individuals and nations, but on the national level, the readjustment to a position of lower rank in the international order may take several generations. If the decline of a nation does not go so far as to require facing up to the reality of its changed position, as was the case in Germany after 1918, then profound status insecurities may permeate the social habitus, belief and behaviour tradition of its members (1996: 359 – I return to this in chapters 6 and 7). The more ingrained the social habitus, the greater the resistance to changing patterns of integration and interdependence. Elias refers to this resistance as the 'drag effect' (1991a: 211), and gives as an example the barriers felt and erected by those living within European nation states to the formation of an integrated European configuration of nation states. Because of the natiocentric socialization of children and adults, emotional identification centres on one particular nation and thus the larger identification with a European unit has more of a 'rational' rather than emotional significance (1994a: 254–5n). As another example, he cites the experience of the North American Indians, who were and are forced to form social units within a developing nation-state context. Their pre-state forms of social relations become 'fossilized' – their older ways of life are retained in their social habitus, so that traces of what Elias calls their 'traditional habitus' survive, if only as tourist attractions. At the same time, the forms of social organization which generate this type of pre-state social habitus, the organization into relations characterized by warriors and hunters, have disappeared as the tribes become unequally interdependent within the United States of America. These transformations are obviously not devoid of conflicts, and these conflicts are not considered by Elias as accidental events: they are a function of a transition from one integration level to another, in this case, from the tribal to the nation-state level (1991a: 213).

As we shall see, all of these ideas on social habitus and national identity underlie Elias's explanation of the mass murder perpetrated by the Nazis which will be discussed in chapter 7. Such ideas are potential tools with which to explain the sociogenesis of violence at both the intra- and inter-state level. The notion of established-outsider relations, to which I shall turn next, is also a conceptual tool of this type in that it serves to illuminate both 'micro' and 'macro' social processes which may engender violent conflict.

Established-outsider relations

The dynamics of established-outsider relations is elaborated upon by Elias and Scotson in *The Established and the Outsiders* (1994).[6] The utility of this concept in explaining the sociogenesis of violence is not dealt with explicitly by Elias in his English publications, although it is implicit throughout his work.[7] It provides a model for social tensions as power differentials between groups which may or may not generate violent conflict: it is developed explicitly as a means of illuminating social processes in which people may be helplessly 'trapped in a conflict situation by specific developments' (1994b: 23). The concept provides insights into the sociogenesis of violence without necessarily *reducing* the explanation of this type of action to the psychological or biological dispositions and attributes of those involved. To this end, Elias focuses on group cohesion and the generation of collective fantasies. As we shall see in chapter 6, these ideas are crucial to Elias's understanding of group cohesion and violence in the German student fraternities earlier this century.

The established-outsider conceptualization avoids reducing the analysis of inter-group tension to class relations, thus allowing for the affective, status-competitive, charismatic (above all group-charismatic) and ideological dimensions of these relations to be incorporated into a synthetic model. It also allows racial, ethnic and gender inequalities to be handled within the same framework. The monopolization of economic resources is not privileged to the exclusion of all others, allowing for the relative autonomy of the struggle for control over other power resources such as the means of violence, the means of orientation and the means of self-restraint (see Elias 1987c: 227–31). The word elite is avoided in order to distance the conceptualization from an implicit identification with established groups. Furthermore, the *established-outsider* phrase is used to conceptualize power differentials at *any* level of social stratification which derive in part from the existence of bonds over time, that is, over a number of generations. The established-outsider formulation allows the power differentials existing between groups to become the focus of attention and in turn enables one to conceptualize how these differentials permeate the habitus of the particular group members concerned.

Established-outsider relations are a universal feature of human societies. Elias gives as examples the black slaves in the American South, the 'Great Unwashed' after the 1830s, or the Burakumin of Japan who are said by the established groups to have a dark birthmark under their arms which marks them as biologically constituting a distinct group fit only for menial, dirty work. Other examples include the relations between blacks and whites, Gentiles and Jews, Protestants and Catholics, women and men or relations between nations.

Characteristic of established-outsider relations is a distorted 'black and white' image which the established have of outsiders. This image corresponds to the 'minority of the worst' (Elias and Scotson 1994: 81). Within the established group's we-image, even those members who are defined as least 'worthy' tend 'to claim for themselves by identification characteristics and values attributed to the whole group and to be found in practice perhaps only as attributes of the "minority of the best"' (1994: 104). In other words they develop a figuration ideal (Van Stolk and Wouters 1987: 484) and tend to identify with the most edifying components of it. This is not simply a matter of individuals' prejudice, but a group stigmatization. When these power differentials are relatively even, the outsiders begin to retaliate and counter-stigmatize. Group charisma and group disgrace play their part here. They act as emotional barriers to non-occupational contact with outsiders, even when the power balance between the groups in question is more even. These images are crucial to the mechanics of group stigmatization. Once the process of reciprocal distortion of group images and identities proceeds, the tensions engendered by it may become exacerbated and even result in violence. This potential is directly related to the level of security felt by the group members concerned:

> The distorting effect which the dynamics of competition within closely-knit groups have on group beliefs in general and on gossip

> items in particular is an aberration veering towards the most favour-
> able, most flattering belief about one's own group and towards the
> most unfavourable, most unflattering belief about non-submissive
> outsiders with a tendency towards increasing rigidity in both cases
> ... [T]he more secure the members of a group feel in their superiority
> and their pride, the less great is the distortion, the gap between image
> and reality likely to be, and the more threatened and insecure they
> feel, the more likely is it that internal pressure, and as part of it
> internal competition, will drive common beliefs towards extremes of
> illusion and doctrinaire rigidity. (Elias and Scotson 1994: 95)

Stigmatization of groups in established-outsider relations
involves collective fantasies. A relatively unequal balance of
power between groups will tend to produce a decrease in the
reality content of the images groups have of each other: their we-
and they-images will each tend to contain a relatively high
degree of fantasy content. However, this would also seem to be
the case with groups who display a relatively equal balance of
power between them, as the example of the Primal Contest
discussed earlier in this chapter demonstrates.[8] Group images
and identities are perpetuated by what Elias and Scotson call
'sociological inheritance': the intergenerational transmission of
social codes and attitudes (1994: 120).

While Elias, like Freud, seeks to conceptualize the fantasy
element of human life, he makes a critical departure from the
Freudian concentration on the I-level of the individual which
neglects the formulation of concepts which might refer to other
levels of the personality: Freud tends to consider these as an
aspect of 'reality' which he implicitly perceived as unstructured,
the dynamics of which have no influence on the 'inner' dynamics of individuals (Elias 1994b: xlii–xliii). For Elias, people's we-
images and we-ideals are just as much a part of their self-images
and ideals as that aspect of themselves which individual people
regard as unique and to which they refer as 'I'. These aspects of
group identity are inextricably interwoven with their personal
identity, just as much as those elements which demarcate them
from other members of their own we-group. While Freud tends
to look at pathology in order to discover normality, Elias suggests that, *mutatis mutandis*, this approach can be applied in the
study of we-images and we-ideals, which are always a mixture
of emotionally laden fantasies and realistic ideas. Imagination
becomes accentuated when the differentiation between fantasy
and reality is increased.

Mechanisms of group coherence including the maintenance of internal ranking in power and status competition through the pressure of gossip are also common features of established-outsider relations. This powerful means of social control serves to hurt and stigmatize members of the established just as effectively as the outsiders. Recognition through internal group opinion presupposes compliance to group norms and the penalty for deviation from them entails a lowering in status and power within the group. The self-image and self-attention of the group charismatic established are bound up with what other members of their own group think. This becomes active in many layers of their own conscience. But to say the individual is autonomous from group opinion is just as misleading as saying that he or she may follow it like a robot (Elias 1994b: xl–xli).

The dynamics of group charisma and group disgrace are particularly important in established-outsider relations (Elias and Scotson 1994: 103–5). The drawbacks of having to exhibit a specific pattern of self-restraint as part of an established group are outweighed by the social advantages of being part of a group which possesses greater social charisma and thus entails higher levels of self-respect. The balance between group charisma and group disgrace involves tensions and conflicts which are central to status competition. 'In fact', Elias and Scotson comment, 'as things are, tensions and conflicts form an intrinsic structural element of status hierarchies everywhere' (1994: 41). But the charisma–disgrace dynamic is not simply a boundary-drawing exercise of establishing those who belong and those who do not:

> It also served the function of a weapon which held outsiders at bay, which helped to preserve the purity and integrity of the group. It was a weapon of defence as well as a weapon of attack. It implied that it was a sign of disgrace not to participate in the grace and the specific virtues which the members of the distinguished group claimed for themselves. (Elias and Scotson 1994: 104).

This dynamic permeates the conscience of the individual members of these groups, another typical feature of established-outsider relations: 'established groups usually have an ally in the inner voice of their social inferiors' (Elias 1994b: xxiv). If the power relations between groups are very uneven, then the oppressed measure themselves with the yardstick of their oppressors and experience themselves as of less human worth, as unclean and/or as law-breakers.

The strength of the social fear of contamination felt by members of an established group towards the outsiders does not seem to depend solely upon differences in physical appearance between the groups. Elias therefore sees terms such as 'racial' or 'ethnic' as symptomatic of an ideological avoidance action which focuses on peripheral issues such as skin colour to the exclusion of what is central, that is, power relations within such figurations. But he does not underestimate the role of economic forces in the formation of inequalities between groups. Economic bases of power superiority are, most of the time, indispensable to an understanding of established-outsider relations (Elias 1994b: xxxi), but these are more likely to come to the fore when power balances are relatively uneven. The more even the power ratios between the groups, the more prominent other non-economic aspects of tensions and conflicts become. Thus, in general, steep power differentials tend to result in quiescent differences; relatively even differentials may result in differences coming out into the open. In these relations, groups are often locked in a helpless double-bind situation and sometimes the established will have no use at all for the outsiders, and in extreme cases they may attempt to exterminate them.

Established-outsider relations go hand in hand with broader social processes of increasing or decreasing functional differentiation and integration. They are 'the normal concomitants of a process in the course of which two formerly independent groups become interdependent' (Elias and Scotson 1994: 17). When the balance of power shifts (however small it may be) in favour of outsider groups and inequalities are increasingly challenged – as has been the case in the twentieth century with workers, women, homosexuals, ethnic minorities, colonial peoples and even children – then feelings of inferiority held by members of the outsider groups will tend to diminish or weaken. This is partly due to the social process of functional democratization in which lengthening and increasing differentiation of interdependency chains lead to a decrease in power differentials within and among groups, as people with specialized functions increase their mutual interdependence and expected self-restraint (cf. Mennell 1992: 124; and Wouters 1990b: 72). Cohesive organization further enhances collective action and thus the ability to increase the power ratio of the group. The differentiation of nodal social power centres results in increasing reciprocal group inter-dependency which in turn brings about new problems and pro-cesses of integration at a new level. These latter processes result from the co-ordination problems posed by the increase in differ-entiation, not least the problem of how to control the controllers (Elias 1978a: 145). New concentrations of power are created in the wider organization of the state and economy. The power that accrues to the state is utilized by complex bureaucracies, the elected parts of which are subject to various controls from below by virtue of that fact. One could say that forms of functional democratization take place within the state apparatus. The overall democratization process is spurred on by increasing global interdependencies on the level of orientation (particu-larly the mass media and forms of electronic communication) and transportation, which allow greater potential for formerly outsider groups (including nations) to influence the decisions of the more established social organizations.

In summary, several distinctive aspects of established-outsider relations can be highlighted (cf. Mennell 1992: 138; and Baumgart and Eichener 1991: 141–42). Within such processes, two or more groups become interdependent and their relations are characterized by an uneven balance of power. The estab-lished groups consolidate their power through various means, one of the most important of which is the level of group cohesion in internal group control. This goes together with the cultivation of a collective identity and group charisma, marking off the established from the outsiders in terms of their group norms and collective behaviour. The established, by virtue of their domi-nant power position, are then able to stigmatize the outsiders and exclude them from their monopolized power resources. Their group charisma is based on the minority of the best in their own group, and the group disgrace of the outsiders is based on the minority of the worst within their number. Group stigma normally enters the self-image or consciousness of the outsid-ers, weakening their ability to develop their own power re-sources of cohesion and internal control. The confidence of the established in their own status and coherence prevents non-occupational interaction with members of the outsider groups. This taboo on association is maintained through social controls in the form of gossip and exclusion. When the power ratio between the established and the outsiders shifts in favour of the latter, or when the established lose their monopoly, the former outsiders retaliate with counter-stigmatization, resulting in rebellion, resistance and sometimes emancipation.

Violence in established-outsider relations: the Maycomb model

Elias considers violent established-outsider relations in only one untranslated publication (1990: 291–314). He focuses on a community in the American South through Harper Lee's novel, *To Kill a Mocking Bird* (1974). The book is set in Maycomb, Alabama, during the time when the Ku Klux Klan was at its height and open hatred of black people was even more firmly institutionalized than at present.

The social figuration includes a poor white class who, along with wealthier white Americans, form the established group in relation to black Americans, the outsiders. In Maycomb, there is a large established group and a smaller outsider group who are relative newcomers, and the established have a long cohesive tradition behind them. The penniless whites count over the blacks in the eyes of the wealthier white establishment: no poor whites have such a low status that they cannot mobilize the sympathies of the rest of the white establishment. Thus wealth is a significant factor in social ordering and group-value ascription.

The book's narrative tells of a family man, a white lawyer named Atticus Finch, whose roots in the area stretch back several generations. Finch is called upon to defend a young black man, Tom Robinson, accused of raping a white woman. He is convinced of the young man's innocence and he makes his views known. For this he is branded a 'Nigger Lover', as he has transgressed the boundary of white solidarity. In Maycomb, if a black man sleeps with a white woman, as the defendant is accused of doing, then he fears for his life. At the trial, the jury takes three hours to find this black man guilty and sentence him to death. The majority of whites do not have the scruples of Atticus Finch. They see the facts which suggest that Robinson is innocent, but in their hearts, they believe he is guilty. Thus, the facts are relatively inconsequential. To sleep with a white woman (whether she was raped or not is irrelevant) is the privilege of other white men which has been infringed by a black man.

In the Southern USA, blacks have been exposed to organized violence from whites throughout their history in the country. The development of the United States was, and to a large extent still is, different in significant respects from that of most European states where the development of the monopoly of violence was highly centralized relatively early on. In contrast, many state institutions in the USA emerged through the struggles of a majority of whites in the absence of clear institutional frameworks. The American people in part developed such frameworks themselves.

In the situation studied by Elias and Scotson the state's monopoly of violence was firmly established and relatively effective, whereas in Maycomb people are relatively more familiar with violence. All the members of the established (whites) have access to firearms, while blacks are largely denied access to these weapons, except in times of war. Physical struggles are customarily controlled by whites. Whites do not consider blacks to be of the same value as human beings: there is a relatively low level of mutual identification between the two groups. The twin monopoly of violence and access to white women is part of white pride. Any weakening of this decreases the family or individual position in the ranking of their own group. In the Robinson case, the broken pride of the whites cannot recover until the taboo-breaker dies, while Atticus Finch, one of the few who stands up for his innocence, represents a threat to the self-respect of the white majority. Thus, the killing of a black man suspected of a sexual crime against a white woman is closely bound up with the decrease in value experienced by a white community if it is unable to avenge the crime, whether real or imaginary, of which the black man is accused (1990: 309). In this way, social pride can be, but is not always, connected with the status or function of a person in society, rather than a static quality in an individual. Social pride is fragile, and this fragility is at least one of the factors which accounts for the universal discrimination of one group by another (1990: 311). The value attributed by humans to their own group(s) is basic to human existence and is central to their search for lineage or national heritage in order to demonstrate a 'higher' rank and to confirm their collectively higher value within group hierarchies.

A fundamental dynamic of potentially violent established-outsider relations here comes to the fore: the fact that most human groups live in fear of the others. Where groups with deeply rooted belief systems become interdependent, one usually finds that one group blames the other for the fear they experience. In such constellations, the 'beginningless' (*anfangslos*) character of fear arousal is quickly forgotten (1990: 310), but in reality there are seldom beginnings to such conflicts, an example being revolutions. To talk of a beginning in such cases is deceptive and reduces processes to static entities.

It is important to bear in mind that Elias's comments summarized here are based on a work of fiction, albeit the semi-autobiographical account of Harper Lee. However, in drawing his evidence from a novel for his example of violence in established-outsider relations, Elias detracts from the force of his argument. It is unclear to what extent this example resembles reality. While he does point to the advantages and disadvantages of using a novel as sociological evidence, he seems to assume it merely reflects reality, and reflects it accurately (1990: 295n). He does not maintain the critical distance from his evidence that one might expect in view of his conscious reflections on the matter: Elias even argues that empirical case studies such as the one he carried out with John Scotson have for sociologists an importance comparable to the experiment for the physicist (1990: 293). In fact, Elias's use of Lee's novel does nothing other than serve as an example of what the generation of violence in established-outsider relations might look like. In effect, it does not provide evidence for Elias's argument at all, but it does serve to clarify Elias's model of such group relations. What does stand out with greater clarity, however, is the idea that relations between groups characterized by mutual fear and suspicion are highly significant for the way in which Elias explains inter-group relations such as those in Maycomb, as well as those at higher levels of integration, such as relations between states,[9] or between state authorities and groups defined as outsiders within national boundaries. All these themes will surface once again in the following chapters in relation to the way Elias deals with historical examples of violence and its controls in England and Germany.

Integration conflicts and the price of violence

The established-outsider model is broad in scope. It can serve as a conceptual tool with which to shed light on the developments of social integration and differentiation at the level of humanity as a whole.[10] The concept of the monopoly of violence is at present reality-congruent only in relation to the intra-state or nation-state level, but of course a higher level of internal pacification in a society does not presuppose that inter-state relations will take the same form. At the global level, Cas Wouters has used the phrase 'competition and intertwining mechanism' as a replacement for the concept of the monopoly mechanism, because at the moment it is difficult to talk of a monopoly formation at all at this level (Wouters 1990b: 75).[11] On the inter-state level, an effective monopoly of the means of violence does not exist, although the United Nations is a rudimentary example of the potential for this development (cf. Elias 1987a: 73–111).

For Elias, in line with his conceptualizations of inter-group dynamics covered above, relations between states are largely characterized by mutual fear and suspicion, while he also describes them as 'double-bind processes' (cf. 1987a: 48, 49ff, 73, 85–6, 96–7, 107, 108, 109, 114). He sees humanity as a figuration of tensions between intra- and inter-state monopolies of violence (or lack of them). Characteristic of relations between states is the way in which they are relatively willing to use physical force in order to achieve their goals and in this respect they are similar to societies at a lower level of integration. However, with increasing global interdependency networks, more and more states, particularly the richer (established) countries, are increasingly forced to take into account the actions of others (the outsiders). This generates an intrinsic competitive pressure within the configuration of states which may spawn conflicts (1987a: 83).

With the decline of colonialism and the spread and tightening of global interdependencies, the 'price of violence' (Wouters 1990b: 72) perpetrated by states against each other increases in direct relation to the growing importance of money in the settlement of international disputes. This is part of a largely unintended social process whereby,

> the rich [countries] are now somewhat less likely simply to settle
> conflicts between themselves and the poor ones by violent means,
> i.e. by dispatching armies or gunboats. They have been compelled to
> show more respect to the people of new states than they had to show
> in the days of colonialism. (Wouters 1990b: 72)

If the price of violence becomes too high, then alliances and
compromises of a non-violent kind will have to be sought.
Confederations of sovereign states and the decline of colonialism will therefore be a relatively more likely possibility. Indeed,
this has proved to be the case in the recent developments within
the area formerly known as the USSR, with all its attendant
instabilities. During the cold war when the USSR was one major
superpower facing another, the USA, Mutually Assured Self-
Destruction (MAD) brought about by the awareness of the
capabilities of nuclear arsenals, generated the formation of
Mutually Expected Self-Restraint (MES) (Van Benthem van den
Bergh 1990; Wouters 1987: 422) in the use of military power, thus
favouring the development of economic activity. In this respect,
the civilizing process has become a global process among humanity as some nations begin to exercise greater restraint on the
use of inter-state violence. That is not to say, of course, that it is
at present anything more than partial and heterogeneous, or
that it will continue. With the breakdown of the Soviet form of
communism – part of an integration process from a global
perspective – the stability of MES is now uncertain. There are,
once again, many more players in the game of world politics. A
process of social disintegration within the new global order has
generated regionalism and claims for nationalistic self-
determination on behalf of many groups previously subsumed
as outsiders under centralized state establishments. On the one
hand, I would suggest that in this more unstable figuration the
competitive dynamic is more likely to result in small-scale wars
and border conflicts. A mess is more likely than MES. This
situation also increases the possibility of outsiders utilizing
parts of the nuclear arsenals previously monopolized by the
established central authorities. On the other hand, this social
process of disintegration at the political level goes together with
ever-increasing processes of interdependence at the levels of
identification, communication and economic developments.
Increasingly, paying the price which the use of violence entails
would then prove to be tragically high.

Elias's work clearly emphasizes the importance of intra- and inter-state tensions which are likely to generate conflicts (cf. Elias 1985b: 36ff), but these conflicts generated within processes of increasing interdependence are not discussed by Elias in great detail. Some potential lines of thinking implied by his approach lead to a broader consideration of the nature of inter-group violence in terms of 'integration conflicts',[12] a theme I shall return to in more detail at the end of chapter 7 when I consider the mass murder perpetrated by the Nazis in 1940s Germany.

On the intra-state level, as we have seen above, democratization processes have occurred in many societies throughout the globe, generating processes of partial integration of the masses in the running of state affairs. During these processes, conflicts may arise when former outsider groups striving for emancipation – the masses, including the bourgeoisie – seek representation within or control over the key monopolies of state power held by the established ruling authorities. On the inter-state level, up until the Second World War, the survival units of humanity had become more and more interdependent and the process had gained a momentum to which we now refer as Europeanization or globalization. Twentieth-century European societies have witnessed a general expansion in the scope of mutual identification between various different peoples (cf. Wouters 1989, 1990b; De Swaan 1995: 25–39; Mennell 1995b: 175–97), in conjunction with increasing state interdependence and the accompanying tensions this generates. At the same time, these long-term processes have been characterized by relatively short-term integration conflicts which may involve violence between the outsider states and the more established states as the former grow in relative power. These changes can also involve intra-state tensions resulting in whole groups being defined as outsiders and excluded from the state apparatus in the name of the *national* we-ideals which gain in significance and strength with the advancing process of inter-state interdependence. And in the context of a collapse of a monopoly of violence over a specific territory, we-identities may contract in scope and become less inclusive in processes of decivilization.

Criteria of civilizing and decivilizing processes

Elias explicitly states certain interrelated criteria specifically for determining 'directions' of civilizing processes in a few places (see 1994a: 443–524; 1992d: 384–6). The first three mentioned here, I would suggest, are the most important or main criteria: a shift in the balance between constraints by others and self-restraint involving the taming, differentiation and increasing complexity of external controls; the development of a social standard of behaviour and feeling which generates the emergence of a more even, all-round, stable and differentiated self-restraint; an increase in the scope of mutual identification between people. Others include increasing differentiation between drives and drive-controls; a spread in the pressure for foresight; psychologization and rationalization; an advance in the thresholds of shame and repugnance; contractions of behavioural and emotional contrasts and expansions in alternatives; and changes in orientation from more involved to more detached perspectives (cf. Mennell 1990a; Wouters 1990a: 35ff, Flap and Kuiper 1981/2: 277). These features are in turn related to the extent to which human beings are dependent upon and control non-human natural processes. These changes in the direction of civilizing processes can be represented with the terms 'progressions' or regressions' in the descriptive sense mentioned in chapter 3.[13]

In several places Elias makes isolated comments which reveal an awareness of the potential results of an increase in social fears and levels of violence. He suggests, for example, that the 'armor of civilized conduct would crumble very rapidly' if former levels of social fears and insecurities re-emerged (1994a: 253n); in such situations the human capacity for 'rational' action 'would crumble or collapse' (1994a: 519), and also that established authority would become increasingly challenged as groups tested through physical struggles the correspondence between actual social power relations and those symbolized in the form of laws (1994a: 531n). These comments undoubtedly reflect Elias's experiences during the First World War and his observations regarding developments preceding the Second World War (cf. Mennell 1992: 14–19). In the preface to *The Civilizing Process* he remarks that the issues raised in the book owe less to a scholarly tradition than to the 'experiences of the crisis and transformation of Western civilization' (1994a: xvi). Much later in his life, he writes in *The Germans* that he first encountered what he calls the Nazi 'barbarization spurt' as a personal problem under his own eyes in the 1930s, which led him to wonder how standards of civilized behaviour could break down. Believing that little knowledge existed about the socio- and psychogenesis of such civilized controls, he set out to investigate this in his two-volume book (1996: 444–5).[14]

But Elias did not develop an explicit theory of decivilizing processes,[15] although his discussion of 'feudalization' in the second volume of *The Civilizing Process* could be seen as an implicit model of the likely conditions under which a decivilizing process might occur (1994a: 273–314).[16] He refers in *The Germans* to the Nazi mass murder of the Jews as a 'decivilizing *spurt*' (1996: 1, 15). The term 'spurt' seems to be used by Elias rather loosely to refer to a phase in which the *pace* of social processes increases, while he uses the term *decivilizing* to refer to civilizing processes which go into 'reverse' (1986a: 46; 1992d: 386). Commenting on the general course of the civilizing process, Elias suggests in an interview for *Der Spiegel* in 1988: 'It has two directions. Forwards and backwards. Civilizing processes go along with decivilizing processes. The question is to what extent one of the two directions is dominant' (1988d: 183). So the relationship between civilizing and decivilizing processes is here clearly conceived in terms of a *balance* between dominant and less dominant processes.

As a provisional model, I would like to focus on three main criteria of decivilization which are logically implied by Elias's criteria of civilizing processes: one would be a shift in the balance between constraints by others and self-restraint in favour of constraints by others; another would be the development of a social standard of behaviour and feeling which generates the emergence of a less even, all-round, stable and differentiated pattern of self-restraint; and, third, we would expect a contraction in the scope of mutual identification between constituent groups and individuals. These three main features would be likely to occur in societies in which there was a decrease in the (state) control of the monopoly of violence, a fragmentation of social ties and a shortening of chains of commercial, emotional and cognitive interdependence. It is also likely that such societies would be characterized by: a rise in the levels of fear, insecurity, danger and incalculability; the re-emergence of violence into the public sphere; growing inequality or heightening of tensions in the balance of power between constituent groups; a decrease in the distance between the standards of adults and children; a freer expression of aggressiveness and an increase in cruelty; an increase in impulsiveness; an increase in involved forms of thinking with their concomitantly high fantasy content and a decrease in detached forms of thought with an accompanying decrease in the 'reality-congruence' of concepts (cf. Dunning and Sheard 1979: 288–9; Dunning et al. 1988: 242–5; Mennell 1990a: 206).[17]

These part-processes may be reciprocally augmenting and fear-inducing: 'double-bind processes' (Elias 1987a: 42–118). However, social processes which may involve decivilizing would not necessarily replicate in 'reverse' processes which are likely to generate civilizing. One reason for this is the relatively large human capacity for social learning which modifies social relations. It is unlikely that people simply forget, although this is of course possible. But they do not simply reverse and go backwards, as it were, down the path along which they have already travelled. It is extremely unlikely that the composite relations of the networks of interdependencies go into 'reverse' to the same degree, resulting in a different composition of the new configuration.

In terms of the three main criteria of decivilizing processes – shifts in the balance of social constraints and self-restraint, changes in the social standards of feeling and behaviour and changes in the scope of mutual identification – such processes would involve 'reversals' of each of these three interrelated criteria in such a way that if a 'reversal' occurred within one of them, a 'reversal' would also be triggered, sooner or later, among the others, together forming a *dominant* overall process. The term 'reversal' thus refers to a collapse or gradual erosion of specific social standards which were previously dominant within particular individuals and among particular groups or societies. A 'reversal' in these interrelated criteria could occur amongst a smaller or larger group; and it may occur within these main criteria *in conjunction* with two other part-processes: a breakdown in the monopoly of violence and a disintegration of interdependency chains, all together representing a societal decivilizing process. During decivilizing processes, these part-processes I have mentioned – that is, the three main criteria, the de-monopolization and disintegration processes – would be likely to 'trigger' each other in what might be called a 'mutually reinforcing spiral'.

Several interrelated dimensions of decivilizing processes, or in other words, the perspectives from which it is possible to view them, can also be specified. First, one can speak of the individual dimension of decivilizing processes, in which a person experiences an erosion of his or her standards of behaviour and emotion management. Second, there is the group dimension, in which significant numbers of members experience an erosion of their dominant social and individual standards of behaviour and emotion management. Third, there is the intra-state dimension, in which the same occurs among significant numbers or even most members of a state-society. Fourth, we could speak of decivilizing in the inter-state dimension, in which this occurs simultaneously within neighbouring states. Finally, there is the dimension of humanity, in which the same might occur among significant numbers or even most of the world's population. All of these dimensions of decivilizing processes – or the perspectives from which they may be seen – can be understood within the time-span of one generation (roughly thirty years) or over several.

Decivilizing in smaller or larger groups may be immanent and simultaneous components of particular phases in civilizing processes. In some situations, less direct, long-distance ties via the state become increasingly more important at the expense of those more direct face-to-face contacts, and this may result in solidarity and controls by others among those who were formally highly dependent upon each other diminishing (cf. Van Stolk and Wouters 1983; Bogner 1992b: 7; Schröter 1990: 72–85; Wilterdink 1993). Under specific conditions, this may result in decivilizing, and this is evident, for example, in some inner-city areas and in the integration processes of tribal societies in nation states. The reported increases in the incidence of inter-personal violence in the latter half of the twentieth century, particularly within large urban conurbations, can be described as group decivilizing processes which may occur in the context of a longer-term process of civilization, or indeed, they may even be precursors of a decivilizing process within the societal and inter-societal dimensions (cf. Pearson 1983; Mennell 1990a: 213–14; Dunning et al. 1987, 1988; Murphy et al. 1990).[18]

The specification of state societal and inter-state societal decivilizing processes, in contrast to those within the smaller or larger group dimension, refers to more encompassing social processes which gain a greater permanence due to the fragmentation of structural ties. In such cases the three main criteria of a decivilizing process would be likely to occur within a society or group of societies in which there is a disintegration of interdependency chains and the breakdown of the state monopolies of violence and taxation. The scope of societal decivilizing processes can contract to the smaller- or larger-group level, or the reverse may occur.

These theoretical comments on decivilizing processes require empirical corroboration through the consideration of particular examples. I have clarified some of the conceptual issues surrounding their specification and various dimensions, and I have also described the probable conditions under which they would be likely to occur, but I have not dealt with the problems of historical detail and explanation, such as the transition between group decivilizing processes and those occurring in more encompassing dimensions of social relations, or between civilizing and decivilizing processes more generally. I shall return to some of these issues when considering Elias's treatment of German history and the Holocaust in chapters 6 and 7.

So far, the discussion has focused on Elias's more theoretical constructions: his theory of civilizing processes, the concepts of violence and civilization, his formulation of 'figurational' process models of social and psychical dynamics and the criteria of civilizing and decivilizing processes. We have seen how these process models shed light on the sociogenesis of and control over violence through highlighting the role of group fantasies and identifications and their place within intra- and inter-state dynamics; how the established-outsider dynamic helps to explain the treatment of outsider populations; the significance of fear in inter-group relations which may generate violence; and the importance of the habitus concept in understanding shifts in civilizing and decivilizing processes. But how do these process models shed light on actual examples of social processes which may stimulate or constrain the perpetration of violence – processes which may tend in a civilizing or decivilizing direction?

The subsequent chapters consider violence and civilization in the work of Elias with a different emphasis. They will present examples he uses from England and particularly Germany, and show how these models can contribute to understanding specific historical instances of the generation and control of human violence.

CHAPTER FIVE

Social Habitus and Civilizing Processes in England

Although rarely seen as a comparative contribution to European history, *The Civilizing Process* is nevertheless a rich source of such historical data. While the book focuses principally on the development of France as an example of monopolization and state-formation processes, there are many comparisons with both England and Germany. Indeed, when Elias mentions either of these two countries, he usually gives an example from the other for comparison. The assumptions of his process models are evident in his discussion of we-identity, public opinion and sport in England, revealing a sensitivity to the formation of social habitus in England compared with Germany. His historical approach is not simply a 'sociology of the past': he seeks to reveal long-term structured processes of development. This chapter begins with Elias's observations on English state formation and social habitus, before moving on to discuss public opinion and national identity in relation to violence. Finally, sport is also discussed, focusing on Elias's comments on foxhunting as a means to demonstrate the relationship between social habitus and controls over violence. We shall also see how the three main criteria of civilizing processes outlined in the previous chapter are relevant to an understanding of the development of the English social habitus.

State formation and pacification

According to Elias, the roots of the English social habitus stretch back to the time of the Norman invasion and the establishment of the island territory as a satellite of Norman hegemony. William, Duke of Normandy, redistributed areas of England to the warriors who accompanied him in a fashion designed to avoid centrifugal tendencies as well as the formation of large territorial units which might pose a threat to his authority. This distribution of land also favoured the development of contacts and common interests among the landed class throughout England *vis-à-vis* the king. The small size of the territory was highly important in facilitating the relatively continuous centralization of managerial and administrative functions (1994a: 358). Inter-group struggles were simpler than those on the Continent which sometimes involved many contestants. At the end of the elimination contest between various families in France and England, which eventually fixed the territorial boundaries of the English crown, two significant processes in the history of England became apparent.

First, England was established as a separate entity from the Continent. The English kings were no longer contenders in the struggle for the French crown. The conquest of Wales in the thirteenth century, parts of Ireland between the twelfth and sixteenth centuries and the unity with Scotland in 1603, marked the peculiarity of the subsequent extra-continental development of British society. National boundaries became fixed at a relatively early stage compared with France or Germany, assisting in the process of internal pacification within the British Isles.

Second, the Plantagenet King John's defeat by Philip Augustus in Normandy at the Battle of Bouvines resulted in a loss of prestige, financial difficulty and therefore an internal weakening of his grasp of power at home. Within this context, the agitation and demands of the barons and clergy brought about the Magna Charta, limiting royal power. The gains of the nobility were further extended under John's son, Henry III, through the establishment of a regular parliamentary system and a monopoly of taxation, differing from the regional estates with a Diet, as in Germany. Thus, the power of the nobility was institutionalized relatively early on and the general trend for the institutions of England was to move from smaller to larger. Overall, we can discern (a) the setting of firm territorial boundaries, allowing for internal pacification and (b) a well-established role for the nobility and gentry in state government, both of which proved highly significant for the subsequent development of the island realm.

Contacts and allegiances between the urban bourgeoisie and the landed nobility developed early on, and in comparison to Germany this encouraged a relatively gradual and continuous merging of upper- and middle-class codes of behaviour, particularly moral codes (1994a: 506). The social barriers between sections of the English upper classes became less rigid and more fragmentary (1983: 68; cf. Stone's counter-thesis 1986). A relatively successful alliance between the landowning nobility and the gentry, and the merchants' and traders' urban interests, further restricted royal power. Tensions between the competing groups were not favourable to the establishment of a 'royal mechanism', not even after the Restoration in 1660. This meant that in England the court society did not become nearly as important as it did in the development of France, since the king and his attendant court did not form the main fulcrum of social power. Instead, 'Good Society' was constructed around 'the Season' (see Davidoff 1973), which had become an institution by the eighteenth century. This involved 'good' families of the nobility and sections of the wealthier bourgeoisie leaving their country houses when Parliament sat, to visit London where they flaunted their social power; a practice which established close links between country life and court life, unlike in France. In doing so, English 'Good Society' served the function of unifying the values and behaviour-codes of the upper classes (1983: 97). 'Good Society' comprised several model-setting centres, among them the court and Parliament, which formed a central politically integrating institution for the upper classes. The right to free assembly for men in the form of 'clubs' was also an important aspect of this process.

In comparison with Germany, the army and a centralized police force were for a relatively long time less important in the moulding of the population, that is, in the enforcement of social control.[1] By contrast, the Prussian/German state, led by its privileged nobility, accorded the military a high status. The army was therefore significant in the formation of a social personality structure which became habituated from early childhood to a strict order of superiority and inferiority. However, the fact that England was relatively isolated as a land mass was also crucial for the development of the English social habitus, since the upper classes placed greater military reliance on the navy (see Elias 1950: 291–309) rather than the army. A dominant code developed in England whereby people became 'integrated in relations of "team-work" based on a high degree of individual self-control and self-attunement to others' (1994a: 512).

The role of the modern Parliament is singled out by Elias as particularly important for the understanding of the development of English society. Parliament emerged as a means by which powerful social groups decided in a non-violent fashion which of them was to have access to the key monopolies of state control through reasoned arguments and persuasion, in accordance with rules accepted by both parties. Elias describes the period of the 'English Revolution' in terms of a 'cycle of violence' – a double-bind process with relatively high violence potential as described in chapter 4 – which afterwards trapped the upper classes on the one hand and the middle- and lower-class Puritans on the other in a position of mutual fear and distrust (1986a: 26).[2] In the late seventeenth century, compromises began to appear between the Puritans and the Jacobite followers of the Stuart quest for absolutist Catholic power. Between them were the landed gentry who were also an intermediary and overlapping group between the urban craftsmen, traders and merchants and the landed aristocracy. The gentry, comprising Whigs and Tories, came to figure prominently in the House of Commons. Accordingly, landed interests were additionally represented in the Commons by a group who did not belong to the peerage – although they often maintained very close family or patronage ties with the nobility – in contrast to many continental countries where landed interests were usually represented solely in the state assembly of nobles, while those of urban groups were represented in the Commons assembly. The relatively weak power position of the English monarchs in comparison to those on the Continent enabled the gentry to assist in the breakup of the peasantry, curb royal powers through increasingly subjecting kings to the control of Parliament, subdue the Puritans and maintain some control over capital and urban corporations (1986a: 30).

The two-tier parliamentary system developed in the eighteenth century in conjunction with the ongoing pacification of the English upper classes. Although internally divided, the gentry, aristocracy and higher sections of the bourgeoisie shared a common code of 'gentlemanly' conduct. The influence of this code helped to dampen down the cycle of violence and bring together conflicting segments of the community. Both Whigs and Tories came to see themselves as representatives of political philosophies or principles, for which they would wage a war of words in competition for governmental office within the context of this gentlemanly code of conduct. Elias conceptualizes this change, with an apology for the neologism (1986a: 34), as 'parliamentarization'. In this process Elias observes some defusing of the distrust and fears which the Whigs and Tories had of each other. Both sides still harboured suspicions, but the general tone of their relations moved in the direction of consensus of argumentation and non-violent forms of conflict (which were not immune to bribery and extortion).

This overall process of parliamentarization involved a 'civilizing spurt' – a period in which the pace of the civilizing process increases – which in this case incorporated the pacification of the upper classes as well as large segments of English society. This civilizing spurt occurred in conjunction with growing commercialization; pacification connected with the expansion or increasing effectiveness of the monopoly of the means of violence by representatives of a country's central ruling authority, the exclusion of the use of violence from inter-group struggles for control of the main institutions of the central ruling authority (parliamentarization). This generated a corresponding conscience formation, which corresponds with the three main criteria of civilizing processes mentioned in the previous chapter: a shift in the balance between constraints by others and self-restraint can be seen through a relative strengthening in the pervasiveness of social taboos over the exercise of violence and the greater frequency and vehemence of guilt feelings associated with the exercise of violence against people and animals with whom a greater mutual identity was felt.[3]

While in France the central civilizing agency was the court, in England, a civilizing spurt occurred in a more fragmentary and gradual fashion in several nodal communities, the most important of them being Parliament. Both social relations forming particular patterns or institutions and the corresponding changes in personality structures of the upper classes prevented attempts to establish absolutism. This unplanned development encouraged the defusion of the cycle of violence and the learning of non-violent forms of conflict resolution in accordance with mutually agreed rules (1986a: 37). The landed upper classes had at least increased their power potential in relation to the king and court and their superiority over the urban middle classes. The king and his ministers increasingly had to take into account the actions of the nobility and gentry: compromise therefore became essential. Within this parliamentary regime it was *necessary* for factional interests to come out into the open, but they did so in a controlled, relatively non-violent fashion.[4] Thus, the nature of this pacification process in the upper classes of English society during the eighteenth century was unique. More specifically, it was an example of a *self*-pacification process which entailed a type of restraint being imposed by a self-ruling oligarchy upon itself and not by a prince and courtly entourage.

National identity and social habitus

In the eighteenth century, the English royal court was dominated by aristocratic codes and there was very little chance of middle-class morality permeating it. But the rise of the middle classes to a pre-eminent position as state representatives in the nineteenth century generated a strong emphasis on humanistic and moralistic concerns in international relations. This influence of moral imperatives formed part of a broader overall transformation of society through the nineteenth and twentieth centuries which included processes of democratization, moralization and the spread of national feelings, consciousness and ideals. With these processes, increasing numbers of the English population, including the working classes, became more aware that they were part of a broader sovereign collective and this became expressed in the formation of their own we-image. Earlier monarchs became symbols of a national continuity.

The English national habitus reflected the gradual resolution of conflicts between the upper and middle classes through a blend of manners and morals (Elias 1994a: 506). A situation arose in England which was, in comparison to the continental countries, highly conducive to civilizing processes, particularly in terms of the three main criteria mentioned in chapter 4: the transformation of constraints by others into more all-round, even and stable self-restraint, together with an expansion in the scope of mutual identification. This tendency was further compounded by the position of England in its relations with other states. The fact that the noble and bourgeois classes stood at the centre of a far-flung colonial empire enhanced the maintenance of a common foresight and a shared pattern of firmly differentiated self-restraint (1994a: 512). These ideas echo the way in which Elias's ideas on social habitus and national-identity formation discussed in chapter 4 apply to England. The first spurt towards the moralization of state images and a 'nationalization' of morality came with the establishment of Cromwell's Commonwealth. Colonial expansion marked the growing importance of England as a sea power and her ability to acquire or rule over other territories. The middle-class intelligentsia could justify their colonial conquests as 'civilizing missions' which they regarded as more or less successful depending upon the degree to which the standards of the conquered society could conform to their own ideal of 'civilization'. Thus, 'what appeared in the eyes of the people brought up in the tradition of middle-class morality to be hypocrisy, deceit and violence was, in fact, a normal distinguishing characteristic of a dynastic and aristocratic warrior tradition' (1996: 458n). Nobles and princes together employed these means as an unavoidable and self-evident necessity in their relations with other states. But the rising industrial middle classes of England, through the process of relative equalization *vis-à-vis* the aristocratic establishment, fought against aristocratic codes with the weapons of morality as they gained an increasing stake in the ruling of their own country. Elias suggests that England provides more examples of conflicts between moral and honour codes than other European countries because in the latter there was greater pressure to conform to the nationalistic credo. At the same time, however, a more homogeneous national belief system spread and came to be seen as an indispensable tool of state power.

By the nineteenth and twentieth centuries, the 'nationalization' of feelings, consciousness, we-image and we-ideal were firmly established in England, due largely to its relative continuity of state formation in comparison with other European states. In the twentieth century, after the First World War, the middle classes decreased in power relative to the working classes who then became the second most powerful social group. Compared to Germany, the English middle classes were far more successful in their struggles against absolutist rule. The structure of power allowed greater integration of social elites and the development among them, and the mass of the population, of an identity with a *moralistic* national tradition, in contrast to the German emphasis on power politics in international relations.

To summarize, Elias highlights several processes which together interlink in the civilizing process of the English social habitus:

- the small size of the island territory which facilitated a relatively continuous and stable process of state formation and pacification stretching back 900 years;
- a weakening of royal power and a corresponding strengthening of competing groups, particularly the gentry, thus mitigating attempts to establish absolutism and rigid hierarchy accompanied by vehement expressions of superiority and inferiority;
- military confidence being grounded in the navy, rather than the army, resulting in the former having greater significance in the formation of social habitus, placing less emphasis on warrior values and rigidly hierarchical chains of command than in continental countries;
- the formation of modern Parliament, facilitating and expressing a civilizing spurt among the upper classes;
- the relatively high degree of integration and pacification of the upper classes, particularly through institutions such as the Season, allowing shared interests, morals and behavioural codes to develop among them;
- the position of the upper classes in the centre of a large and powerful empire which generated a characteristically individualized, self-reliant and stable social habitus;
- the rise of the middle classes bearing a moral norm-canon which gained national and international significance;
- a strong process of democratization allowing broad sections of the working classes to develop a national identity.

Before considering public opinion in England, the nature of the 'self-pacification' of the upper classes mentioned by Elias deserves some consideration. It is unclear whether this process is a refinement of, or an *ad hoc* justification for, his theory of civilizing processes based on evidence derived from medieval societies. This notion encapsulates a dynamic of a civilizing process which does not seem to fit with his earlier model. The idea of a self-ruling oligarchy pacifying itself seems to go against Elias's notion of 'courtization' in which more peaceful modes of behaviour are generated within the context of greater density of interdependencies and face-to-face contacts in court society (see 1983: 119). Self-pacification, however, suggests that the movement in the sociogenesis of more civilized forms of behaviour- and feeling-codes, in which the balance between constraints by others and self-restraint tips in favour of the latter, can occur within a group of relatively equal social rank. It can be seen in terms of a self-ruling oligarchic establishment avoiding violent in-group competition which could permeate other areas of social life and lead to a more general process of social disintegration or revolution, as in England in 1645–50. Although it remains unclear in Elias's work as to how the dynamics of this self-pacification process operate in contrast to his model of pacification in the context of court societies – to my knowledge he does not mention the concept in any other publication – the implication is that Elias's theory of pacification clearly includes 'courtization' *and* self-pacification. Both can be seen as varying degrees of the same process which occurs differently depending on the context.

Public opinion and national ideals

Two untranslated and little-known essays on public opinion reveal Elias's concept of social habitus in greater detail, primarily in relation to England, although again with some reference to Germany (1960 and 1961).[5] These essays give an insight into the ways in which Elias accounts for English public reactions to two issues involving violence. They further prepare the ground for greater contrasts and similarities to be drawn with Germany in the next two chapters of this book. Before considering Elias's essays on English public opinion, some brief comments on the context in which they were produced are necessary. Both of them were written in the late 1950s, before immigration had decreased the relative social homogeneity of the British Isles, and before the 'permissive sixties' and the Thatcherite reaction both to that era and to the institutions of the welfare state. Within these bounds, much of what Elias says still retains some interest and value. Through the picture he paints of dominant features of English social habitus, it is still possible to discern many aspects of behaviour- and feeling-codes which can be described as 'typically English', whether as a current ideal, or the heritage of previous generations whose influence can be felt and seen today. Also, it must be remembered that Elias's essays on English public opinion were written for a German audience. They therefore stress aspects of public life which are largely 'taken for granted' to a far greater extent than in continental societies, particularly Germany. In continental countries, questions concerned with 'the thought of the masses' were (and still are) more intellectualized. There, a greater differentiation existed between estates, resulting in a restricted forum through which the majority might seek to express ideas with a view to influencing decision-making within the state apparatus. Correspondingly, philosophers and other intellectuals on the Continent gained greater prominence in such discussions. In contrast to the plethora of publications serving as the mouthpiece for political debate in England by the end of the eighteenth century, the forum of German public political debate took place largely within private gatherings among bourgeois circles, within the context of a 'salon' culture. A similar flowering of the public forum of debate did not occur in France until after the Revolution. Thus, when referring to England, Elias often mentions the 'moral' binding character of English public opinion to express this more 'taken for granted' dimension of a critical public forum.[6]

Elias specifies certain characteristics which he thinks are typical of the English, such as their subtlety, indirectness and tolerance. He suggests that these traits are indicative of a strong communal integration and mutual trust, which in turn are symptomatic of the extraordinarily high degree of unification of the English nation. Despite class and regional differences, one finds a 'lasting intimacy, a deep and secure feeling of mutual trust, of togetherness and belonging' (1960: 8). More generally, while the tone and strength of national identification differ from nation to nation, in all countries the sense of national pride is expressed in various ways: through poetry, hymns, holy writings, solemn speeches, parades. While this is of course also the case in England, the English allow themselves to poke fun at their own national identity, but within certain loosely defined limits. This ability is indicative of and is based upon a strong sense of security, a belief the English hold in their own self-worth which is relatively stable and assured. This has found subtle expression in magazines like *Punch* which reflected the intimacy of an English elite who formed the majority of the magazine's readership. The English sense of humour also reveals a particularly strong sense of moral feeling which is often expressed in the English national consciousness. Also characteristic of 'the English way of life' is a strong emphasis on idiosyncratic behaviour, which is justified more in terms of moral feelings than by any necessarily 'reasoned' principle.

Elias gives other examples of the constitution of the English social habitus, such as the institutionalization of rivalry and competitive struggles. While this is also ubiquitous, Elias attempts to elucidate its norms and rituals, and the balance between competition and co-operation in relation to other nations. In England there are 'built-in' restrictions on the severity of public competitions, for example in politics or sport. But whilst friendliness and respect are accorded to others, this does not necessitate blindness to weakness – a sense of reality is maintained regardless. For example, an incompetent general may be liked, but is required to retire on 'health grounds'. Career rivalry, commercial rivalry and political struggles are not characterized by the same bitterness as may be found in many continental countries. Ambition is not openly declared, except within clearly defined boundaries, resulting in shame or embarrassment if these silently maintained barriers are transgressed.

National ideals and public opinion in England

Elias's primary intention is to shed light on the problems surrounding the differences of reciprocal perception between nations, in particular between England and Germany. He sees his task as not only to translate words, but also, as far as possible, to 'translate' attitudes and dispositions (1961: 23). In other words, he wishes to point out the differences in national habitus, the different standards of feeling and behaviour regulation and the observable balance in their operation between constraints by others and self-restraint. Differing national developments are expressed in forms of speaking and thinking, which in turn provide insights into the way in which people relate to one another within a particular nation (1961: 1). The forms and perceptions of behaviour which are coloured by this national influence are often overlooked because they are so pervasive, frequently leading in Europe to stereotyped misunderstandings between nations, blocking, for example, the movement towards European integration. A major obstacle to the mutual understanding of nations is the obsession of European nations with their own past – at the expense of considerations of their future. This past has given them unusually strong nationally contrasting 'physiognomies' and deeply ingrained prejudices against each other, not to mention a resource in providing proof of their own value on a tacitly assumed ranking-scale of states.

As we have seen in the first section of this chapter, English national pride and tradition are largely unbroken in comparison to the continental nations due to England's relative insularity. In the papers on England, Elias once again highlights long-term trends which help to explain why the line of these developments in England has been relatively continuous. He mentions the fact that no enemy armies had successfully invaded English soil since 1066; and that the process of state formation and societal development had been generally continuous, especially compared with the great discontinuities in the development of Germany (see chapters 6 and 7 below). He also points to England's relatively high level of urbanization which integrates large sectors of the population. This high level of unification, he suggests, has a great deal to do with the fact that there is no peasantry (*Bauernschaft*) in the German sense of the word. This group disappeared partly through the enclosures movement and partly because of the peasant migrations to the towns in the eighteenth century when people sought work in the growing urban centres. This peculiarity of the English social structure has had a strong influence on the formation of English public opinion and party structure. In continental countries, peasants as well as workers and employers form separate social classes –

a split between town and country exists which in England disappeared a long time ago (1960: 9). In England, farmers form one interest group among others. They do not stand as a 'culture-class', or a 'manner-class' in their own right.

Elias observes that a large proportion of the population of England is concentrated in London, in the relatively small area of a capital city, an important fact for the formation and dissemination of public opinion. He points out that while in England social stratification is quite firmly entrenched, there also exists a relatively strong integration and uniformity of interests and of basic thoughts and reciprocal understanding. Among the larger European nations, he suggests, the English are the most unified 'in manners, socialization, the way in which they understand each other through small movements, through small nuances of the voice, and in the reconciliation of people with each other over the whole country' (1961: 6). Despite the local differences emphasized by England's inhabitants, a relatively strong mutual feeling overrides all social and local differences. This uniformity can be expressed as a 'we-ideal' (1960: 8 – to my knowledge, the first time Elias uses this term in print) held in common with the majority of those within the nation. In comparison with other nations, the English we-ideal, or what it means to be an English person, including one's self-conduct, is relatively unquestioned. By contrast, what it meant to be German after the Second World War, for example, was more or less uncertain and a residue of that uncertainty remains today.

For Elias, the structure of the British press is characteristic of English unity, with greater importance given to national, rather than provincial newspapers. The former usually attract a widespread readership throughout Britain. When Elias wrote his articles on England, these papers were printed mainly in London and often tended to run similar stories, expressed in their headlines. As an example, Elias cites the *Daily Telegraph*: 'Dame Margot in Panama Jail'. Margot Fonteyn, who was married to a Panamanian involved in a conspiracy, was held in a Panamanian gaol for one day. Other papers, for example the *(Manchester) Guardian* and the *Daily Mirror*, ran with the same story and had similar headlines. 'Think what it means when this is the object of a headline!', exclaims Elias to his German audience (1960: 5), suggesting that this was evidence of an extraordinary uniformity of interests, as well as expressing surprise that readers throughout Britain were expected to know in advance the identity of this prima ballerina. The Sunday papers, of which there were sixteen in the late 1950s with a combined circulation of thirty million, were all printed in London and read throughout Britain. Few of them had direct party ties. Ideologically, they tended to left or right, but did not form direct party platforms, tending instead to express a particular world-view rather than party allegiance. Of course, different social circles tended to read different papers, but they frequently formed a focus of discussion, for example in the workplace, which Elias sees as another example of the level of integration of the British and their public opinion formation. But how does English public opinion operate in practice and how does it function in relation to violence?

Violence and public opinion: two examples

In order to illustrate the operation and effectiveness of public opinion in England, Elias concentrates on two examples: a small incident of face-to-face violence, and the role of violence at the inter-state level in the Suez crisis of 1956. This second example is also bound up with Elias's more general comments on inter-state rivalry and feelings of national superiority and inferiority considered in chapter 4, and in particular, with problems of national identity and the relative power of England *vis-à-vis* other states. Elias sees the crisis itself as a function of problems encountered by nations in coming to terms with their changing power positions. This discussion bears similarities to the way in which Elias traces developments in Germany up to the Third Reich, but while his references to Germany are few in this context, some elements of his approach to that country can be sketched in order to provide an introduction to his consideration of these themes in relation to the rise of Nazism in the following chapter.

The first example concerns a case reported in the national press which commanded the attention of the English public for roughly sixteen months. Attention focused on an incident which took place in a small Scottish town where some young people were sitting in a café. When two policemen entered, one of the youths, a sixteen-year-old named John Waters, made a cheeky remark. As a result, the boy was beaten up by the policemen outside the café, leaving him with bruises, a bloody nose and a torn jacket. While this may appear a relatively insignificant event, except of course for those involved, it had the effect of an avalanche. There was an outcry in the national press that the police could use violence against a young man in such a situation. The boy's local MP raised the issue in the Commons and demanded an enquiry. Eventually, the Prime Minister appointed a special tribunal. The sequence began with the public outcry which led to newspaper reports, generating further interest, leading to MPs asking questions in Parliament, spurred on by the Opposition, and eventually resulting in the government being forced to take some action through the strength of public opinion. Political allegiance was also set aside. Although the youth's father was a Labour voter, the local MP who supported his case was a Conservative, but this did not prevent the father publicly thanking him for his support. Elias seems to express amazement at this whole affair, commenting to his German audience that the whole process of the mobilization of public opinion in this case was like trying to 'crack a nut with a sledge-hammer' (1960: 13).

The Suez crisis is the second main example Elias employs to demonstrate the operation of public opinion with respect to violence in England. As I have said, Elias's use of this example ties in with the first section of this chapter and with his ideas on national identity and the problems faced by states in processes of inter-state competition. Elias suggests there are two poles on the broad spectrum of the value stance and character system of each nation: at one end, a narrow egoistic patriotism and national solidarity bound up with feelings of superiority over other peoples; at the other, a moral claim to the general validity of humanity and a rejection of this 'daydream' (1960: 11). The form of expressing these feelings tends to change throughout history, particularly according to the shifting power balance between nations, but while English politics and public opinion also swing within these broad confines, they are more constrained by moral norms. These moral feeling standards, suggests Elias, are deeply ingrained in the population as a whole and keep the national pride and the national hubris of the English in check. As democratization advances, the statesmen and women of the nations concerned are increasingly bound to the dictates of domestic public opinion, and this also makes moral feelings perceptibly stronger as a counter-balance and a barrier to what these leaders can do in the name of national interests. Within Parliament, public opinion can be seen to play a similar role to various pressure groups like trade unions or entrepreneurial associations, as a sort of unorganized, or not particularly organized, pressure group which has the potential to influence the decisions of those in government. Certain events 'open the floodgates of public opinion' which forces its way along the pre-given institutional channels established within a democratic country (1960: 12). In general, public opinion helps to form a clear moral code, and as such, is potentially very powerful, as was demonstrated during the Suez crisis, when the actions of the British government aroused wide moral condemnation from large sections of the public. The fact that their government threatened another country with physical force brought shame on their nation and thereby themselves. These actions were seen as 'un-English':

> In the eyes of the English at the time of the Suez Crisis, the United Nations was seen as the personification of neutral humanity and therefore also of the English conscience. It was unheard of, so felt many English people, that their government was ready to use violence without the approval of the United Nations. (1960: 14–15)

It was the implicit demand for self-respect which generated the strong negative reaction of public opinion against the government in the Suez crisis. Many feared the loss of respect of other nations, but above all, the loss of self-respect, which according to Elias, was one of the strongest leitmotivs of the growing opposition to the government at the time (1961: 16). Another major theme of protesting public opinion during this period involved the feeling that the whole proposed undertaking was based on a profoundly unrealistic assessment of the power relations existing between states. The proposed use of violence was considered outdated. Not only did it seem immoral for Great Britain and France to attack Egypt, but it was not sanctioned by other states, including the United States and the Commonwealth countries. The power balance between nations had changed, as well as that within them. The English masses had become less bound to the dream of the upper classes whose world-view was still, to a large extent, associated with an

outdated empire. Leading statesmen were more than ever constrained by the dictates of domestic public opinion in the realm
of international politics. The reaction against the government
can be seen as the reaction of broad masses of people against 'the
old school' tradition, 'typical for the way in which *Realpolitik* can
become unrealistic and power-politics non-power-politics' (1961:
17).

As we shall see in more detail in the following chapters, the
rise of National Socialism in Germany provides a further example of how changing power relations bring changing 'adaptation crises'. The Germans suffered such a crisis after their defeat
in the First World War when they were forced to relinquish their
dreams of becoming a significant world power and to adapt to
a position of lower rank in the status hierarchy of European
nations. With this came a transformation of their own self-
image: their we-ideals and their own sense of value, their social
habitus. The rise of National Socialism involved the search for
an identity to re-establish Germany as a 'great power', even a
world power, but this was doomed because its representatives
lacked a realistic appreciation of inter-state relations. Even if
Germany had won the Second World War, their colonial rule
over other European states could not have been maintained.
Indeed, rule by these countries themselves over others outside
Europe was proving increasingly difficult throughout this
period

In the adaptation crises of European inter-state competition,
England was relatively cut off, but it was the Suez crisis which
regenerated the outmoded feeling-codes of a former world
power.[7] England has had a tradition of yielding to adaptation
crises in a non-violent fashion, inherited from the old aristocratic upper classes. Slow compromise characterizes the relations between the powerful (established), and the rising, relatively
less powerful (outsider) social groups. This ethos was extended
to crisis adaptation in national public life more generally. 'The
desire', writes Elias, 'to prove their own greatness and value as
a nation to the whole world seldom overwhelms the English
sense of reality' (1961: 19). The peculiar tradition of English
politics holds this impulse in check. A particular sense of humour, manners, morality and reality prevalent in the English
social habitus all serve to dampen the quest for national self-
assertion, a tradition highlighted by the example of public

opinion reacting to the foreign policy of the governing authorities during the Suez crisis.

The effects of the Suez affair had particular ramifications for those in power. The Chatham House Report, produced by a cross-party group which investigated the interests of Great Britain in relation to Europe and the Middle East, had the following to say:

> The Suez Affair was a valuable education of conscience . . . It is necessary to clarify how English public opinion brought an end to the situation. One must show the nation that adventures of this kind are only harmful to the country. We must learn other ways of behaving . . . we can no longer act alone, without allies, as a great power in the same sense as in the nineteenth century. (1960: 15)

The report concludes that 'Britain . . . does not need to be particularly powerful to be great' (1960: 15). For Britain, as for other European countries, the central issue then became one of how it could maintain its pride as a nation, despite its changed power position. This similar problem of adaptation was also to place severe strains on the national self-image of Germany after the First World War, as will be seen in subsequent chapters.

Problems with Elias's picture of England

Elias is able to utilize his outsider status in painting this picture of English social habitus, public opinion and national ideals in that he is able to discern patterns that are taken for granted: the English may be only dimly aware or even unconscious of them. However, there are disadvantages in such a portrait. This view of the English seems quite simplistic *because* of this outsider perspective. Even during the 1950s when Elias wrote these two articles, the images of social habitus he conjured up were quite stereotypical and idealistic. Also, he often, but not always, conflates the national boundaries of England, Scotland and Wales when referring to 'England'. This effectively downplays the tensions between the various regions and over-emphasizes their harmonious relations, despite Elias's disclaimers that such tensions are exaggerated by natives to these areas. He also seems to neglect the differences between Welsh, Scottish, Northern Irish and English national identities, as well as the extent to which the we-images of these other countries are constituted in reaction to English hegemony. Indeed, it would seem that the harmonious image of England which Elias evokes is more characteristic of the self-image of elite groups within the south-eastern regions of that country. Nor does he comment upon the so-called North–South Divide which cuts an economic and cultural swathe through the middle of England. And in suggesting that the process of urbanization brought together large sections of the population, Elias appears to downplay the deeply rooted class conflicts involved in this integration.

In his discussion of public opinion, Elias also seems to over-emphasize the extent to which the social habitus of the English is dependent upon the continuity of state formation, rather than simply to do with the small size of the region. In other words, the fact that English newspapers share similar headlines may well have a great deal to do with the expression of a high degree of uniformity of interests, but, more simply, it also reflects the ease with which information can be moved around such a relatively small modern country utilizing modern social organization and mass media technologies. In connection with this, Elias does not consider the organization of the media industries themselves or the institutionalized practices of journalists in creating and exaggerating 'public opinion'. All of these aspects are crucial in the construction of public debate surrounding various issues which appear in the national papers. Nevertheless, what Elias does highlight is significant: the fact that certain issues are, for whatever reason, taken up in public life in England and discussed according to shared principles. A similar issue such as the Waters case cited by Elias would hardly have caused such a commotion in Germany, where it is highly unlikely that such a story would have reached the national papers, but would perhaps have been reported only in the regional news sheets, suggesting a more fragmented and regionalized social structure (see chapter 6). Once again, Elias was writing for a German audience, and the examples he cites show what he wishes to demonstrate: namely, the relative unity of the English in comparison to the Germans.

The presentation of Elias's ideas above clarifies his notion of national identification and how this is influenced by what he calls 'adaptation crises' in the context of European integration. These crises tie in with the earlier discussion in chapter 4 of

Elias's notion of the 'reality shock' felt by nations in the process of coming to terms with a lowering of status *vis-à-vis* other nations. The significance of established-outsider relations in intra-state processes is also evident. Elias's ideas on public opinion in England highlight the way in which certain acts of violence or the threat of its use were perceived by the English as a nation in terms of their we-ideal and the changes in national we-identity. This highlights those features of Elias's models which emphasize the role of collective identity as well as behaviour- and feeling-codes. These themes will now be continued through presenting Elias's discussion of sport, again in the context of England, but with comparative reference to Germany.

Sport and violence: the example of foxhunting

The development of sport as an expression of social habitus and the implications this has for an understanding of violence controls and civilizing processes in England forms a major focus of Elias's work,[8] although here I focus on Elias's consideration of violence in civilizing processes in the context of one specific example: foxhunting. A more general outline of his ideas on the emergence of sport in England is followed by a consideration of his comments on violence, 'parliamentarization' and 'sportization'.

English sporting life is characterized by specific controls over competition. It was England that developed the peculiar tradition that, though one should try to win, winning is not the main goal. For the English, at least as an ideal, to lose in sport does not preclude equanimity.[9] Losing performances are therefore often accorded appropriate dignity with expressions such as 'he is a good loser', 'well played' or 'bad luck'. This ethos, which developed first among 'gentlemanly' circles, permeates the whole of public life, particularly in sport and politics, and as we have seen in the previous section, emerged as a dominant trait in the English social habitus.

The English term 'sport' incorporates the notion of 'playing the game', differentiating it from other types of leisure activity. Sport is defined by Elias as 'a competitive exertion of human beings that excludes as far as possible violent actions which can seriously hurt the competitors' (1986a: 23).[10] For Elias, such an activity usually attains the label 'sport' when it has reached a 'mature' stage, an unplanned social discovery in which an equilibrium develops within the confines of its structure: a pleasurable tension balance is achieved between winning, losing and 'playing the game'. Those forms of activities to which we now apply the term 'sport' are generally derivative of pastimes developed in England within, or in close conjunction with, the aristocracy and gentry, including horse-racing, boxing, foxhunting and ball games such as football, rugby, tennis and cricket.

Together with processes of industrialization and urbanization, but above all with state formation and parliamentarization, Elias highlights a process of 'sportization'. This itself is an expression of underlying directional changes in European societies whereby individuals increasingly cultivated regularity and differentiation of conduct. It is bound up with the lengthening and differentiation of chains of interdependence. Along with models of industrial organization and production, England also exported models of sports throughout the world, mainly between 1850 and 1950: pastimes involving strenuous activity which became increasingly subject to more precise, explicit and differentiated frameworks of rules, particularly those surrounding the idea of 'fairness'. This was accompanied by an increased efficiency in supervising the application of these rules. In short, a previously unknown level of self-restraint in game-contests emerged, the outcome of which was an increase in the level of pleasurable tensions, while at the same time minimizing injuries to the participants.

The process of sportization went hand in hand with the broader process of parliamentarization and bore some similarities in terms of its overall direction to the civilizing spurt outlined by Elias in relation to the 'courtization' of warriors in *The Civilizing Process* (1986c: 151). These sports had a very different character from the earlier forms of 'game-contests' which existed prior to the eighteenth century. As an example of a game-contest which involved high levels of violence in comparison to modern combat sports, Elias cites the pancratium of Ancient Greece (1986b: 136–9). These contests, unlike the development of sport in England, were derivative of a warrior ethos. Elias explains the relatively high level of tolerated violence within these game-contests by pointing to the lack of an effective, stable monopoly of violence in the Greek city-states of the time, which in turn did not lead to the inculcation of more civilized restraint upon witnessing violence which developed later. The example of Greek city-states is intended by Elias to illustrate the theoretical connection he seeks repeatedly to establish between levels of violence in sports and in the wider society of which they are a part: corresponding to the balance between self-restraint and constraints by others existing in a particular society, one would expect to find specific levels of violence. In short, the less stable and effective the state monopoly of violence, the more likely it is that higher levels of violence will be tolerated by most members of that society in their sports and games. In Elias's comments on modern societies, this relationship between social habitus and state formation is clearly revealed in his discussion of foxhunting in England.

Foxhunting in a civilizing spurt

Elias's comments on foxhunting are instructive in that he elaborates upon the characteristics of a 'civilizing spurt'. The way in which English foxhunting emerged from earlier types of hunting provides evidence of a process involving increasing restraint upon killing and the use of violence (1986c: 163), and the displacement of pleasure experienced in perpetrating or witnessing violence as an expression of this restraint.[11]

In the more recent past, there has been an observable change in attitude within large segments of the English population, particularly among the middle classes, towards the 'blood sport' of foxhunting. The idea that it is itself an activity which has undergone some kind of civilizing process may not find currency among the many who protest against it on the grounds that it is cruel to foxes. Not only have people now developed a type of conscience formation which does not sanction the use of violence against other humans with whom they identify, but they have also extended this sensitivity to the lives of animals. However, it could be argued that the reasons for this development had less to do with the social mechanisms outlined by Elias than with the campaigns of Evangelical Christian groups in the early nineteenth century. Cock-fighting, dog-fighting and bear-baiting (as well as bare-knuckle boxing between humans) were popular pastimes among the English working classes which were made illegal during the 1820s and 1830s. Such activities were considered vices by Evangelical Christians, not so much because of any revulsion against the violence involved, but because of a dislike of disorderly, unproductive and unpious behaviour which was opposed to the virtues of thrift, hard work and just reward. But it is unlikely that these campaigns would have made an impression without the level of state formation prevalent at the time and therefore the argument in fact complements Elias's theory.

According to Elias, the pleasures involved in earlier forms of hunting were derived primarily from killing and eating the prey. The chase was more of a preliminary. Hunting also formed a type of pest-control function as wild animals were often a menace to the peasantry and gentry alike. Foxes in particular were regarded as vermin and also, in times of famine, as a source of food. But for those of higher social rank, hunting was often seen as a substitute for war involving 'seventy percent of the excitement with only thirty percent of the danger'. As such, it imposed relatively fewer constraints on its perpetrators and went hand in hand with the increased enjoyment felt in the killing and chasing of wild animals.

As foxhunting developed there emerged a peculiar constellation of relationships within the configuration of people, hounds and prey; a specific and elaborate code of conduct surrounding the hunt and the training of the hounds. This was a means of killing by proxy through the hounds (1986c: 164). It therefore required a more sophisticated mediation of relations which would function in accordance with a specific form of socially constructed precepts surrounding the types of emotional self-restraint deemed acceptable in the context of the hunt. For example, a form of affectionate bonding emerged between the hounds and their masters; hounds which performed well were highly valued and praised. The hunter was no longer directly implicated in the destruction of an animal, but merely followed and watched or controlled, while the skill and restraint necessary for the development of an efficient means of killing by proxy served to increase the pleasure and excitement involved. Three kinds of contest were thus enacted during a hunt: the first was between the hounds and the fox, the second among the hounds themselves, and the third among the people engaged in

the hunt. Such was the status rivalry between the human participants that they frequently risked serious injury through
goading each other on.

During the phase which saw the emergence of modern
foxhunting, suggests Elias, people (primarily within the aristocracy and the landed upper classes) did not automatically possess a high degree of revulsion towards the killing of animals,
but they did with regard to the spilling of human blood. The
pleasure of killing existed, but in an attenuated form. The *pursuit*
of the prey became a major focal point of the hunt which
developed into a specific way in which people could allow
themselves a pleasurable release of emotions with a minimum
of physical harm: a quasi 'mock-battle'. In comparison with
medieval times, what in the eighteenth century became known
as 'sport' was a much more specialized technical term which
'represented a profound sublimatory transformation' (1986c:
167) within specific pastimes developed by the aristocracy and
the landed upper classes. The peculiar form of foxhunting
developed as an expression of this. Duelling, or any other form
of violence, was no longer a primary means of resolving issues
of status rivalry among these groups, but rather, conspicuous
consumption and prowess, and a sometimes fanatical outlet for
the latter could be found in the hunt (1986c: 171).

For Elias then, it is no accident that the sportization of pastimes developed at a particular time and among a specific social
group in English society. The sophisticated, wealthy leisure
class who were instrumental in the development of sport imbued it with a particular 'ethos' which became a characteristic
shared with all sports. There was a shift from 'consummation-
enjoyment' to 'tension-enjoyment' characteristic of a civilizing
trend (1986c: 170). The standards of conduct and the ideals of
courtiers and citizens in the seventeenth century (with the
exception of Cromwell's Commonwealth) were relatively exclusive. 'With a slight exaggeration,' Elias comments, 'one might
say that manners without morals stood on one side, morals
without manners on the other' (1986c: 174). In the early eighteenth century the two divergent standards began to converge
and the effects on constraints regarding the use of violence were
felt throughout the social hierarchy. As we have seen, during the
eighteenth century the behavioural codes of the landed upper
classes became relatively more refined along with their relative

pacification and domestication in the process of parliamentarization. This occurred within the context of increasing
security brought about by growing commercialization and economic growth, which also generated a greater regularity in the
personal conduct of everyday life, both within the occupational
sphere and within the psyche, through the development of
different standards of self-restraint. However, increased regularity in social life also generated an increase in general dullness.
Life became less exciting and therefore new forms of excitement,
palatable in terms of existing canons, needed to be devised in
order to satisfy the need for pleasurable excitement which,
according to Elias, 'appears to be one of the most elementary
needs of human beings' (1986c: 174). A specific type of tension-
management emerged within the social institution of foxhunting
which marked this activity as 'sport': 'the fine run, the tension,
the excitement, not the *fricandeau*' (1986c: 160).

Keith Tester (1989: 161–72) argues that Elias was too selective
in his interpretation of the historical evidence of foxhunting and
seeks merely to confirm preconceived notions consistent with
his theory of civilizing processes. I would like to comment on
Tester's two main criticisms: that foxhunting is a 'sportized'
version of earlier pragmatic activities of pest control, and that it
is a restrained form of earlier hunting patterns.

With regard to Tester's first point, Elias describes how deer
and foxes were hunted indiscriminately by people, sometimes
using hounds. Foxes were regarded as vermin, but also as food
in times of hardship. In contrast, Tester says that wolves and
foxes 'were merely pests to be eradicated' (1989: 165), whereas
the hunting of other animals like deer and hare was always a
pleasure, suggesting the 'sport of hunting has always been a
pleasure whereas the labour of eradication was a necessity'
(1989: 165). However, this tends to equate hunting with sport,
and thus denies that eradication can be and is a type of hunting
which can also be experienced as pleasurable. Foxhunting can
indeed be seen as 'the fusion of pleasure and pest-control under
the aegis of sport', as Tester claims, but Elias does not suggest it
can 'be understood as the sportization of the quest for food'
(1989: 166). Tester's second major point, that Elias suggests
foxhunting is a restrained form of earlier hunting patterns,
seems to be based on a misunderstanding. Elias does not claim
that previous forms of foxhunting were unrestrained, but ar-

gues that restraints were fewer, less differentiated and involved fewer codifications. Nor does Elias suggest that the method of killing foxes prior to the eighteenth century was hunting in the modern sense of foxhunting. Instead, he compares foxhunting with hunting generally before the rise of the specific type of foxhunting as a sport peculiar to the eighteenth century.

Tester does add details which are certainly lacking in Elias's account but, unlike Elias, he does not see the relevance of the formation of the modern English Parliament to the development of foxhunting as a pleasurable pastime or sport. Instead, Tester contextualizes the development of foxhunting in terms of class relations and traces the meaning the activity may have had for those land-workers, the 'poor', who were barred from joining in the hunt except in certain marginal, low-status roles. He shows how important facets of early foxhunting were incorporated from deer- and hare-hunting, such as the need to start early in the morning in order to find the scent of a fox weary from its night-time activities, and how the fast, southern stag hounds were selected as favourites over their slower, northern, harrier counterparts in early forms of foxhunting. Later, hounds were bred to have both attributes of speed and olfactory sensitivity. For Tester, therefore, the development of early foxhunting is discontinuous with what came before. He adds further detail concerning the breeding of the hounds by Hugo Meynell in the mid eighteenth century and his 'bending of nature's will' in the search for more challenging forms of entertainment in the hunt. The control of the hounds (embodied in the huntsman and his assistants) became increasingly important. Also, Tester correctly highlights the legitimizing function of foxhunting in maintaining the power and status of the landed classes in the aftermath of the Civil War, forming 'an attempt to naturalize the power of the ruling classes' (1989: 169). The privileges surrounding hunting were designed as a mechanism of social exclusion and were maintained by certain economic practices and experiences of exploitation – 'the appropriation by the gentry of a surplus produced by tenant farmers and the work carried out by the landworkers' (1989: 170).

Elias's remarks on foxhunting are undoubtedly problematic, not least for the simple reason that he relies on a very limited selection of historical data. And as Tester's comments reveal, Elias's account is simplistic and is too reliant on a model of a civilizing spurt which is derivative of his analysis of courtization in *The Civilizing Process*. He also ignores the exploitative social control functions of the ritual. Another commentator, Ruud Stokvis (1992: 125), argues that Elias overlooked the highly ritualized and civilized form of hunting first developed in the court society of France in the sixteenth century, adding force to Tester's claims that the emergence of modern foxhunting had little to do with parliamentarization. On the one hand, as Stokvis points out, this questions only the relationship Elias draws between parliamentarization and foxhunting, not the more general theory of civilizing processes itself. On the other hand, it must be pointed out that in drawing these unusual connections Elias does not argue that parliamentarization in England *caused* sportization, but that the growing effectiveness and stability of the monopoly over the means of violence by a central authority is crucial to the understanding of a civilizing spurt within the English upper classes. Sportization was *bound up with* the non-violent exchange of governmental power in competitions for control of state organs as the seventeenth-century cycle of violence calmed down, and included a civilizing of personality structures within those groups involved. In drawing these connections, however, it seems that Elias over-estimates the extent to which macro-sociological developments impinged upon the development of modern foxhunting, thereby overlooking the more discontinuous elements of its history. Indeed, the relevance of his comments on parliamentarization and foxhunting in England may well be restricted merely to an explanation of the emergence of 'killing by proxy' and the formation of clubs in which a more standardized version of foxhunting became popular, rather than to the civilization and sportization of the hunt in particular (Dunning 1992: 269; Stokvis 1992: 126). So Elias's comments on the relations between sportization and parliamentarization, while partially flawed, still retain some explanatory force, but with respect to a more limited scope of historical data.

This chapter has presented Elias's reconstruction of the development of England and in so doing has emphasized a comparative aspect to his work on civilizing processes which is frequently overlooked. State formation and pacification took a distinctly English path and this had observable results in terms of certain dispositions described by Elias as constituting the English social habitus, national we-identity and the development of sport. This peculiarly English social habitus was also highlighted in his discussion of public opinion and the nation-wide reaction to two events involving violence or the potential threat of it. Together they demonstrate that the three main criteria of civilizing processes outlined in chapter 4 – a shift in the balance between constraints by others and self-restraint in favour of the latter, the emergence of a more even, all-round and stable self-restraint, and an enlargement in the scope of mutual identification – became dominant features of the English social habitus.

In a collaborative essay, Elias and Dunning have traced the transformation of sensibilities in England with regard to violence in sport (1986b: 175–90). The authors show how 'folk football' in medieval and early modern England involved high levels of violence often resulting in fatalities, whereas today the game is a highly controlled sport with sophisticated rules to ensure 'fair play' and penalize (violent) misconduct. For Elias and Dunning, the example of 'football' also serves to demonstrate the way in which the relative social instability and ineffectiveness of violence monopolies are reflected in the relative instability of internalized self-restraint which results in the more spontaneous expression of emotions involving a greater propensity and strength towards showing cruelty or kindness (Elias and Dunning 1986b: 180). In Germany, such a development in the field of sporting activities would have been unlikely because of the widespread tendencies generated in the direction of hierarchy and non-compromise internalized and intergenerationally transmitted in the social habitus. There, an ethos of 'playing the game' and 'fairness' was alien. With some exaggeration, one could say that in Germany an ethos developed which emphasized 'playing to win', while at the same time it was considered unrealistic to 'pretend' that fairness was important in such competitions. Because of this, the particular development of German social habitus is not considered by Elias through the 'lens' of sport. Rather, he focuses on other social institutions such as the imperial court, nationalism, war and student duelling fraternities, all of which will be considered in the following chapter.

CHAPTER SIX

Nationalism and Decivilizing Processes in Germany

The path to National Socialism in Germany is dealt with by Elias in a broadly sweeping developmental analysis which integrates psychological and sociological insights. While this chapter considers Elias's comments on the historical roots of the Nazi disaster, the following chapter focuses on the Nazi era itself. In the first section Elias's comments clarify the dynamics of his sociological process models through considering national and group we-images and ideals in the context of German state formation. This forms a historical backdrop to a more detailed discussion of violence and social habitus among the imperial German establishment. Elias traces the continuity of a culture of violence stemming from the imperial German bourgeoisie, through the Weimar era to the formation of the Nazi state. This and the following chapter make frequent and detailed reference to *The Germans* in particular, in which Elias elaborates further upon interweaving themes of violence and civilization, but this time with more of an emphasis on decivilization, or what he sometimes calls 'breakdowns' of civilization.[1] The three main criteria of decivilizing processes introduced in chapter 4 will help to clarify the directional trends Elias seeks to highlight. Some of the quotations from Elias's work in this and the following chapter include words like 'barbarism' or 'barbarity'. I will comment on his use of these terms in the concluding chapter.

State formation and national identification

The social development of the Holy Roman Empire was quite different and much less continuous in comparison with that of England. A significant reason for this was the large size of the territory involved, which meant that geographical and social divergences within it were considerably greater, facilitating the development of centrifugal forces and making centralization more difficult. The probability was low that a dominant power would emerge, in comparison to the smaller territory of England, because of the low level of economic integration and the greater effective length of distances (1994a: 342). But centralization did eventually occur with the victory of the Hohenzollerns over the Habsburgs, and this integration hastened the *disintegration* process of the old empire which, up until the Middle Ages, had spread to the west as far as the Meuse and the Rhône.

From the Middle Ages, in direct contrast to the development of England, the general trend was the 'constant attrition and diminution' of the German Reich (1994a: 343). After the Thirty Years War (1618–48), the Germanic territories were threatened from all sides, heightening inter-group struggles for resources and survival within the area and in the process emphasizing the means of distinction and exclusion of the constituent groups. Thus, the fragmentation of the Germanic regions, which was marked by a very long phase of absolutism with a large number of relatively small and relatively poor courts, in conjunction with the isolation of the middle classes from the nobility, meant that no central model-setting society could emerge (1994a: 18). Only a moderate civilizing of warriors took place, because borders were vulnerable and constantly threatened by invading armies. The prominent position of the warrior establishment in the development of the area allowed their social habitus to override that of the courtly civilian (1996: 63).

Among other European countries, the 'collective memories' of France and England depict the seventeenth century as a period of major cultural creativity, increasing internal pacification and 'civilizing' of people (1996: 6). In contrast, Germany at this time was economically and culturally poor, and was characterized by a relative coarseness of people's conduct. In the seventeenth century, and probably earlier, the seeds were sown for the beer-drinking traditions of later student groups in the nineteenth and early twentieth centuries. Among 'Good Society' circles, loss of self-restraint through heavy drinking was typical. A greater emphasis was placed on the type of self-restraint expressed in the ability to hold one's drink. Drinking formed an effective way of escaping from the pain of social catastrophe, of protecting one's self from the dangers of the world, or at least making them tolerable. The weakness of their own states compared to others in Europe and the crisis in which they found themselves – the physical uncertainty, doubts about their own self-worth and the generation of feelings of humiliation and disgrace – inclined the upper classes towards wishful dreams of revenge for their situation.

The eighteenth and early nineteenth centuries saw the elimination struggles between the kings of Prussia and the Habsburg rulers in Austria, and the victory of Prussia meant the removal of many old functions of the Kaiser and of Austria from the federation. In the nineteenth century, the revolutionary armies under Napoleon invaded Germany in an attempt to unify Europe under French rule, a fact which clearly shows the lack of an effective, centralized state within Germany in comparison to neighbouring states. It was during this time that German students founded the Freikorps which harassed the occupying French troops. The structural weakness of the German state, which allowed constant invasions from neighbouring states, stimulated an attitude among many Germans whereby the use of military action was idealized and highly valued (1996: 7).

In contrast to England, lack of access to key monopolies of power generated a compelling habituation to a strong external state authority, particularly among the middle classes. Within the vulnerable land frontiers of the Germano-Prussian empire, the nobility-led army was highly significant in the formation of the social habitus of the population in general. A form of conscience or 'Over-I' was reproduced in individuals among the bourgeois classes over several generations. Elias suggests that this development generated a type of social habitus

> which was disposed to relinquish to a separate, higher social circle the specific kind of foresight demanded by the ruling and organization of society at large . . . This situation led . . . to a very specific type of bourgeois self-image, a turning away from everything to do with the administration of the power monopolies, and to a cultivation of

inwardness, and the elevation of spiritual and cultural achievements
to a special place in the table of values. (1994a: 512)

As we saw in chapter 2, in France, the tension between both
estates was relatively great because the warrior nobility and the
bourgeoisie had roughly the same access to power chances. The
king was able to manipulate factions to his own advantage: he
could distance himself from the aristocracy without denying his
membership of it, while at the same time he could demand the
compliance of the nobles. Again, as noted earlier, in England,
tension between parts of the nobility and bourgeoisie was
already reduced in the course of the seventeenth century and
together they were able to restrict the king's power. Thus the
king and court formed only one centre of power in eighteenth-
century England, while the aristocracy and gentry formed another, at least equal in power, while in Prussia, despite its
relative poverty, there was a gradual transition from a warrior
nobility to the use of standing armies, the former then becoming
officers in the service of a central ruling prince. The power
balance between the aristocracy and the bourgeoisie was tipped
strongly in favour of the nobles. A tacit compromise-pact arose
between the nobility and the king, the nobility supplying the
king with officers and courtly and administrative services,
while the king undertook to maintain the nobility in their
position of highest rank (1996: 63). In this way the top positions
within the establishment were reserved for the aristocracy.

In 1870 a successful war against France pushed the relatively
weak German state up into a higher status bracket within the
configuration of competing European states and made up for
past losses. At this stage however, Germany still remained
'in core' an absolutist monarchy and there was an 'overgrowth'
of various socially inherited models of military order and
obedience which subdued the municipal models of negotiation
and persuasion. Within this context, sections of the bourgeoisie critically appropriated these aristocratic models of 'power
politics'.

As Elias clarifies in *The Civilizing Process*, the Classical period
of German literature and philosophy represented a phase in the
social development of Germany in which there were strong
antagonisms between the bourgeoisie and courtly nobles. Correspondingly sharp was the rejection of military values and

conduct by these bourgeois groups, because they were largely cut off from political power, although they may have aligned themselves with the monarch. The two broad streams of bourgeois politics in the nineteenth and early twentieth centuries – idealist-liberal and conservative-nationalist[2] – both sought an end to the multiple states which characterized Germany in the first half of the nineteenth century. However, the failure of these plans was of decisive significance for the development of the German bourgeois habitus. Unification was in fact achieved by the Prussian king and his adviser Bismarck through violence: a victorious war against France. But the victory over France can also be seen as the victory of the German nobles over the German bourgeoisie (1996: 14).

The Hohenzollern state was characterized by a militaristic ethos. Its leading men urged an increase in industrialization and modernization generally, but bourgeois industrialists and capitalists were not the most powerful classes in the country. This position was held by the nobility and higher civil servants. The victorious wars of 1870–1 not only preserved this situation but also strengthened it. Most, but not all members of the bourgeois classes accepted their second-class status as dependants in the social ordering of the *Kaiserreich*. Broad sections of them were won over to the strong military ethos and critically appropriated these models and norms, thereby distancing themselves from the German Classical ideals in favour of a power strategy which seemed more realistic. 'In this situation', writes Elias, 'a strange and significant (from the viewpoint of the civilizing process) thing happened' (Elias 1988c: 183).[3] Segments of the bourgeoisie became more accepted among the higher ranks of the nobility. In the process they internalized its characteristic military ethos while at the same time giving this ethos a peculiarly bourgeois stamp. It was advocated with the 'zeal of a convert'. This represents another relative discontinuity in German history, a decisive transformation of the German habitus. In this case the break was important because the appropriation of nobility models frequently depended upon a misinterpretation. Noble officers usually stood in a rather 'civilized' tradition, but this feeling was often lost in the appropriation of nobility models by the bourgeois groups who supported a boundless use of power and violence in conjunction with a rigid adherence to hierarchical forms of social organization. Elias comments:

this pre-eminence of the military in the time of the second German empire was extremely closely associated with a low point in the value-scale built into the new German self-awareness, which accorded power in social life a very high, if not the highest place, and social weakness, from which Germany had escaped only shortly beforehand, the lowest place. (1996: 118)

The appropriation of these nobility canons by the German bourgeoisie led many of them to develop a somewhat distorted image of the unification process. In many European states, as in Germany, the rise in middle-class self-awareness went hand in hand with the development of dynastic states into nation states. But in Germany, the 'Third Estate' remained relatively power-less *vis-à-vis* the autocratic establishment. Germany's previous fragmentation made it more difficult for the middle and work-ing classes to unite in organizations spanning even the major cities, while there was no large capital city to provide the focus for action. The middle classes also felt themselves threatened on two fronts: they feared the rising social power of the workers and their representatives, while at the same time they were opposed to the traditional aristocratic and civil service elites. As a result, they could not focus their actions against the establish-ment who effectively fulfilled the national dreams of the middle classes for them. Their political power was still limited, even in the early phases of industrialization. For them, the reality of unification did not quite sink in. It seemed unreal because the national ideal was not linked to reform movements in the name of broad sections of the population. German national unity, in a sense, was only nominal. Thus, for the middle classes, national unity materialized 'as a gift from above' and 'preserved its strongly autocratic character, bathed in the twilight of fantasies' (1996: 339).

For the mass of the population the 'state' was perceived more in terms of 'they' than in terms of 'we'. The two perceptions began to merge after unification, but the self-image of the nation did not shed its association with autocracy. The masses had become deeply habituated to this form of social control and a change in their own political favour would have meant an increase in self-reliance. But Elias remarks that since such a change is usually gradual, while emerging from autocracy there is a tendency to revert to it in times of crisis. The German social habitus and images of autocracy, lacking counter-images, developed into a national code and image which embodied in the national we-ideal the trappings of hierarchical and oppressive autocratic rule. The *extent* to which this was the case in Germany was unusual, but not its actual occurrence.

For those members of the middle classes who did identify with the aristocracy, the frustration inherent in their position as secondary representatives of the nation and Reich did not find expression in relation to their social superiors, but in relation to their past. While the aristocratic groups based their claim to particular status on inherited traits and family traditions, these sections of the middle classes based similar feelings of pride and claims to status on an image of their national ancestors, their past deeds, merits and achievements (1996: 133). This national reorientation took on a particular significance in inter-state policy. In contrast to England, where various social groups sought compromise for differences, compromise in Germany was seen by the middle and upper classes as 'unclean': it was even considered to be illegitimate. This attitude informed their relations with other states, an orientation which mirrored the unreflective acceptance of national thought traditions frequently held by members of a nation to be uniquely legitimate. The German middle classes did not compromise in their stance on nationalistic norm canons, which they had appropriated from the norms of the aristocracy, who in turn stood in a tradition of violent norm canons inherited from the rulers of dynastic states (1996: 154–70).

In line with his comments on inter-state dynamics outlined in chapter 4, Elias suggests that Germany's projection to the status of a great power brought increasing rivalry with other states; it even pushed the Kaiser into another war in 1914. This action was not open to question for him, despite the strength of the Allies, including America later on, severely limiting his chances of success. The largely unexpected defeat of 1918 brought great humiliation and trauma for broad sections of the German people. This return to the previous days of weakness, with foreign troops on their own soil, constituted a crucial point in the development of the German social habitus. Many of the middle and upper classes felt they could not live with this humiliation and sought to prepare for the next war with great expectations of German victory, in a sense to 'make up' for what had been taken away. This was important in Hitler's rise to power. The

Weimar Republic found many supporters among the Social Democratic workers and small groups of liberal bourgeoisie. But the majority of the middle and upper classes were on the other side. A broad movement developed with the aim of removing the Versailles Treaty and waging a war of revenge. Hitler was able to renew hopes of greatness. He mobilized large parts of the masses, whose support gave him a chance to harness these feelings, with tragic results. The end of the Third Reich marked yet another break in the formation of Germany.

Thus the development of the area now known as Germany was characterized by cycles of defeat, lamentation and dreams of revenge and greatness. Compared with the development of other European states, particularly England, Germany shows more breaks and discontinuities. The capital cities of both countries serve as examples of this. London has for centuries been a relatively secure city, a fact which mirrors the relative continuity and stability of the state-formation process in England. By comparison, Berlin is a relatively young city which gained its importance as a capital under the Hohenzollerns. A peculiar constellation of historical trends and psychical dispositions were involved in the German *Sonderweg*, and the characteristics of social habitus which emerged among the German establishment after the 1870s continued a culture of violence, as we shall see in the following section. However, what is clear from this interpretation of the development of Germany was that in comparison to England the dynamics of social processes were not as conducive to the transformation of contraints by others in favour of self-restraint, the development of a more even, all-round and stable habitus, and the widening of the scope of mutual identification between groups. Within the German civilizing process, the social habitus did not develop as far in the same direction as that characteristic of the English.

Violence in the imperial establishment

Having outlined Elias's reconstruction of the broader structural developments and the emergence of national we-feelings and images in Germany in contrast to England, attention now moves to the more specific dynamics of this process outlined by him which generated a particular emphasis on violence and controls by others. As we have seen, the nationalist emphasis on power and violence had particular effects among the bourgeois members of the imperial establishment. Elias's discussion of social habitus in the imperial establishment centres on the growing importance and social significance of certain institutions from around the turn of the century. In particular, he focuses on German 'Good Society'. Such social groupings, he suggests, form as part of establishments that are capable of maintaining their position of monopoly longer than a single generation (1996: 49). They serve an integrating function. 'High Society' in London and Paris tended to dominate over the local ones, while in Berlin it succeeded only briefly in achieving this central role. In Germany, other institutions served this integrative function as well as, or as a complement to, 'Good Society'. Apart from the court, these social formations traditionally included the army and the universities. At the same time, the student associations gained particular significance because of duelling: the duelling fraternities in Germany allowed access to the establishment and served a binding function through this particular form of violent contest.

As we have already seen in the previous section, with the growing power of the industrial workforce and the demands of its representatives, significant parts of the bourgeoisie shifted their allegiance to the side of the aristocracy, so much so that 'between 1871 and 1914, the majority of the German middle classes made peace with the privileged high-status group' (1996: 60). The middle classes, in aligning themselves with the aristocracy, became increasingly focused on demarcating themselves from those below them. Therefore the court and the nobility, with their attendant rituals and signals of social demarcation, gained in importance. Among the aristocracy, the Prussian values of the warrior predominated. As the bourgeoisie became increasingly powerful, the warrior codes they had appropriated came to be expressed in the standardization of duelling and honour codes found among the student organizations and then later developed into a national cultural tradition.

The 'Good Society' of imperial Germany did not possess many traditions. It could not claim a long line of continuity. From 1871[4] it developed from a group with a relatively modest self-esteem to one with exaggerated power feelings. Nevertheless, the imperial establishment felt itself 'threatened and was correspondingly insecure' (1996: 81), and therefore required clear forms of social demarcation. Despite informalization processes,[5] the imperial establishment remained relatively formal and hierarchical. It not only comprised the courtly, military and civil service aristocratic estate, but was also a hierarchical configuration which integrated aristocrats with bourgeois strata. The latter did not belong to trade or capitalistic entrepreneurial groups, but were primarily high civil servants, including university professors and various types of academics. The aristocratic groups drew on a tradition of contempt for tradesmen in their stigmatization of some sections of the bourgeoisie. This more traditional means of social demarcation also incorporated the duel, which played a special role in the 'Good Society' of the imperial era.

Satisfaktionsfähigkeit and the student associations

Although the upper classes differed amongst themselves in Germany, they were distinguished in their adherence to a code of honour and behaviour by which members were 'entitled to demand satisfaction' (*satisfaktionsfähig*) in relations with one another. If a person's honour was questioned, he[6] could demand a duel as compensation. This tradition flourished in the student associations. Membership of such a group marked a young man out – both locally and throughout the Reich – as a member of the establishment. Certain ways of thinking, feeling and behaving were characteristic of this membership. This social habitus had its functional counterpart in the gentleman's code of the English establishment, a code that was gradually transmitted over many centuries to other social classes lower down the status hierarchy. In Germany this was not possible, largely because of the steep formality–informality gradient tipped in favour of formality. Part of the reason was that the warrior code of the army officers played a smaller role in the roots of the English national canon than in Germany, and in England even the obligation to duel had largely disappeared from the army officers' canon by the mid nineteenth century. In Germany, the honour code and the duel retained a crucial significance because of the importance attached to the military in a fragmented country which had frequently formed the arena for war in Europe.

Duelling was traditionally an aristocratic means of defending a man's blemished honour in armed, one-to-one combat. This was not ratified by the state, it occurred outside the law and the courts. It was also transmitted to the upper sections of the bourgeoisie. The tradition itself stems from dynastic states when central rulers attempted to pacify territories and, in the process, robbed the warrior nobles of their most respectable means of exercising power whilst dealing with the socially weaker, the lower rank and with their own peer group. Duels were an infringement of this violence monopoly. Often the police were not summoned in such cases of infringement since they themselves were bound by the same law-breaking code of the elite (1996: 52). The aristocratic infringement of a royal monopoly of violence in the form of duelling was the expression of a particular self-definition. They saw themselves as somehow above the law. For the lower classes, fists had often to suffice, because if they were caught using weapons they were liable to be locked up, or even executed if they shot someone. Duelling among members of the establishment was not subject to similar punishment. If a fatality did occur, the survivor would often simply disappear abroad for a short time. Thus, the aristocratic code of honour took priority over the laws of the state and this went together with the notion that the Kaiser and his surrounding courts formed the 'real Germany', while the rest of the 'masses' were regarded by those within the establishment as 'outsiders'. For their part, these outsiders saw the state as something external: the overall configuration was one in which feelings of superiority and inferiority flourished, generating a social habitus in the masses which became attuned to autocratic rule. Even though the members of 'Good Society' saw themselves as the only rulers of Germany, increasing industrialization after 1871 weakened the privileges of the establishment with the rise of the 'masses', while at the same time, national unification strengthened the regime.

Within the German imperial establishment *Satisfaktionsfähigkeit* permeated social life. It raised members of these *satisfaktionsfähige Gesellschaften* above the masses. In doing this, the participants bound themselves to a norm which called for the use of formalized violence under specific circumstances, thus echoing the warrior code which emphasized ability and skill in the use of physical force over and above that of talking and persuasion. Elias comments:

> The immanent dynamics of human groups where the use of physical violence, even in the formalized shape of duelling and fencing contests, is accorded a central place in social life lead again and again to the same outcome. Types of people rise within such groups who are distinguished not only by their physical strength or skill, but also by the pleasure and enjoyment they take in smashing down other people with weapons or with words whenever the opportunity arises. As in simpler, less pacified societies, there are even in more pacified societies enclaves of ritualized violence which give the physically stronger or more skilful, the more aggressive person, the bully and the ruffian the chance to tyrannize others, and to win great social respect by doing so. (1996: 71)

Compared to fist-fighting, for example, the duel was highly formalized violence. It served three main functions: as a means of social distancing, of differentiation from others, and as a means of integration among the upper classes. Duelling went hand in hand with group-specific denials and frustrations which the members of the upper classes imposed on themselves by adopting this canon. This was also bound up with the colonial aspirations of a nation and formed an important instrument of rule, as well as being crucial to fuelling status competition between groups within the establishment itself. The court rituals and *Satisfaktionsfähigkeit* remained highly important in Germany even up to the first decades of the twentieth century.

Duelling became a symbol for bourgeois students of access to the establishment, the most visible sign being a scar on the face or head received during a bout (*Gang*). The student associations also served the function of 'rounding off' a young man's education at university. He would gain a subject orientation from his formal classes and lectures, while his more 'social' education was provided through membership of a student association. These associations inculcated traits regarded as desirable for entrance to the professions – especially the academic professions in service of the state – in keeping with the main training function of the universities, rather than for work in the economy, as is generally the case today. At the beginning of the nineteenth century, the student fraternities (*Burschenschaften*) were primarily agencies of reform, pushing for greater liberalization and equality. But once the national goals for which they strove had been achieved – unification and nationhood – their political aims were abandoned and they accepted their inequality and social existence as second-rate bourgeois contenders, receiving 'the fulfilment of their wishes and hopes as a present, so to speak, from the hands of their social opponents' (1996: 91). This was the price they paid for the retention of privileges which demarcated them from the rest of the 'masses'. However, greater standardization of the party organizations and thus the political power of the masses also developed with national unification. The German upper classes feared this increase in power from below and sought means to close ranks and increase their group cohesion. The fraternities were one of the means of achieving this.

The student associations were integrated into the 'Good Society' of the establishment, but they were below the status of the officers' duelling corps. In the process, the associations increasingly incorporated 'Good Society' values. With the loss of communal goals for the future, an increase in meaning was bestowed upon the formalities and rituals of the day in the status competition between groups, which among the student fraternities gave a strong impetus to cultivating an entitlement to demand satisfaction – previously the province of the officer duelling corps – as well as increasingly standardized compulsory duelling competitions for their members. A clearly defined status hierarchy operated within the whole duelling culture establishment, but the officers' duelling corps and the student associations shared the same characteristics of rigid internal hierarchies and a strong culture of rituals, such as communal beer-drinking and singing in pubs. The training of these young men served as an important symbol of their relations of power and rank *vis-à-vis* the lower classes and women. While it was regarded as acceptable to sleep with women of a lower social rank, marriage was considered impossible. The converse was true for women of equal social standing. Thus, 'rigid formality and precisely delimited informality [was] typical of the code of conduct of the student duelling corps and the nationalist fraternities' (1996: 106). The young men internalized a particular set of public behavioural norms: they were trained and trained themselves at the same time.

The training provided by these groups was also unintentionally orientated towards the formation of a social habitus which

favoured control by others (1996: 95) and their conscience formation was therefore similar to that of the officers in their
duelling corps. This code played a key role in the formation of
a specific we-group orientation. Formerly, warrior classes legitimized themselves through honour which emphasized traits of
violence and courage. This was increasingly seen in opposition
to bourgeois values of morality. The latter, with its stronger
emphasis on individualization, represented an increase in the
degree of self-restraint in comparison to an honour code integ-
rally bound up with the fear of losing self-esteem in the eyes of
others. In accordance with his figurational approach to established-outsider relations, Elias points out that, not surprisingly
in such circumstances, transgressions from established group
norms could bring forth severe stigmatization or even expulsion. This proved extremely effective in maintaining norms
because expulsion usually extended into the future and affected
the individual's career prospects. After 1871, as more and more
sections of the German middle classes moulded with the aristocratic upper classes, 'even the predominantly middle-class
nationalist fraternities more and more lost all earlier elements of
the moral code' (1996: 97). This permeated their educational and
social goals. A pure canon of honour emerged in conjunction
with a rigid hierarchical organization. The ritualized drinking
sessions were also permeated with hierarchy and custom and
formed arenas in which the power of superiors could be demonstrated over junior members less experienced in consuming
alcohol. The most characteristic activity, however, was the practice of duelling. During the Imperial era, this practice under-
went somewhat of a coarsening in its rituals connected with a
formalization of violence. The honour code served the double
purpose of a selection process favouring those with specific
personalities and of their inculcation with specific attitudes. The
former, suggests Elias, emphasized physical size and prowess
and encouraged fighting, while the latter was orientated towards hierarchically organized group structures.

More than for any other similar social group in Europe, the
great significance of ritualized violence ('real' violence as
opposed to the 'mock' or 'play' violence embodied in English
sport) among the German upper class served as a symbol of the
power and superiority of its own members. This, combined with
the strong reciprocal competitive pressures on members of the

hierarchically organized student associations, together with the precarious position of the imperial establishment (despite its external appearance of brilliance), served to generate an intensification of the practice and coarsening of duelling. Selection for membership of these student associations on the basis of aggressive skills with a sword shows a movement in a similar direction (1996: 102). Fighting for one's own association meant one could increase one's sense of self-pride, but it also allowed for the generation of feelings of remorselessness in the judgement of the comportment of every opponent. The student associations cultivated 'a pitiless human habitus' (1996: 107). This was an emphasis on toughness, an 'untamed warrior ethos' in a bourgeois form. It served as an influential model of behaviour and feeling which spread to other areas of social life in which physical fights did not occur at all (1996: 109). The extent and depth of people's mutual identification and the corresponding depth and extent of their ability to empathize, one of the central criteria of a civilizing process (see chapter 2 above), were almost completely omitted from the student associations. Here we find the crystallization of a type of social habitus which is symbolized by the German expression, *Schadenfreude* (malicious glee or, more accurately, malicious gloating) (1996: 112). The cultivation of this ethos was intimately bound up with the honour code and the feeling of solidarity it entailed. The entire social habitus reflected the individual's membership of the establishment. The whole constellation operated in a kind of 'unconscious' fashion, without the character of 'a logically thought out philosophy, but rather an unplanned tradition of behaviour and feeling produced by the blind fate of history' (1996: 112). With the inclusion of large numbers of the previously 'outsider' bourgeois groups into the court-aristocratic 'established', the uncompromising warrior tradition became a national tradition.[7] While there was no lack of people bemoaning the rise of a militaristic ethos and the denigration of a 'classical' past, in many ways the overall social process seemed to develop its own dynamic. It is the continuation of this enthusiasm for violence which Elias traces through the Weimar Republic and into the Third Reich, where it became an all-embracing instrument of state policy operating not only against other nations, but also against its own population and those defined as outsiders within it.

Elias is clear that National Socialism and what he refers to as the 'decivilizing spurt which it embodied', cannot be fully understood without reference to this spreading of nobility-models (1996: 15).[8] The duel can be seen as a model of the habitus-moulding influence of institutions in Germany. In other countries the duel generally lost importance with the rise of the bourgeoisie, but in Germany, it developed in the opposite direction. Together with the appropriation of nobility models by sections of the bourgeoisie after 1871, and possibly before, the duel readily became an influential institution for bourgeois students. The duel is an example of the societal regulation of violence, in this case mainly among students and officers who became accustomed to a strong hierarchical ordering as well as an emphasis on the inequality between people. This spreading of socially sanctioned models of violence and social inequality forms one of the continuities of this time which can be traced through to the Hitler era.

Comments on duelling in the student associations

It would seem that Elias over-emphasized the extent to which physical force and size play a crucial role in the duelling of the student associations. While carrying out research for this book at the University of Bochum in Germany, I was invited to attend a *Pro Parti* meeting of *Studenten Corps* and *Burschenschaften* and therefore had the opportunity to witness the rituals and methods of the duel at first hand.[9] I was told that these had remained largely unchanged over the last 150 years, but this is highly questionable as the great changes in German society at large during this time would lead one to expect changes in the social habitus and settings of the people involved in duelling. A major difference between then and now, however, is that the practice is legal and has been since the mid 1930s.

One immediately striking aspect was the amount of protective clothing worn by the combatants. This includes heavy black steel goggles which are buckled tightly at the back of the head with a leather strap; chain-mail covering the upper body and upper arms; leather padding over the same area, as well as the groin and thighs; a thick ribbed leather brace protecting the larger veins in the neck; leather ear-coverings; and thick leather detachable sleeves for the exposed sword arm (the combatant holds his left arm behind his back, gripping his chain-mail) on to which a suede glove is buckled.[10] Only the top of the head and the cheeks are uncovered. However, a wound to the cheek region is quite difficult to inflict, although certainly not unknown, because the action of the sword arms takes place above the heads of each opponent. This means that wounds are more usually inflicted on the top of a fighter's head or at the temples.

It is also interesting to note the detailed and specific rules of the duels. The opponents, each with a Second, similarly dressed, to their left-hand side, stand facing each other exactly one sword's length from shoulder to shoulder. They are not allowed to move any part of their body apart from their sword hand and arm. A bout lasts for no longer than six strikes from each opponent – executed at high speed – but they are usually interrupted after only a few strikes by a Second who then appeals to a judge standing nearby. The Second attempts to prove the failings of the opponent by referring to mistakes in his stance or technique. A potential forty bouts can be fought, with a pause after the twentieth. However, it is unusual for a duel to last this long as one of the duellists is usually wounded after the first or second bout, whereupon his Second formally thanks his opponent and the attendant officials for their time and the opportunity, and leads his charge away with the help of his other corps members.

From witnessing these duels, it is clear that a powerful taboo exists, both for the combatants and the spectators, against the expression of any emotion or feelings, as in the form of wincing. For example, I was told that if a duellist cries out in pain when hit, the fight is immediately halted by his Second and he is then ushered away in disgrace. Opponents frequently fight on with blood dripping freely over their goggles and on to the floor – they have no choice in the matter – without any overt expression of pain. Only if the wound is deemed sufficiently dangerous by an ever-present corps doctor is the bout halted and honour satisfied.

Furthermore, when there is a large difference in size between the opponents, this is rectified with the aid of large wooden platforms on which the shorter combatant stands. A great deal of time is spent at the beginning of each bout making sure that each opponent is precisely positioned in order to avoid any unfair advantage on either side. My impression, in this specific respect, is that a strong emphasis is placed on carrying out the procedure – both in preparation and during a bout – with the utmost precision. Thus, contrary to Elias's description, very little room is left for the physically stronger or larger to exert his strength and aggression simply in order to win. Indeed, the duellists are specifically matched by experienced senior corps members according to technique, speed and how hard they are able to strike in order to avoid wide discrepancy in competitions, a component feature of what Elias would refer to as 'sportization'.

All these controls mean that not only is movement highly restricted, and indeed requires a great deal of skill and practice in order to execute manoeuvres with any degree of accuracy, but that such controls also have the effect of allowing each bout to be highly regulated and monitored. In short, on one level, these duels are relatively civilized forms of combat. What remains unclear, however, is whether this 'fair play' element of the duelling fraternities was added after the Second World War, since the members of such associations traditionally claim unchanged descent from a distant past. More research is needed to clarify this, but it seems that Elias is right to point to the role of these associations in the inculcation of an attitude of nonchalance towards inflicting physical injury and a relative lack of identification with others suffering physical pain. In other words, it is highly likely that the duelling culture in Germany during the time considered by Elias was instrumental in generating a decrease in sensitivity among segments of the bourgeois classes towards perpetrating and witnessing acts of violence. Together with the fact that these associations inculcated a strict code of obedience and hierarchy, these features represent a decivilizing process among specific groups in terms of the three main criteria mentioned in chapter 4.

Ute Frevert (1991) criticizes Elias as being too one-sided in his suggestion that the duel was an element of feudalization and a simple copying of noble canons or the blind obedience to socially institutionalized controls. She also argues against what she calls Elias's 'compensation theory' in which he suggests that a major purpose of the duel was to make up for the long-term loss of traditions and prestige of the establishment through emphasizing this ritual. She suggests that a positive emphasis

towards duelling can be found among the German establishment before 1871, that is before the practice became hidden in
England and France. Furthermore, Frevert counters Elias's
claim that the duel was not a civilized form of behaviour but
the embodiment of a war canon grounded in the struggle for
superiority in social honour. Rather, and this is confirmed by my
own observations, she claims that it was not the winning that
was important, but primarily the manner in which one com-
ported oneself in the execution of the duel. Above all, everything
has to be done 'properly'. However, duellists must visibly draw
blood and hide their pain, and this, together with the fixed, rigid,
face-to-face stance, is very different from the English forms of
combat-sport, even boxing, thus representing a form of social
habitus which clearly results from very different historical
antecedents.

Violence in the Weimar Republic

In Elias's work, individual forms of behaviour are always seen
as intertwined with broader social interdependencies and this
interconnection is again evident in his discussion of the Weimar
Republic. For Elias, even where a monopoly of violence in the
hands of the state is relatively effective, it is still vulnerable (Elias
1988c: 182). Those not authorized to employ violence within
states can become involved in violent struggles with those who
are. Focusing on the Weimar era as an example, Elias seeks to
establish an 'understanding of the problematic of state monopoly of violence and how it is related to collective changes in
behaviour, whether in a more civilizing or more barbarizing
direction' (1996: 221).[11] In connection with this, Elias discusses
the many evidently popular contemporary novels which glorified power and violence and which reflect the culture of violence
found among the bourgeoisie from the imperial Reich through
to the Weimar period.

The novels Elias cites elevated the honour code of the nobles
and bourgeois student associations. One book, R. Herzog's
Hanseaten (*Hanseatic Merchants*, 1909), provides many examples
of common traits of personality structure prevalent at the time.
When, for example, an employer talks to his workforce and
appeals to their strength of spirit in the face of a cut in wages, he

evokes a particular manner of thinking and feeling (1996: 205). Elias suggests that this gives some indication of a strong militaristic tradition which was also bound up with industrialization and extended to the behaviour of entrepreneurs and workers: it permeates all levels of society. 'Discipline' and 'honour' were words frequently used by both sides in relations between employers and employed. While Elias does not suggest that the book necessarily reflects the relationship as it actually was, he points out that the author held certain expectations which he quite possibly shared with his audience.

In Germany around this time, certain everyday key words surfaced in novels alongside a 'cult' of hardness, severity and unyielding attitudes prevalent among parts of the imperial bourgeoisie. While such attitudes may be typical of established-outsider relations in which there exists a marked power differential between groups, it is rare that such severe orientations are actually put into practice, held as an ideal and imbued with a strong positive value (1996: 206). 'Iron' was one of these key words during the Weimar era. It was a symbol which rallied against the expression of any kind of weakness and revealed a fear that Germany might revert to its formally weak position. The cult of severity was a type of 'hyper-compensation', an extreme reaction to the fear of failure. Great emphasis was therefore placed on the importance of becoming both economically and militarily more powerful. 'Emotionalism' was stigmatized, while 'false sentimentality' and suspicious morality were opposed to positive values such as 'iron will', 'guts' and 'hard behaviour'. The overall tendency of this process was in the direction of anti-humanism, anti-moralism, and anti-'civilization', along with an increasing emphasis on state power. In other words, these traits were justified in terms of a national ideal.

To repeat a key theme of the previous section, members of the upper bourgeoisie found themselves in a paradoxical position. Being largely composed of people with peaceful occupations who were socially inferior to the noble groups they yearned to become – a wish that was impossible to realize in one generation – the bourgeoisie adopted an aggressive 'action' approach, particularly in foreign policy, derived from noble circles. They actually elevated brutal actions by portraying them in popular novels as positive, acceptable standards of behaviour, breaking with the classical German idealist tradition, representing a 'reversal' of a civilizing process in terms of the main criteria of decivilizing. Elias comments with reference to one such novel published in 1912, depicting violence in the 1870–1 wars:

> The ultimate identification of human beings with each other, a goal which was perhaps exclusively idealistic, [was] denied intentionally and emphatically in favour of an exclusively national identification. During war, the common people on the enemy side need no longer be treated as people . . . The popular bourgeois authors obviously expected their readers to share and approve this attitude. (1988c: 185)

The novels of Ernst Jünger also give a positive emphasis to violence, both in the *Kaiserreich* and the Weimar Republic. The brutality of war is glorified and held up as something which should be accorded a high value. Anxiety, fear or weakness in battle are not mentioned. Instead, one reads of glorified violence and hardness. In most modern Western societies, it is rare for people to experience severe levels of brutality and violence, but in his novels Jünger describes it with detail and enthusiasm. The polar opposite of Jünger's work was Remarque's *All Quiet on the Western Front*, which was regarded as treachery by those who read literature in favour of war.

Elias points to a contrast in the war literature written from the perspective of the aristocratic officers and from that of the ordinary men and non-commissioned officers. Jünger's, *Storm of Steel: A War Diary* (1937) describes the way in which the internalization of the aristocratic officer ethos is developed by the bourgeois officers in a quite different fashion. Jünger was a living example of this bourgeois officer ethos, a tradition which emphasized anti-moralism, anti-humanism and anti-civilization. War for these bourgeois groups, rather than being perceived simply as a social fact, became desirable as the expression of 'an ideal manly behaviour, so that its violence and brutality appeared to be something great and meaningful' (1996: 211). While the Republican Reichswehr, the official army allowed by the Versailles Treaty, was led by an elite of aristocratic officers, paramilitary organizations such as the Freikorps[12] were generally led by officers of bourgeois origin who were generally against the noble canons of 'civilization'. They also held strong images of a better past which were fused with the wish for a better future. For Elias, the war literature of the Weimar Republic reveals unstated ideological propaganda, namely: internationally, to restore Germany to the position of a great power, through war if necessary; and intra-nationally, to restore a hierarchical society with clear demarcations between the rulers and the ruled (1996: 212).

The literature of the early Weimar Republic essentially provides a mirror of the pro- and anti-war sections of the population. On the one hand, there was the anti-war faction consisting of a large part of the industrial classes, parts of the liberal bourgeoisie and many intellectuals. These people were tired of war and believed Germany could enlarge its power without resorting to fighting. They were glad to see the back of the Kaiser and the establishment of a Republic. Also, although they as Germans were defeated in inter-state struggles, they were on the winning side in intra-state struggles for supremacy and control over the key monopolies of state power. On the other hand, there was a group comprising the German nobility, with its extension into the officer corps, higher bourgeois civil servants and administrative juridical servants; most entrepreneurs, merchants and bankers; and also a large section of the young people of bourgeois origin who were officers in the war, including many of those who joined the Freikorps and other paramilitary organizations (1996: 213; see also Steinberg 1977: 5). Internally, within the state, they wanted an end to the parliamentary system and the re-establishment of a formal hierarchical system of subordinate and superordinate relations. Externally, with or without war, they sought to win a greater power position for Germany and a return to a form of absolutist state. It was the active paramilitary groups who sought to undermine the state monopoly of violence in the Weimar Republic.

The infringement of a violence monopoly

The First World War not only brought humiliation in the face of unexpected defeat. It also saw the disappearance of the throne and court of the Kaiser, the centres of German 'Good Society' with its associated honour codes of *Satisfaktionsfähigkeit*. The effect was 'like someone running with full force into a brick wall. A traumatic shock resulted' (Elias 1988c: 186). But the old imperial establishment could not come to terms with this defeat, either domestically or internationally. The Freikorps and the ethos they cultivated encapsulated many of the frustrations of this establishment and they sought to vent their anger using violent means. They were the main agents of 'extra-governmental' political violence, which they employed in an attempt to overthrow the newly established Republican government in the failed Kapp Putsch of March 1920. Prominent among the troops responsible were the Erhard Brigade who later formed the secret Organization Consol.[13] They used terror activities, particularly between 1919 and 1923, against ministers of the Republican government, several of whom, including Erzberger and Rathenau, were murdered. However, it is significant that these terrorists were largely drawn from bourgeois backgrounds, officers or students from the imperial period, and they apparently took it for granted that the murdering of political opponents was acceptable (Elias 1988c: 189). These reactionaries elicited a vehement counter-reaction from the working classes, whose representatives now largely formed the government. They were also highly resentful of their previous leaders who, it seemed, had duped them into believing the war could be won.

A strong tension emerged between the Freikorps members and the majority of working people. Both groups were caught in a double-bind process in which each side sought to advance their own political goals through the use of violence. The Freikorps, however, with their superior discipline, training and group cohesion, not to mention access to weapons and occasional support from the Reichswehr, were in a far more favourable position in comparison to the groups they opposed. Inevitably these factors resulted in the balance of power between them and the workers tipping in their favour. Another aspect of the greater cohesion characteristic of the groups orientated towards the old establishment was that, since the war, the German officer corps had remained fully operational with its own *esprit de corps*. The Allies had restricted the size of the German army, and therefore the number of officers. Thus, many young officers returning from the war were effectively made redundant. The Freikorps were their answer. They also shared common enemies: first the Bolsheviks, and then the parliamentary Republic itself.[14] All this meant that a successful workers' uprising was doomed to failure: two main mitigating factors being the cohesion of the old officer corps and the Allied powers' fear of spreading revolutionary zeal from the Russian borders.

Indeed, fear of the Bolsheviks legitimized the very existence of the Freikorps (Elias 1988c: 192). This fear was also an important element in the rise of Hitler, who was able to mobilize broad sectors of bourgeoisie, united in this aversion towards any type of 'communist' orientation. The Russian Revolution provided a tacit model for weaker outsider groups in the use of violence for the pursuance of political aims (1996: 216). Non-state violence aimed at overthrowing the state monopoly of violence had proved itself in this revolution, generating double-bind processes of violence in many countries ever since. Germany was one of the first countries where this occurred. However, there, unlike in the Russian Revolution, the working classes were more highly educated, and therefore generated greater fears among the upper classes during the course of the power shift which tipped in favour of the workers.

The German noble establishment had laid claim to power primarily through military successes, but because they were largely agrarian classes, their power base had become eroded with industrialization. After the departure of the Kaiser in 1918, with the exception of their military establishment, they fell to the rank of social inferiors relative to the bourgeois classes. In this way, the latter gained in power by the nobles' loss of privileges rather than by revolutionary struggle, as in France. But the 'gains' of the bourgeois classes were counteracted by the increased power of the workers, the disintegration of the absolutist regime and the establishment of a parliamentary government. For their part, the workers' organizations were split largely into those who favoured and those who were against the use of violence, which corresponded to a similar division within the bourgeois classes; the difference was that the former groups fought each other and were thus less effectual overall. The latter developed a tacit agreement in defining their common enemies. Even those segments of the bourgeoisie who were anti-violence were still against the Republic and thus gave implicit, if not explicit, support to those who *were* willing to engage in violent activity in order to maintain their own self-respect and sense of collective and individual integrity.

All this had significant results: 'After 1918 the high value placed on physical force among sectors of the German middle class which had already been encountered in the Wilhelmine era was accordingly strengthened; but now it acquired a new character and tone' (1996: 217). In imperial Germany, the aristocratic establishment did not question the use of violence in the settling of internal conflicts. Later, however, bourgeois groups adopted a far more conscious attitude in bringing violence to bear in class conflicts. The stability of the state is dependent upon the degree to which its monopoly of violence can be compromised, and the maintenance of this monopoly is in turn dependent upon the extent to which the economic development of a nation state is secure and stable. But a major problem in the early Weimar Republic was that the government effectively controlled only a small section of the police and army. Its monopoly of violence was not strong or stable and was thus open to challenges from any group who could muster weapons and organize them-selves. With the old establishment still able to command alle-giance from the military forces which remained intact, the new Republic was anything but secure. An added complication arose because the representatives of the new government (particularly liberal bourgeois sympathizers such as Beer, Scheidemann and Noske) held a deeply felt aversion to the utilization of violence in the interests of the workers. They were just as hostile to the workers' violent outbursts as were those groups opposed to the very existence of the Republic itself. Thus, a 'marriage of convenience' emerged between the politi-cians of the Weimar Republic and the high command of the armed forces, including the Freikorps. The weakness of the state's monopoly of violence becomes evident through its de-pendence on these anti-Republican military groups. The Repub-lican state structure had a Janus-head. On the one hand, there were non-violent, public party struggles within a parliamentary system. On the other hand, there were violent, military and conspiratorial struggles which occurred outside the parliamen-tary system. These struggles, suggests Elias, were neither less significant, nor less structured, than economic processes, while being intimately bound up with them.

It was terrorist acts such as these which contributed signifi-cantly to the gradual erosion of the German state. Elias attempts to make a direct connection between these violent acts and what came later, arguing that it is possible to 'establish . . . a continu-ous development in a subculture and in circles of people that led from the terror acts of the guerrillas in the first years of the republic to the brawling at public meetings and street fighting in the early 1930s' (1996: 221). This continuity is mirrored in what he suggests was a typical sequential pattern in the life of many men within the establishment of the 1920s: officers in the Wilhelminian wartime army (or, if they were too young, cadets in the Prussian Cadet Corps); members of one of the Freikorps, often participants in their unsuccessful Baltic campaign; members of a conspiratorial secret society of a terrorist kind; and finally, members of the Nazi Party (Elias 1988c: 193). Opposing the terrorists, the Republican defence associations lacked three main things according to Elias: money; officers (most of whom were on the other side, which meant that they did not have the military expertise in leadership and organization; and a military tradition with a strong orientation towards war-like activities. With both sides locked in a double-bind generating violence and hatred in a reciprocally augmenting spiral, the state's monopoly of violence was increasingly paralysed, while the state itself was increasingly undermined from within (1996: 222).

Of course the Freikorps themselves consisted mainly of men whose sympathies lay with the pre-war establishment. After the defeat of Germany, however, they were the outsiders and their members felt disillusioned with the whole situation in their own country. Their resort to terrorism was only one form of expressing their sense of disorientation. Another was their involvement in the Baltic campaign. This ostensibly involved fighting back the Russian threat which was gradually encroaching on these regions, while promises of land for resettlement may have spurred some to engage in the fighting. Elias suggests that one of the major motivations of the men was compensation for the lost war, for a lost way of life and even for lands lost in the West. In short, they sought meaning in their lives, but that meaning was bound up with a mode of social relations which was now impossible. Eric von Salomon, a Freikorps member and later novelist, reveals all these feelings and hopes in his work. He wrote 'like a detached outsider in relation to a society that appears to be completely rotten' and which is dying. The irony was, however, that it was the old society that was dying (Elias 1988c: 194).

Two significant events brought the shock of reality home to these men in the Baltic. The first was the signing of the Versailles Peace Treaty in June 1919 which finally broke all psychological and emotional links they may have had with their homeland.

The experience of this shock may have varied from individual to individual, but for the freebooters in the Baltic it was particularly significant. For many, the final break came when the German government ordered the withdrawal of their troops from the region. The freebooters would not give in. They fought on regardless, against mainly Latvians and Estonians, rather than Russians. The second significant event was their defeat. Many of the freebooters had never experienced retreat on the battlefield. They reacted with an explosion of rage. The following passage from von Salomon's *The Outlaws* (1931) gives a flavour of the basis for Elias's comments:

> We made our last thrust. Yes we got up once more and charged on a wide front. Once again, we drew the last man out of cover, poured over the snow-covered fields, and charged into the forests. We fired into surprised crowds, and raged and shot and struck and hunted. We drove the Latvians across the fields like rabbits and set fire to every house and blasted every bridge to dust and cut every telegraph pole. We threw the corpses into the wells and threw in hand grenades. We killed whoever we captured, we burned whatever would burn. We saw red, we no longer had any human feelings in our hearts. Wherever we camped, the ground groaned under our destruction. Where we had stormed, where formerly houses had stood, there now lay rubble, ashes, and glimmering beams, like abscesses in the bare fields. A huge trail of smoke marked our paths. We had ignited a huge pile of wood, which burned more than dead matter. On it burned our hopes, our desires: the bourgeois tablets, the laws and values of the civilised world, everything that we had dragged along with us as moth-eaten rubbish, the values and faith in the things and ideas of the time that had abandoned us. We pulled back, boasting, exhilarated, loaded with booty. The Latvians had never stood their ground. But the next day they returned. (Quoted in Elias 1988c: 196–7)

This kind of 'path towards barbarity and dehumanization', writes Elias, 'always takes a considerable time to unfold in relatively civilized societies. Terror and horror rarely appear in such societies without a long process of social disintegration' (Elias 1988c: 197). But this decivilizing process described by Elias was not simply the result of the conscious choice of the individuals involved. It was generated within a long-term, largely unplanned social process.

The violence of this earlier era, however, had a different form to that within the later Republic. Under the vigilant eyes of the

Allies, paramilitary groups were forced into clandestine, conspiratorial activities.[15] Allied fear of the German military was gradually replaced by their fear of Russian militarism, and this in turn strengthened their sympathies for any groups publicly opposed to communism, allowing the Freikorps and similar groups to come out into the open. If their actions contradicted public opinion, they could then blame the weak Republican government. Whereas in the earlier days of the Republic, extra- and intra-parliamentary struggles took place alongside each other, in the later days, they were fused together through the parliamentary legalization of paramilitary organizations supporting extra-parliamentary violence (1996: 223). From 1929, the economic crisis fuelled a double-bind relation in a political crisis that resembled a kind of civil war.[16] The extra-governmental violence of the Weimar era formed the precursor of the state-sponsored violence of the Third Reich.

Hitler actually succeeded where the Freikorps and groups like them failed. He destroyed the Republican regime. His success was based upon an ability to mobilize the masses 'through extraparliamentary violence and extraparty propaganda' (Elias 1988c: 198). But while the Freikorps shared many of the aspirations of the Nazis, they remained loyal to the 'old guard' noble–bourgeois honour codes. Hitler, who was himself an 'outsider', was able to break through this elitist conservatism. In a peculiar way, his appeal was far more democratic. Membership of the German 'race' was open to many more people than was membership of an elite 'Good Society' (1996: 197). It was much later that the Freikorps' loyalty was repaid in characteristic fashion. On 30 July 1934, the so-called Night of the Long Knives, many of the former freebooters affiliated with the National Socialist organization, who had seen many of their hopes fulfilled with Hitler's rise to power, were murdered by Hitler's own men (1996: 227). Jünger had written that he wanted nothing to do with the monarchy, conservatism or bourgeois reactionism of the Wilhelminian period, but with the Nazis in power, the negative connotations of these aims were transformed and given a legitimate face.[17] Out of the political tumult of the Weimar Republic emerged a grand inversion of the former values which stemmed from aristocratic tradition. 'In the end, the destroyer triumphs – Lucifer upon the ruins of the world' (1996: 226).

Long-term trends and short-term crises

Hitler fits in to broader long-term sweeps of history outlined by Elias intertwining with shorter-term processes which together form the conditions for the generation of National Socialism. But while few of these conditions were specifically German, their coincidence in time and the resulting patterns often were specific to that country (1996: 317). Elias highlights several threads of a broad social process which came together in Germany in the Weimar Republic revealing a directional trend towards 'barbarity and dehumanization' which allowed the myths put forward by the Nazis to come to the fore and grip the German popular imagination.

The Weimar era provides an example of the 'lag' between social habitus and political developments, as mentioned in chapter 4. While the workers and their representatives gained in power, those within the upper classes experienced a diminution in their power potential. At the same time, however, the national beliefs and behaviour traditions of the middle and upper classes were not as affected by the rise of those groups who had previously been outsiders to the affairs of state as were the political institutions themselves, which changed radically. This is because these beliefs and traditions were less amenable to conscious intervention. Institutions and power relations developed abruptly, along with a spurt in the development of national habitus, but the latter still retained autocratic tendencies. Thus, the establishment of the democratic regime did not necessarily entail a democratization of attitudes and beliefs. Habituation to autocratic rule and the internalization of this external compulsion had heightened the difficulty with which the social habitus of many Germans could keep pace with the rate of change generated within political institutions. Various processes intertwined in creating this difficulty: a long period of discontinuity combined with autocratic rule; philosophical modes of thought combined with an unconditional acquiescence to ideals; and the rapid rise of Germany to the status of an industrial power within Europe after unification in 1871, which increased the power potential of the industrial middle and working classes (1996: 338).

As we have already seen, centuries of fragmentation of the

area, with its attendant wars and social disintegration, resulted in a longing for unity which permeated the self-image of the German people and proved remarkably continuous in the face of a relatively discontinuous state formation. This longing found expression in a deep-seated desire to place trust in the hands of a powerful leader who could bring about unity, someone who could save the Germans 'from themselves no less than from their enemies' (1996: 318). In the Weimar Republic, the heightened sensitivity of Germans to quarrelling amongst themselves was expressed in the vehement hatred that many directed towards the parliamentary system itself. This democratic system necessarily involved tensions and conflicts in the course of its everyday business. With no traditional models, such as the English had, for delineating the parameters of actions without betraying inner convictions, struggle and compromise did not sit comfortably in the social habitus of many Germans of the time. Implicitly, people were scared of the conflicts getting out of hand because they did not know their own limitations.

This crisis situation added impetus to a national behaviour tradition which set great store by the virtues of a strong leader. In cases where the we–I balance tips in favour of the former, or, in other words, when constraints by others predominate over self-restraint, actions perpetrated in the name of the collectivity attain a high value and frequently override those ideals which are not orientated towards the nation. This is precisely what occurred in Germany among large segments of the population from the end of the nineteenth century, gaining momentum and culminating in the Nazi dictatorship. National identity was then so firmly rooted in the conscience of individuals, in their we-image, that it overrode their more personal sense of meaning and purpose. Elias comments,

> it is never the immediate situation of one country alone which determines the strength and particular character of national sentiments or the degree of the barbarity of which a country is capable in its relations with those earmarked as its enemies . . . As determinants of behaviour, past, present and future work together. Lived situations are, at it were, three-dimensional. (1996: 355)

As we shall see from the following summary, longer-term trends came together with shorter-term trends from the time of imperial Germany to the end of the Weimar Republic, some of which can be described in terms of the main criteria of decivilizing processes:

- the slow but steady diminution of the German empire from the Middle Ages;
- poverty and fragmentation of this empire into small absolutist courts and the idealization of military values;
- the isolation of the middle classes from the monopolies of state;
- dreams of unity and feelings of humiliation among 'Good Society' circles;
- a victorious war against France, unification and restoration of pride in the self-image of Germans;
- a rift among the middle classes, breaking with the classical tradition in conjunction with their increasing 'nationalization' and critical appropriation of violent aristocratic norm canons;
- a shift in the we–I balance in favour of the we throughout a population habituated to autocratic rule;
- the national identity of the middle classes in their rise to power with dreams of greatness and restoration;
- the general insecurity of the imperial establishment in the face of the rising power of the lower classes, emphasizing rigid hierarchy and court ritual as a centre for the integration of the *satisfaktionsfähige Gesellschaften*;
- within the *satisfaktionsfähige Gesellschaften*, a tipping of the balance between self-restraint and restraints by others in favour of the latter;
- a spurt in the appropriation, glorification and idealization of military tradition and violence among segments of the bourgeoisie, involving a contraction in the scope of mutual identification, and the infringement of the state's monopoly of violence particularly through the student duelling associations in the Wilhelminian period;
- the further 'nationalization' of feelings and thoughts of particularly the middle classes, but also of the masses;
- the disintegration of the imperial 'Good Society' with the abdication of the Kaiser after the First World War;
- a shift of the overall power structure of society in the Weimar Republic to favour the previous outsider (workers') groups

and their representatives, increasing social tensions between them and those who identified with the old establishment (noble and bourgeois groups);

- a 'lag' problem of habitus adjustment whereby people found it difficult to come to terms with the operation of a parliamentary democracy;
- the instability of the Weimar republican state's monopoly of violence involving an infringement of the state monopoly by the Freikorps, a double-bind process between the supporters of the Imperial establishment and those who supported the Republic, escalation of violence and social fears through the use of police and military violence, retaliation of communist and fascist groups against each other, and general economic crisis;
- the republican government's acceptance of the Versailles Treaty, something many Germans could not forgive, fuelling tensions between established and outsider groups.
- the collapse of the republic and the rise of Hitler and the Nazi Party.

The 'path towards barbarity and dehumanization' described by Elias gained momentum within specific groups at a specific time. This path represents a breakdown of social standards which had once existed. In this respect, it constituted a 'regression' from these dominant social standards and thus a change in the direction of the civilizing process in Germany: a decivilizing process. All of these elements summarized above are in fact precursors to Elias's main aim, which is to focus on the 'breakdown of civilization' – what he refers to as the 'decivilizing spurt of the Hitler epoch' (1996: 1), to which I turn in the following chapter.

CHAPTER SEVEN

Genocide and Decivilizing Processes in Germany

This chapter focuses on certain violent events in Germany and considers Elias's texts on anti-Semitism (1994c: 121–30), the Nazis, mass murder and what he sees as the 'breakdown of civilization' (1996: 299–402). I present Elias's reconstruction of the rise of the Nazis before considering his comments on the Nazi mass murder and German national we-identity. The final section draws together themes of decivilizing processes and inter-state configurations discussed in previous chapters, and suggests how the criteria of decivilizing processes presented earlier may be useful in adding to our understanding of the Nazi era. As in chapter 6, some of the quotations from Elias's work include words such as 'barbarism' or 'barbarity'. Again, I will return to this issue in the concluding chapter.

National ideals and the rise of the Nazis

As we have seen in chapters 5 and 6, German national pride and self-respect did not develop the level of stability that it did among the people of France and particularly England. Indeed, in this respect England represented almost a polar opposite to Germany. In comparison, the German ideal did not allow for compromise or concessions. A firmly established centuries-old tradition of absolutist rule had generated an implicit requirement for national ideals, beliefs, principles and standards that could be obeyed absolutely. In short, this tradition generated an ideal that was almost impossible to live up to. Democracy, with its attendant demands on self-restraint, was not part of this tradition and did not engender a sense of pride, as was evident in the Weimar era. Democracy had a tinge of 'everyday hum-drum life' and associated connotations of sordidness, in contrast to the national ideal which was seen as 'a brilliant star high up in the sky' (1996: 326), an 'exalted we-ideal'.

The longing for greatness inherent in this tradition, suggests Elias, for the 'spectacular, extraordinary hour', also meant that people were less firmly supported by common norms and aims in their individual self-restraint in everyday life, which made it more difficult for them to develop their own ideals. Elias argues that this increased the tendency to grasp at unusual occasions which had the potential to lift them out of themselves through the generation of a feeling of collective devotion to ideals held in common. In pre-Nazi Germany this was often latent and often half-conscious, but it complemented a marked contrast which existed between the traditional national ideal and the everyday life of an industrial parliamentary society. This feeling of long-ing was then tapped into by the Nazis – who of course also experienced it – in their ascent to power. National ideal and reality were separated by a wide gulf, with a belief in greatness and perfection in the Reich on the one hand, and apathetic emptiness on the other: 'if the ideal could not be reached, it was hardly of importance what one did and how one did it' (1996: 327). People therefore strove to establish a common ideal which transcended everyday life, one which was intimately tied up with their image of the past.

In crises, suggests Elias, idealistic aspects of belief are more likely to come to the fore and predominate. The deeply con-ditioned responses of aggressiveness and destructiveness in crisis situations prevalent in Nazi Germany were the result of a long intergenerational tradition bound up with successive defeats, a decline in power, uncertain national identity and an orientation towards the past. The Nazi ideal was also more exclusive than other national ideals in emphasizing the pri-macy of one race and one nation: it was not moderated by a more general belief in the advancement of humanity, which informed Russian and Chinese communism or American capitalism. It had a compelling character, but 'the constructive side of their beliefs was massively overwhelmed by its destructive and barbaric aspects' (1996: 330). The Nazi movement fed on this tradition which emphasized unconditional submission to a highly demanding discipline in the name of a national ideal. The songs and poetry of the German nation reflected this – they often spoke of imminent death in enticing tones suggesting a 'morbid' fascination. A leitmotiv of the German national tradition included the theme of heroic death in the name of the national ideal, a theme Hitler himself took to its nihilistic conclusion in a new form. The fatherland ideal promised enchantment, but with a foretaste of disaster, an orientation which is significant in understanding the sociogenesis of the Nazis. In comparison to the dominant tendency in England, this resulted in a self-fulfilling prophecy:

> While the British, in accordance with the lessons of history, seemed to be convinced at the deepest level that they would win the last battle, even if they suffered a defeat (a conviction which helped them, in fact, to win), the Germans, even when they were victorious, never seemed quite able to silence the feeling that they would lose the last battle (which contributed in no small measure towards their eventually losing it). (1996: 332)

This particularly demanding and severe German national identification included a high level of fantasy embedded in the national ideal. It fed into what Elias calls a 'vicious circle', a notion that bears direct similarities with his ideas on double-bind processes presented in chapter 4 (see also Elias 1987a: 98–9). Increased fantasy impulses in the demands of conscience lead to a decrease in the ability to modify actions through testing of factual evidence. This in turn leads to a reduction in the ability to escape from these fantasy demands, increasing the levels of strictness and discipline which add to the oppressive character of the demands themselves. The latter become increasingly compulsive, making it all the more difficult to escape or modify the fantasy demands which are 'internal' as well as 'external'. Social reinforcement of the fantasies makes the internal pressures all the more compelling, and this mutual reinforcement generates a spiral or 'spin' dynamic. For those involved, this 'spin',

increasingly stresses their collective fantasies, leading them into
increasingly reality-blind behaviour until, finally, the great crash
comes which – usually with a high loss of human life – brings them
back down to earth, more clearly revealing in retrospect the emptiness of their compulsion. (1996: 343)

One of the most characteristic expressions of the German
belief and behaviour tradition which expressed itself as a willingness to use violence in threatening situations was the emphasis on *Realpolitik*. This attitude assumed that the only realistic
basis for political action was that which rested upon the use of
force. But the Germans felt that they were only different from
other nations in this respect in that they were more honest in
admitting it, an attitude that was inherited from the older war
strategies of the pre-industrial dynastic states. More so than in
other nations, suggests Elias, where traditional rules and limitations developed surrounding when and where to use force,
'power' politics and the role of violence came to be emphasized
over other forms in Germany because of a greater sensitivity to
their former situation of weakness and uncertainty over their
own strength. The Germans tended to underrate these restraints
on violence, even to the extent of perceiving them as an expression of hypocrisy. This generated a paradox: 'the same people
who followed an absolute, unconditional and often highly
unrealistic national idealism', writes Elias, 'at the same time
boasted about what they believed to be their realism, their
Realpolitik' (1996: 365). In a world of increasingly interdependent nation states with growing restrictions on the overt use of
force in the conquering of other territories, this was no longer
appropriate.

We saw in chapters 5 and 6 how Elias argues that changes in
national self-image and reorientation were common problems
for nations in Europe at the time (and of course still are). For the
English, despite a strong desire to restore their former greatness
as a nation, the shock of the nation's decline from one of first
rank was absorbed more slowly. But the Germans experienced
greater difficulty because their national reality had rarely risen
to the level of their expectation of their own ideal as Germans.
The Nazis sought an empire within Europe, rather than overseas like other European states. A point of realization was
reached: the traditional dream of a Reich was threatened and
Germany was not the centre of an extensive overseas empire.

Thus, '[w]hatever else was responsible for the barbarity of the Hitler period,' writes Elias, 'one of its grounds was certainly the refusal to see and accept this development. The strength of the downwards trend was reflected in the extreme brutality of the means with which people sought to check it' (1996: 346). Writing before the Falklands War, Elias suggests that apart from the Suez affair, which for him represents a short-term 'lapse', the English did not react to their decline as a world power with a last-ditch attempt to influence the course of international events through violence. To some extent, the British claim to world-leadership status was at one time close to the reality of the situation. In the British case, their justification for superiority over other nations had a great deal to do with being standard-bearers of 'civilization', resulting in a 'quiet superiority'. In contrast, the Germans' national ideology was, metaphorically speaking, an inversion of the case in Britain. German superiority feelings came to be justified, among other ways, in terms of exclusive *racial* membership. The Nazi belief system served as an instrument with which to build, consolidate and control an empire, but it differed from that of the pre-Nazi rulers who ruled by a 'caste allegiance' without the need to appeal to a national creed. The Nazi creed, on the other hand, had the potential to win followers from all sections of society. Like other national creeds it required the participation of the now powerful masses who could identify with a nation. But this was taken to extremes, opening access to active participation for greater numbers. 'Race' became the criterion of membership of the German nation, rather than privilege or birth.

While the traditional German elites had viewed the problem of ruling as primarily a military or policing problem and second-arily as an economic one, the Nazis, as representatives of a democratization process in common with other industrialized societies, added a third: 'rule and disciplining by means of a social belief' which encouraged the masses to control them-selves (1996: 375). But the National Socialist belief existed in the international context of other deeply rooted national belief systems and therefore had a limited appeal. The Nazi leaders were also not very tolerant of other national traditions. In the decline of the German nation, fantasy and reality parted com-pany. The latter came to be seen as unimportant and trivial and was not admitted in any significant way to conscious reflection.

At the same time, an attempt was made to force the mould of reality into the increasingly fantastic national ideals. A recurring theme, then, which led to the extremism of the 1930s and 40s, was the attempt to avoid the shock of a changing position, and especially the desire to reverse the trend towards a decrease in German national power and stature: 'In part, the attempt turned out to be so wild and barbaric because, in comparison with the ideal, with the dream empire which the National Socialists set out to restore, the factual resources of Germany were already very small' (1996: 349).

Even if the German war aims had succeeded and a pan-European empire had been established, argues Elias, it would have been impossible for them to maintain it for very long. The Nazis had no qualms about exterminating populations in countries they had invaded, but the task they set themselves was an onerous one because they simply did not have enough people to replace the subjected countries with a population of their own nationality. They also underestimated the difficulties of conquering other highly industrialized countries with relatively educated populations. If their empire had become a reality, it is likely that it would have faced increasing pressure from guerrilla warfare and national resistance movements, not to mention 'a powder keg of suffering and hatred surpassing by far all the consequences of the Second World War' (1996: 376). Had the Nazis been successful in their empire-building, Elias estimates the ratio of imperial rulers to subject populations would have been something like 70–80 million to 500–600 million, but it seems that the Nazi leaders' awareness of this great disparity was distorted by their social beliefs. Despite instigating a number of incentives encouraging and hastening 'Aryan' breeding, the Nazis could not realize that their belief system had many flaws which undermined these attempts, such as those strategies which led to the imprisonment and death of millions of Germans.

Hitler's appeal: identification with the oppressor

Within a 'spin' process, such as that which occurred in Nazi Germany, leaders play an important role. They may tend to emphasize or radicalize the more extreme elements of beliefs, but, according to Elias, they are not simply 'father-figures' because they also exhibit or possess certain of the attributes which characterize the ideals and conscience of the people they lead. In some respects they carry the imprint of their nation or group and are therefore in many ways similar to those over whom they hold sway (see Scheff and Retzinger 1991: 140–64). When Germany became involved in one of these 'spins', the likelihood was high that the establishment and the masses would drive each other to a radicalization of ideals and beliefs and the autocratic tendencies would tend to increase. A transition from stern to hard, tyrannical behaviour, from fairly fantastic to wildly fantastic beliefs, became very marked. The Nazi belief system was effectively a 'pseudo-scientific varnish spread thinly over a primitive, barbaric national mythology' (1996: 315). Elias suggests that this type of 'varnish' is common in the social and national myths of our age, but the Nazi version accentuated these myths, revealing their common features, particularly those it shared with religious movements: the Nazi movement began as a sect with a messianic mission.

Elias points to an extreme form of the wider phenomenon of 'identification with the masters' which became manifest in Nazi Germany. A simple example in the context of the Nazi era was the identification of certain prisoners with the concentration camp guards. In industrialized nation states, however, this identification can be highly complex. The social bonding of members through a national creed effectively creates a unified outlook between the ruling established groups and the ruled. The latter, in adopting this creed, identify themselves with their masters. If the regime happens to be autocratic, then they are identifying themselves with oppressors. Ironically, an impulse to break this identification, even if the oppression is felt, is paralysed by identification with the national ideal.

Elias highlights how in Germany this 'lust for submission' exhibited by the ruled became a marked tendency in times of crisis. Even in the face of defeat, this tendency held sway. In the absence of a relatively integrated system of thoughts and values to form the basis of resistance against oppressors, it is virtually impossible to remove them. If one identifies with the oppressors, argues Elias, feelings of opposition which cannot be openly expressed towards them may become internalized. Alternatively, the 'lust for submission' may be expressed externally, for example in the hatred of inferior and weaker groups. Elias refers to a German simile for describing such people – *Radfahrer* (cyclists): 'they bend their backs before those above them and tread on those below' (1996: 380). The Nazis made extremely effective use of several techniques, including terror, which was a short-term instrument of rule, concentration camps to remove dissenters and to intimidate the rest, and a belief and behaviour tradition which reinforced the effectiveness of these techniques. But without the cultivation of a conscience formation which encouraged a 'dependency on the oppressor', the Nazi regime could not have been so successful in its aims. Nor could its propaganda techniques have achieved what they did, techniques which also contributed to the relative lack of resistance, which cannot be explained simply through fear of reprisals.

This identification with the oppressor was so strong that no major breakdown in the morale of the German forces occurred during the war, while the majority of the population maintained their faith in Hitler. Despite drawing a negative reaction from some Germans, he was accepted by most of them as the representation of their own conscience and embodiment of their own we-ideal (1996: 388). Hitler's role as the German leader was far more important to the vast majority of the population during the war than the fact that he was a Nazi. He dovetailed into the emotional needs of the population in a way that no Weimar leader could. Elias likens Hitler's function at the time to that of a rain-maker, a witch-doctor or a shaman in simpler tribal societies. He 'was in essence an innovative political medicine man' (1996: 389). Like a primitive leader, he demanded sacrifices and victims. He provided 'semi-magical' solutions to problems of the social universe, filling gaps in knowledge with myths and half-truths. This 'supreme sorcerer', together with his band of henchmen, was able to attract the adulation of the German people not only through coercion, but through providing magical solutions which appealed to the needs and beliefs of the populace. Generally, says Elias, these magical operations and mythical beliefs serve as a 'balm which protects people against the full impact of awareness, the shock of recognition of their own powerlessness in the face of a course of events which threatens both their physical existence and their sense of the meaningfulness of life' (1996: 389).

These beliefs in turn made worse the conditions which they

were designed to ameliorate, contributing to the vicious circle in which the German people were ensnared under the Nazi regime. Elias points out that the notion that someone is a 'convinced National Socialist' does not fully explain the nature of the attraction Hitler had for the German population. Their belief in the *Führer* was

> grounded essentially in the simple needs of simple people whose helplessness in the face of great events of world politics made them turn to someone who, in their imagination, had the aura of a saviour, whose attributes and characteristics dovetailed with their needs and who, fortified by a machinery of external coercion, facilitated them in making all the sacrifices and bearing the oppression of a society geared for war without a serious breakdown of their weak and dependent self-control. (1996: 390)

As evidence of the thoughts and feelings of ordinary Germans, Elias quotes from private letters written during the Nazi era (1996: 391–8). They reveal to him the fact that most Germans were more or less passive objects in the hands of a minority. For most people, their private lives became increasingly important: the only stable things were their family and friends. This 'privatization' of interests developed in the face of a worsening military position, but despite the strong emotional pressure under which the letters were written, they do not contain a great deal of moaning or accusation. Only comments about 'the poor people who have lost everything', referring to those who have lost loved ones in the war, speak of the underlying tension (1996: 399). It is clear to Elias that these people were little or not at all prepared for these experiences. Nor were they conscious of the damage inflicted on other cities by the bombs dropped from German aircraft. Propaganda kept this from them and so all the greater was the shock experienced when news reached home from those returning from battle. Elias is given the impression of an obedient and stunned people who lack the ability, initiative and possibility to organize themselves in unified action against the state authorities. 'Privatization' was the complement of this retreat from public affairs, but the façade was difficult to maintain as enemy armies approached from east and west. Only gradually was the idea of defeat entertained, with all its associations of lost hopes and wishes. For the Germans it meant catastrophe and the realization, for those who thought about it deeply enough, that Germany would no longer play an important role in world affairs for generations to come. In quoting from these letters, however, Elias seems to underestimate one significant feature of the context in which they were written: under a regime where letters were regularly opened by the security services, so that notes of dissent would hardly figure prominently. Elias's analysis therefore reveals superficiality, although his approach attempts to cover a broad time-spectrum and this lack of depth is perhaps an inevitable result. In general, however, his analysis makes the internal dynamics of the National Socialist state more comprehensible with reference to the broader dynamics of inter-state relations (more on this in the final section of this chapter).

To summarize then, Elias highlights several interrelated processes which come together in the 'breakdown of civilization' in Germany during the Nazi period:

- the gradual decline of a long-lost Reich as the symbol of its greatness and the realization that the idealized aim of its future restoration may be lost;
- the exalted we-ideal which gave subjective meaning to the lives of many Germans;
- once again, the longing for restoration of the Reich which was related to a tradition of 'heroic death' in the name of an ideal;
- the 'spin' effect or double-bind as the result of inter- and intra-national entanglements;
- an adaptation crisis *vis-à-vis* growing interdependence with other nation states together with an emphasis on power politics;
- the radicalization of racial membership as a national ideal;
- the Nazi leaders' reliance on magico-mythical forms of thinking and the conjuring tricks of its charismatic figure-head;
- a compelling tendency of identification with the oppressor generating a *Radfahrer* dynamic;
- a strong line of aristocratic, autocratic tradition demanding absolute obedience in which the large mass of the German population acquiesced in the conduct of public affairs.

These processes did not necessitate a 'breakdown', argues Elias, but they prepared the way for the particular form of the 'breakdown of civilization' which occurred in Germany. Many

Germans, under the pressure of a worldwide economic crisis in the 1930s, were afraid that the former imperial greatness of their country would be lost: it had to be avoided at all costs. 'Hitler', writes Elias, 'the gifted shaman with his magical symbol, the swastika, invoked once more for the German masses the *fata morgana* of a superior German Reich' (1996: 402). With their backs against the wall, the *Führer* and his closest followers threw overboard entirely the established norms of decency, honesty and identification with large numbers of human beings in the name of recapturing Germany's lost glory. Thus, Elias comments of those in power during the Third Reich:

> The degree of oppression, violence and barbarism which they used corresponded to the degree of effort which was necessary to give Germany once more the appearance of greatness and to avoid the shock of discovery that the days of the German pre-eminence and the dream of a Reich were over. (1996: 402)

Mass murder and national we-identity

With respect to the Nazi perpetration of mass murder, Elias seeks to establish the 'conditions of twentieth-century civilization which make for barbarities of this kind and which can recur' to reveal once again 'the darker side of civilized human beings' (1996: 304). He asks:

> How was it possible that people could plan and execute in a rational, indeed scientific way, an undertaking which appears to be a throwback to the barbarism and savagery of earlier times – which, leaving aside all differences of population size and provided one is allowed posthumously to grant slaves the status of human beings, could have taken place in Ancient Assyria or Rome? . . . But in the twentieth century one no longer expected such things. (1996: 302)

While there were certainly aspects of the Nazi mass killing which were unique, there are also aspects which it shared with other episodes. History gives many instances of the group perpetration of mass murder (cf. Chalk and Jonassohn 1990). In the Ancient world, the destruction of the Sybarites by the citizens of Croton is one example. In such a situation, genocide was a calculated action which served to reduce the enemy's military strength, as in the case of the Spartan destruction of all men who could bear arms in Argos, the Athenian massacre of the male population of Melos in 416 BC (1986b: 144), or the mass killings recorded in the Bible (see Judges in particular). But it would seem that today's mass killings in wars, revolutions and other violent conflicts mainly differ in terms of the *techniques* employed and the *numbers* of people involved (cf. Elias 1987a: 111). They also differ in terms of the participation of those who are not members of the warrior classes, that is, the ordinary people, because of the development of nations which entails the identification of large numbers of people with each other and with a certain territory. What also differs is the relatively high level of revulsion expressed towards such violent actions and the widespread moral condemnation of them (1986b: 143; Mennell 1992: 248).

The Nazis' perpetration of genocide led many in the highly industrialized nation states of the West to question their own identities as inheritors of 'civilization', expressed as an ideal. The mass killing of the Jews was carried out in the name of a nation, a fact which does not seem to square with the self-image of those living in modern developed nation states who implicitly see themselves 'as if their standards of civilization and rationality were far beyond both the barbarism of earlier times and that of the less developed societies of today' (1996: 302). This self-image derives from feelings of pride associated with progress on the one hand and despair at the 'barbarities' of the twentieth century on the other. A major problem, then, in coming to terms with the mass murder perpetrated by the Nazis is that people simply cannot believe that such a thing could have happened in a 'civilized' country. As a consequence, various means of coping with this knowledge are developed which implicitly take this assumption on board, such as seeing the Hitler period as exceptional, unique, or viewing the Nazis themselves as madmen. Such coping mechanisms, suggests Elias, may provide comfort but do not explain. They prevent people from coming to terms with the idea that it might happen again, 'that such things could happen again, that such an outbreak of savagery and barbarism might stem directly from tendencies inherent in the structure of modern industrial societies themselves' (1996: 303). While Elias comments that, for these people, '[e]very war was clearly a regression to barbarism', within Europe at least, these wars have so far been relatively limited 'regressions' which do not involve

a complete dissolution of mutual identification between combatants or prisoners and their keepers (1996: 309). But this is
precisely what occurred in relations between the Nazis and the
Jews.

> It was not by any means the only regression to barbarism in the
> civilized societies of the twentieth century ... But of all these
> regressions, it was perhaps the deepest. Hardly any other example
> shows the vulnerability of civilization so clearly or reminds us so
> strongly of the dangers of contemporary growth processes and the
> fact that the latter can also predominate relative to the former. (1996:
> 308)

A common belief permeated the national consciousness of
people in other nations in which many, among them statesmen,
assumed that in other 'civilized' countries a more or less 'civilized' belief system would be genuinely held by its adherents
(1996: 315). An underlying disbelief was shared by these national leaders who would not recognize that the Nazis, while
they *spoke* of brutal and murderous behaviour, might actually *be*
brutal and kill people.

The mass murder of the Jews and other groups

In a recently translated essay (1994c: 121–30) Elias places the
Nazi mass murder of the Jews in the context of inter-state
processes and the dynamics of established-outsider relations.
Where groups become interdependent and a socially stigmatized group gains in relative power, the latter are perceived by
the established to be in direct competition for resources: a
regularity of established-outsider relations (see chapter 4). The
outsiders are tolerated so long as they keep to those activities
and positions which are befitting to their low status. But when
they rise in power, extreme difficulties of identity can arise for
both groups. This has been the case for the Jews throughout
Europe for centuries, but with regard to Germany, Elias focuses
on two issues which formed part of the tension within the
established-outsider dynamic.

First, Germany's rise, in relation to the established states
of Europe, to a relatively high position since 1870 meant
that awareness of status and identity was particularly acute, un-

stable and vulnerable in comparison to these other states. The Jewish minority were perceived with some irritation and eventually hostility by a Christian established group that was in fact unsure of itself. An increase in status uncertainty added to the generation of a dynamic of anti-Semitism. Second, within imperial Germany, Jews were generally excluded from many opportunities and positions within the establishment, but in those areas to which they did gain access (primarily economics and culture), Jews themselves did not accede to the low status attributed to them. They took their legal equality seriously and behaved like other Germans (1994c: 124). Disregarding the second-class image attributed to them by the established was a reaction that was closely connected with their strong academic tradition, but in imperial Germany they were certainly made to feel as if they were second-class citizens. Although stigmatized, they were legally, physically, economically and culturally safe. But during a transition to a new level of integration of a nation state, tension usually increases between the majority and the minorities within it (1994c: 127). Assimilation is one answer to this problem, but it is always a long process which may take at least three generations, suggests Elias, and depends on the readiness of the established to allow it. Other alternatives include expulsion and annihilation (Elias 1994c: 128). In keeping with the relative instability of the we-identity and sense of self-worth encoded in the German national habitus, acceptance of outsiders such as the Jews proved not only extremely difficult, but tragically impossible.

Before the decision was taken to exterminate the Jews and other minority groups sometime after the invasion of Poland in September 1939, these outsider groups were already being killed in concentration camps. The main drives against the Jews in particular were focused on their income and employment, the aim of which was the dispossession of assets. However, the effective economic advantages of the Jews were small: they amounted to only 1 per cent of the population. For a time, they were allowed to leave Germany of their own will. Later this was made increasingly difficult through bureaucratic controls. Eventually, with the aid of an immense bureaucratic machine, they were herded into cattle trucks and taken to extermination camps where they were systematically murdered (see, for example, Dawidowicz 1987).

The National Socialist state then comprised several 'semi-independent' and 'semi-feudal' government departments which were each headed by a second-rank *Führer*, in turn dependent on organizations in the country at large. The prestige and status of each leader was dependent upon the utility he was deemed to have for Hitler and the Nazi Party. But the power ratio between the leaders was unstable: they were suspicious of one another and always uncertain as to whether violence would be used against them, since this was for them a normal means of dealing with political opponents. While the party organization was rife with tensions and status rivalries behind the scenes – the social dynamics of 'Hitler's court' were anything but smooth[1] – it was all held together by a common allegiance to the one man at the top, as well as by a shared common belief system.

The 'Final Solution' effectively strengthened the prestige of some significant second-rank *Führer*. Their utility to Hitler had become enhanced by the special task assigned them. Various well-documented means of extermination were tried, ranging from shootings, such as in Poland during the eastern advance in 1941, pogroms, which aroused some negative public opinion and required considerable effort to obtain support in the wider community, to gassing in purpose-built chambers disguised as shower rooms. The latter resulted from the need for more efficient, rational and bureaucratic means of murder: that which 'required only a minimum of direct violence for an execution' (1996: 307). A few centres of extermination emerged which came to be administered in a more controlled fashion. Other questions of administration arose as well, such as the problem of how to determine 'Jewishness'. This was resolved at the Wannsee Conference held on 20 January 1942, which further bolstered the official authority of the now infamous bureaucrat Adolf Eichmann. The programme of mass extermination operated until the end of the war: it was only Germany's defeat which brought an end to the attempt to wipe out the Jews.

But what were the 'reasons' for this hatred and why did it express itself in the attempt to exterminate the Jews? On the surface, suggests Elias, this hatred was unrequited. The mass murder perpetrated by the Nazis was not a war operation. It did not result in the provision of land for German settlers. In short, it added nothing to the political power of the Nazi state, either domestically or internationally. Nor, in hindsight, did it seem

worth all the effort of utilizing scarce resources in perpetrating
the mass extermination of millions of people. Elias's answer is
plain and to the point: 'it was simply a question of the fulfillment
of a deeply rooted belief that had been central for the National
Socialist movement from the beginning' (1996: 310), namely that
German superiority required 'racial purity' which called for the
removal of what they defined as inferior contaminations within
the racially constituted national boundaries. The Nazis believed
that the Jews' own biological make-up predisposed them to hate
the Germans and to wish them destroyed. The Jews therefore
became the main focus for Nazi hatred, the 'logical' corollary of
which was their physical elimination. The war removed the
restraints of international public opinion which the Nazis previously felt to exist against the execution of their aims. Foreigners
could no longer monitor what went on in the German towns
with their ghettos and in secret behind the barbed-wire fences of
the camps.

Elias argues against explanations of group action primarily in
terms of underlying 'group interests' at the exclusion of what
might secondarily be seen as the professed aims and actions of
groups. 'Rational reasons' play their part, and may frequently
be the primary source of an explanation for group behaviour,
but sometimes professed beliefs themselves are more important
to an explanation. Thus, 'the attempt of the National Socialists
to destroy the Jews belongs to this category. It was one of the
most striking examples of the power which a belief – in this case,
a social or, more properly, a national belief – can gain over
people' (1996: 313).

The mass killing of the Jews also had something to do with a
dilemma experienced by Germans: they needed to keep their
enemy alive as a potential source of labour should they win the
war, but at the same time they felt they were surrounded by
enemies and were therefore compelled to kill as many of them
as possible. But the Jews could hardly be said to have been a
'real' threat to the Nazis. They were among the least powerful of
those the Nazis regarded as enemies. Thus, Elias comments:

> the extermination of the Jews was far less significant than the
> elimination of enemies from other foreign groups. The Nazis acted
> like a man who, prevented from destroying his real enemies, dis-
> charged his pent-up rage against enemies who represented a pre-
> dominantly imaginary danger for him. (1996: 371)

While Elias considers the genocide perpetrated against the Jews to be a relatively 'minor episode in the rise and fall of peoples', he points to its symbolic significance:

> It shows what the leaders of a civilized nation are capable of doing in their struggle for the restoration or preservation of their imperial role when a chronic feeling of decline, of being encircled by enemies and driven into a corner, awakens the conviction that only absolute ruthlessness can save their fading power and glory. It also makes clear to what extremes of behaviour people can be driven by the exclusiveness of a national belief system against those whom they experience as 'foreigners', as 'outsiders' who do not belong, as members of a different, potentially hostile group. (1996: 360)

The killing of the Jews and other groups was a function of what the Nazis perceived as their desperate international situation, one in which they faced the threat of having to relinquish Germany's position as a first-rank nation. But their deeds were perpetrated in the name of a national (fantasy) ideal, not a national reality.

The *Radfahrer* dynamic became accentuated in the relationship between the Nazis and the Jews. Elias rejects the idea of 'scapegoats' as too simple, pointing out that the Jews were the favourite hate-objects of those lower sections of society who were experiencing considerable pressure from above. So in the concentration camps, the cruelty of the guards was directly related to their own identification with an oppressive authority. Most of these camp guards were drawn from the least educated members of German and East European societies, such as the peasantry, and were therefore quite used to being on the bottom of the social hierarchy. Then, relatively suddenly, they had people below them for perhaps the first time in their lives, while at the same time they were compelled to exhibit *Kadavergehorsam* (blind obedience) to the *Führer* and his representatives. The resulting tensions were let loose with cruel consequences:

> Hidden impulses which had previously been curbed by the need to repress all hostile feelings towards superiors and to submit cheerfully to the strict discipline demanded by the regime in the name of a harsh and oppressive idol, together with their self-protective identification with this regime, broke out with terrible force like steam released under high pressure in their behaviour against people whom they had to view as inferiors and who were utterly powerless. (1996: 382)

Here a distinction must be drawn between the *Angriffslust* of knightly lords described by Elias in *The Civilizing Process*, and the mass murder perpetrated by the Nazis. This is important in view of the seeming contradiction between Elias's notion of a civilizing process and institutions such as Auschwitz. Face-to-face and mechanized violence at a distance are clearly differentiated for Elias, as I made clear in my discussion of violence in Elias's work at the end of chapter 3. Given the character of the bureaucratic mass extermination of outsider groups in Germany and other countries under the tentacles of the Third Reich, the actual motivations of those at the 'other end', the people who carried out the killing, were comparatively irrelevant (Kuzmics 1988: 157), although the perpetrators' deeds may well have exacted a psychical cost upon them.[2] However, as the quotation above suggests, Elias speculates that the camp guards themselves may well have enjoyed inflicting this cruelty, as a kind of liberation: the chance to inflict on the prisoners what they secretly wished to inflict on others. But he warns against seeing these actions simply as those of sadistic individuals. Rather, '[t]hey are indicative of the enormous pressure of the tensions and conflicts (inter- as well as intra-personal) behind the monolithic facade of a social system whose leading men embarked, as it were with clenched teeth, on a gigantic task for which their resources were scarcely sufficient' (1996: 382).

The whole regime encouraged a categorical imperative of action, with the *Führer* serving as the embodiment of individual conscience, condoning vicious persecution of outsider groups regarded as weaker and inferior in the name of the nation. The balance between external and internal controls was tipped firmly in favour of the former: when individuals had to rely on their own conscience, they often lacked the ability to control their forbidden urges. The *Rechtsstaat* of the pre-Hitler era established a rule of law which was ultimately based upon what are commonly called 'civilized' standards. In contrast, the Nazis discouraged individual conscience to a greater extent than any other German regime. When they took over the state monopolies of state power, they encouraged what was previously regarded as criminal. According to Elias, in this situation, the individual conscience of most people comprising the German masses was not sufficiently independent or strong enough to enable individually guided action which would openly contra-

dict the directives of state representatives. And so when knowledge of the concentration camps was eventually widespread,
many Germans experienced a deep conflict between their own
conscience and that of the state on which they had relied for
reinforcing the former. In this way, Elias once again highlights
the interconnections between psychical dispositions and the
developments of broader social processes. In his discussion,
however, we have also seen that Elias uses words such as
'barbarism' and 'barbarity' in a way which can only be described
as normative, but I would like to save my comments on this issue
for the conclusion. Here, I would like to consider the question of
how we can further our understanding of the 'breakdown of
civilization' outlined by Elias in the context of the 'civilization'
of modern twentieth-century societies.

Civilization, 'modernity' and decivilizing processes

The mass murder perpetrated by the Nazis was an unintended
consequence of the civilizing process, involving increasing control over and dependence upon technology and bureaucratic
efficiency combined with the utilization of a state violence
monopoly against outsiders or perceived enemies. The destruction unleashed in Germany was a potential inherent within the
sort of society Germany had become. This is certainly recognized by Elias, as the quotations above demonstrate, in comments which hint at an awareness of the tendencies inherent in
contemporary growth processes. But those specifically modern
aspects of social interdependencies which might have contributed to the Holocaust do not feature prominently in his discussion of the Nazi perpetration of mass murder.

Zygmunt Bauman (1988) addresses the issue of Nazi mass
murder in the context of modern twentieth-century societies
while at the same time commenting on Elias's theory of civilizing processes. It therefore seems appropriate to focus on
Bauman's work in order to highlight aspects of Elias's approach.
I would like to suggest that Bauman's ideas can complement
those of Elias in moving towards a more adequate understanding of Nazi genocide. Bauman argues for the moral responsibility of sociologists to take on board the implications of the
Holocaust. He also rightly suggests that certain features inher-

ent in 'modernity' came together in triggering this social disaster. But throughout his book on the subject, Bauman uses the terms 'civilization' and 'civilizing process' sometimes with and sometimes without reference to Elias. When he does acknowledge Elias's use of these terms, Bauman seems mistakenly to attribute to him a use of the terms which can only be described as normative. It is therefore unclear as to what these concepts may refer in Bauman's own work, while at the same time he is highly critical of that which he implicitly and explicitly attributes to Elias's use of these terms. After a brief discussion of these misunderstandings, this section shows some characteristic features of Bauman's views on the relationship between 'modernity' and the Holocaust before considering the potential usefulness of his perspective in relation to that of Elias.

Bauman discusses the meaning of the 'civilizing process' which he says is an aetiological myth, a 'morally elevating story of humanity emerging from pre-social barbarity ... most recently illustrated by the burst of prominence and overnight success of the [*sic*] Elias's presentation of the 'civilizing process' (1988: 12). For Bauman, the most common of the many images of the 'civilizing process' involves a suppression of irrational, anti-social drives and the gradual elimination of violence from social life and its concentration in the hands of the state to defend and define national units (1988: 27). This image, he suggests, is not necessarily misleading, but in light of the Holocaust it is one-sided. In the 'myth' of the civilizing process, the Holocaust represents a failure of civilization, that is, of purposive, reason-guided action, while the civilizing process is deemed unfinished and still to be concluded (1988: 13).

As I have already said, there seems to be some confusion surrounding the way in which Bauman uses the term civilization (and by implication the notion as used by Elias) to represent the expression of an ideal, and the term civilizing process to mean a teleological progression towards a predetermined goal. He also attributes to Elias the notion that civilization is the opposite of barbarism, an accusation that is not without foundation (more on this in chapter 8). But all in all, Bauman seems to give a partial and misleading interpretation of the meaning of civilization in the work of Elias.[3] He has blended together aspects of the term described in chapter 3 above as normative, with the more detached meaning of the term developed by Elias.

Elias explicitly states that civilization is an ongoing process which is never concluded, a question of balances and degrees to which people's aggressive tendencies are always locked in some form of tension-equilibrium with more peaceful attitudes and behaviour. He is also highly sensitive to the 'shell' of civilized restraints, implying its fragility. However, despite Bauman's largely mistaken interpretation of Elias's theory of civilizing processes (he does use the concept of civilization himself, but in ways which differ from Elias), his approach can stand alongside Elias's as an important complement to an understanding of the Holocaust.

According to Bauman, modern forms of social organization divest humans of their 'natural' ability to take responsibility for their actions through lengthening chains of command and a highly specialized division of labour which restricts individuals' scope of action and at the same time increases their reliance on means–ends rationality within their own sphere of competence. In short, the capacity of people to act morally is restricted because they are no longer fully responsible for all of their actions. Therefore modern genocide has certain peculiarities compared with the mass murders of pre-modern times, such as a specifically modern form of exterminatory racism (1988: 31–82; cf. Elias 1996: 310); typically modern patterns of technological bureaucratized action with their concomitant mentalities allowing for the dehumanization of bureaucratic human objects (1988: 15, 105–6; cf. Elias 1996: 307); and the acquiescence of victims through the cultivation of their own rationality (1988: 203; cf. Elias 1996: 375, 386). For Bauman, the Holocaust represents a failure or even a lack of any 'modern safeguards' (1988: 88, 108–10). Indeed, for him, 'civilized' traits exist alongside and push on the dynamic of mass murder: 'most bystanders reacted as civilized norms advise and prompt us to react to things unsightly and barbaric; they turned their eyes the other way' (1988: 111).

Bauman goes on to point out that in modern societies violence is increasingly divested of moral calculus and rationality is emancipated from the constraints of ethical and moral considerations (1988: 28).[4] In the course of the 'civilizing process', violence is in fact redeployed and access to it is redistributed: it is removed from view rather than forced out of existence (Bauman 1988: 97, 107), a point which overlaps with Elias's argument. For

Bauman, the Holocaust is the result of primarily, if not exclusively, modern phenomena and he suggests that these phenomena are usually separated in modern societies. However, in Germany towards the end of the first half of the twentieth century they came together in a particular situation which allowed the amoral deployment of violence by the state in conjunction with a lack of safeguards against its perpetration. 'Certain universal features of modern civilization' allowed for the possibility of the Holocaust, but its *implementation* . . . was connected with a specific and not at all universal relationship between state and society' (1988: 82). In emphasizing the role that 'modernity' plays in causing the Holocaust, Bauman argues that modern civilization is not the Holocaust's *sufficient* condition, but its *necessary* one (1988: 13).

Two basic assumptions seem to underlie Bauman's argument, each appearing to have the character of a Kantian *a priori*. First, that human beings have a 'well-nigh instinctual aversion' to perpetrating violence against other humans and a 'universal inhibition' against killing.[5] Second, they have an innate, pre-social moral capacity. These two assumptions interweave with Bauman's presentation of certain features of modern societies which contributed to generating the Holocaust. From Elias's perspective, both of these assumptions would represent misconceptions, or even ideals. Regarding Bauman's first assumption, that human beings are 'naturally' averse to perpetrating violence, Elias shows in *The Civilizing Process* that in some circumstances, as in medieval Europe, people openly enjoyed perpetrating acts of violence and killing. Indeed, the experience of some soldiers in modern wars such as in Vietnam, the Falkland Islands or Bosnia would seem to suggest the opposite to Bauman's claim. But Elias would not go the other way and argue that people are 'naturally' violent (see my comments on drives and aggression in Elias's work in chapter 2 above). The second of Bauman's claims, that humans possess an innate moral capacity, can also be questioned. For Elias, precepts represent the intergenerational tipping of the balance between constraints by others and self-restraint in favour of the latter. In Nazi Germany, the balance tipped the other way (Bauman and Elias concur on this point) because of the changing dynamic of social interdependencies over many generations (here Bauman would deny the importance of historical developments).

Bauman's assumption concerning innate moral capacity seems
to be a variant on what Elias might call '*homo clausus* thinking'.
Those capacities which humans may experience as innate may
well be nothing other than the result of compulsions they exert
over one another in their networks of interdependency. Elias
employs a model of social processes which is a theoretical–
empirical synthesis (a process theory) in his attempt to understand the Nazi mass murder, and because of this, he is not
constrained by reference to the failure of a hypothesized innate
human capacity to triumph over an imposing 'outer' social
reality which divests humans of a 'natural' moral disposition. In
short, Bauman seems to rely upon spurious philosophical assumptions. In contrast, Elias develops his ideas in constant
cross-reference to evidence and his arguments seem preferable
in this respect. Furthermore, in emphasizing the constituent
features of modern societies in generating the Holocaust, Bauman
neglects those aspects of German history which are relevant
to its explanation – that is, features of more recent German
society which are conditioned by events occurring many
generations ago. Bauman's discontinuity thesis therefore
restricts the explanatory scope of his comments on Nazi mass
murder in particular and mass murder in general. In contrast
to Elias, Bauman focuses on the discontinuities rather than the
continuities.

From the previous two sections of this chapter it is clear that
Elias shows awareness of the issues raised by Bauman: he
remarks that the attempted mass murder of the Jews was part of
tendencies inherent in the structure of Germany and of twentieth-century societies themselves and that such an exercise was
rationally and scientifically organized, requiring efficient,
rational and bureaucratic means (1996: 302, 303, 307). But Elias
does not deal with these issues in as much detail. From detailed
description of the patterning of action fields through bureaucratic organization Bauman argues that moral decision-making
is removed from these forms of interdependence. Elias's explanation, however, accounts for the crucial long- and short-term
changes specific to Germany in terms of his concepts of we-
image, state formation and the internalization of controls in
relation to norms of violence within specific social figurations
over time. Elias shows that, particularly in comparison with
England, Germany lacked a *stable* process of state formation,

thereby decreasing the likelihood of controls by others being transformed into self-restraint largely because of the discontinuities of the development of Germany and the resulting insecurities felt by people within its boundaries. Elias's theory of civilizing processes is therefore not falsified by the events of Nazi Germany, as Edmund Leach claims when he comments that Elias's book on civilization was being refuted by Hitler 'on the grandest scale' at the very time of writing (1986: 13). Of course, the decivilizing process of the Nazi era was not the necessary outcome of the German *Sonderweg*, and here Bauman's emphasis on discontinuities is significant, highlighting those aspects of modern societies which 'came together' at that particular historical crossroad. However, Bauman's argument remains somewhat of a truism, since it is of course difficult to imagine how the mass murder of the sort perpetrated by the Nazis could occur in a pre-modern setting. The utility of his approach in relation to that of Elias lies primarily in the fact that he provides greater detail of the dynamics of particular social processes in modern societies which contributed to the human catastrophe of the Holocaust.

Nazi Germany, integration conflicts and the model of decivilizing processes

There is considerable evidence to show that among large numbers of Germans during the Second World War there was a contraction in the scope of mutual identification, a process which in Germany involved the stigmatization and dehumanization of 'outsiders', particularly the Jews, in the name of a national ideal (cf. Manvell 1969; Dicks 1972; Merkyl 1975; Fischer 1982; Bessel 1984; Elias 1988c). Also, millions of Germans acquiesced in the authority and constraints imposed by others, particularly those in positions of political power. In this context, social standards were likely to, and indeed did, allow for the emergence of a relatively less all-round, even and stable habitus. Thus, in the Nazi era, all three of the main criteria of a decivilizing process became dominant: a shift in the balance between constraints by others and self-restraint in favour of the former, social standards of behaviour and feeling which allowed for a decrease in the evenness, stability and differentiation of habitus emerged, together with a contraction in the scope of mutual identification between groups. But these part-processes would be likely to occur in conjunction with the part-processes of the disintegration of interdependence chains and an established violence monopoly. However, in Nazi Germany they occurred in conjunction with a consolidated state monopoly of violence and an economy which was not in decline, but part of a highly specialized division of social functions and long chains of interdependency utilizing rationally planned and organized bureaucracies. In other words, it would appear that these processes occurred in conditions which are not anticipated in the model of decivilizing processes as I have presented it in chapter 4 above.

This could lead to the conclusion that the model either needs to be revised, or is falsified by contradictory evidence, since a configuration of part-processes which would be *likely* to generate decivilizing was not dominant in the Nazi era. In answer to this, a historical, developmental frame of reference must not be forgotten. In other words, in order to understand the Nazi perpetration of mass murder, the sequential development of certain social processes specific to Germany must be taken into account. Particularly the period between 1871–1918 (cf. Feldman 1992; Kocka 1984) and, as we have seen from chapter 6 above, events in Weimar Republican Germany represent a social dynamic that can be described as a societal decivilizing process which had indeed become dominant among certain groups at that time. A specific pattern of part-processes – including the three main criteria of decivilizing and the processes of demonopolization and disintegration – had been dominant in the period immediately prior to the National Socialist rise to power.

To summarize once again, the disintegration of the imperial Good Society[6] with the abdication of the Kaiser after the First World War occurred together with a shift in the overall power structure of society in the Weimar Republic to favour the previous outsider (workers') groups and their representatives, increasing the social tensions between them and those who identified with the old establishment (noble and bourgeois groups). Many Germans could not come to terms with the operation of a parliamentary democracy and they felt betrayed and humiliated through their government's acceptance of the Versailles Treaty. Moreover, the Weimar Republican state's monopoly of violence was gradually infringed by terrorist groups including the infamous Freikorps. The violence was fuelled by a double-bind process between the supporters of the imperial establishment and those who supported the republic, and by increasing social fears through the use of police and military violence. Communist and fascist groups retaliated against each other amid a severe economic crisis which was instrumental in the collapse of the republic and the rise of Hitler and the Nazi Party (cf. Hiden 1977; Nicholls 1979; Berghahn 1962: 82–128). In this situation, inter-group tensions increased, a contraction in the scope of mutual identification with the Jews and other outsider groups occurred and there was a general shift in the balance between constraints by others and self-restraint in favour of group loyalty and the constraints of hierarchical commands.

The group-specific decivilizing processes of the Weimar era tended in the direction of a societal process of decivilization, occurring in the context of a breakdown of a violence monopoly and a fragmentation of economic and personal chains of inter-dependence. In 1933, the decivilizing process which had gained momentum in the Weimar era was transformed by a group of people who openly used violence to achieve their aims: it became once again specific to particular groups. Having gained power, the Nazis took it upon themselves to perpetrate violence and murder, especially against outsider groups, through the efficient use of the state bureaucratic apparatus which remained intact and was consolidated by them, all in the name of an extreme national group identity.

A recurring theme of Elias's explanation is that this mass murder was to some extent a function of the Nazi's reaction to their declining power position in relation to other European societies. But how does the broader context of inter-state tensions in which this genocide occurred help to explain it? On the intra-state level, Nazism was predicated on and made use of the democratization process which had also occurred in other European societies. Italian and German fascism constituted mass movements, their leaders were not reactionaries who sought to maintain the old power structures (in contrast to Franco in Spain): they stood for an integration of the masses, including the petty bourgeoisie from whose ranks many Nazi leaders were recruited. Hitler made it possible for anyone to become an officer in the army and broke up parts of the old elite society by eliminating sections of the Junkers. This integration process occurred in conjunction with democratization. The state apparatus was taken over in the name of a mass movement and then used against its own population.[7] The state's Janus-head character is revealed in greater relief in the case of the Nazi era: it is both protective *and* repressive, inclusive *and* exclusive. The national we–they identity dynamic can be directed inward as well as outside the social boundaries of the nation. The violence and mass murder in Germany was, at least in some ways, bound up with differentiation and integration processes which generated integration conflicts. In Germany, such a conflict arose when former outsider groups striving for emancipation (the masses, including the bourgeoisie) sought representation within or control over the key monopolies. But as we have seen, for many Germans throughout the Weimar period and the Third Reich, their unstable we-identity and sense of worth were experienced to be endangered to the point where acceptance of outsiders in this context, particularly the Jews, proved impossible.

On the inter-state level, as mentioned in chapter 4, up until the Second World War the survival units of humanity had become highly interdependent. Together with the general expansion in the scope of mutual identification within and between twentieth-century European societies came an increase in tensions within and between those states involved. These long-term processes have been characterized by relatively short-term integration conflicts, and Germany during the first half of this century represents an extreme form of this. The Holocaust provides a sociologically interesting case in that ties of national identity outweighed those of identification with outsider groups within the socially defined parameters of the nation. In Germany, intra-state tensions resulted in whole groups, particularly the Jews, being designated as outsiders and excluded from the state apparatus in the name of a *national* we-ideal. The monopolies of state power, utilizing all the technological and bureaucratic organizational possibilities of the mid twentieth century, were turned against specific minorities within and later outside its own national boundaries (see Bettelheim 1979: 189).

Combining the intra- and inter-state perspectives on integration conflicts, the Second World War and the Nazi mass murder can be interpreted *in part* as the result of a dual integration conflict in Western Europe: the integration of the German state

within the configuration of increasingly interdependent Western European states; and the growing integration within them of
the masses (or at least their representatives) in the running of
key monopolies of state power. While the mass murder perpetrated by the Nazis was not, of course, the inevitable result of this
process, broader dynamics of inter-state relations served to
facilitate extreme nationalism and a fear of outsiders among
many Germans at the time. With respect to violence, this state-
sponsored dehumanization of outsiders can be seen to result in
part from an integration conflict involving a societal decivilizing
process within the Weimar era which then narrowed in scope
and became a group-specific decivilizing process within the
Third Reich, generated within a long-term process of advancing
inter-state interdependence.

Many of Elias's critics have implicitly or explicitly assumed
that his perspective is incapable of addressing issues such as the
rise of Nazism and the Holocaust. My reconstruction of Elias's
position in this chapter therefore stands as a corrective to these
views. What I hope to have clarified is how the model of
decivilizing processes sketched in chapter 4, in conjunction with
the notion of integration conflicts, can be used to add to our
understanding of the dynamics of 'reversals' in civilizing
processes more generally and the events of Nazi Germany in
particular.

CHAPTER EIGHT

Elias on Violence, Civilization and Decivilization

I have tried to show that the juxtaposition of the concepts of violence and civilization in Elias's work is only an apparent contradiction. The whole project of *The Civilizing Process* can be seen as a means of developing a more detached perspective on social processes in general and the social crises of European societies in the 1920s and 30s in particular, stemming from Elias's experiences in Germany and his resulting desire to understand them. The first half of this book considered how Elias develops his theory of civilizing processes, the significance of the concepts of violence and civilization in his work, and the way in which he outlines the 'figurational' dynamics of violent social processes. It was then shown in the second half how Elias's concepts are woven into explanations of historical examples, referring to his work on England and then with more detailed reference to his publications on Germany.

Elias's texts reveal that he is aware of the ideological, normative connotations of the word civilization and he makes this a central part of his problematic. Indeed, he offers a plausible account of the way in which the term attained these connotations over many generations. As he suggests, 'civilization' also refers to a 'factual core'. He develops a type of analysis which focuses on the changing behaviour and personality structures – or habitus – of people living within the secular upper classes of Western European societies and on the changing terms these people used to describe socially desirable behaviour. In other words, civilization is used by Elias to signify specific changes of social and individual habitus tending in a particular direction. This transformation of behaviour is observed by him in documents.

Although Elias's theory of civilizing processes is modelled most centrally on the development of France, there is also a clear comparison with Germany and England. From this, he derives more general conclusions concerning the development of social habitus throughout Western European societies. Various critics, anthropologists in particular, have suggested that some dominant behaviour patterns common in the West are to be found outside extended networks of interdependence and effective centralized monopolies of violence. I have argued that the importance of the development and stability of this process is significant and that the issues raised by these anthropologists do not refute the theory. But they may demonstrate that the scope of Elias's approach is restricted to particular levels of social size and complexity, or indeed, relevant only in the European context. Further research is needed in this area, but the problem of the transferability of the theory of civilizing processes remains (cf. Mennell 1992: 232–3).

Having established the way in which Elias constructs an empirically founded theory of civilizing processes, in conjunction with the term civilization, I pointed to some ambiguities in his use of this concept. I argued that those critics who have implied Elias was naive and ethnocentric in his use of this term are largely mistaken in that they have frequently misunderstood how it features in his work. While Elias has shown sociogenetically how the word civilization came to have associations with colonialism and ethnocentrism, he could have been clearer on this point in order to avoid such misunderstandings. The term civilization was therefore discussed in more detail in order to differentiate the various meanings of the word from Elias's employment of the concept: aspects of the term which include normative assumptions and which can be said to be more detached. Elias's notion of civilization does not refer to a homogeneous entity, nor to a necessary, teleological process, but to a beginningless, ongoing and never-ending process.

I have introduced a definition of violence which I believe to be implicit in Elias's work and clarified the ways in which various forms and meanings of violence feature in his writings. Violence is not conceived by him to be antithetical to civilization – both concepts are interwoven aspects of overall processes of social development. Patterns of individual self-restraint with respect to violence are bound up with the patterning of social relations within which the means and use of violence is controlled. The process of civilization involves the gradual, partial and un-planned long-term pacification of human societies within, and increasingly between, states – a process which is 'never com-pleted and constantly endangered'.

Three main themes – figurations and interdependence, social bonding and identification, and established-outsider relations – served to elaborate upon and to clarify the conceptual relation-ship between violence and civilization through Elias's construc-tion of sociological process models. Criteria of civilizing and decivilizing processes were also presented and I singled out three main criteria that can be used to determine decivilizing. As there is no explicit theory of decivilizing processes in Elias's work, I deduced from what is implicit the possible symptoms of such processes that would follow logically from the theory of civilizing processes. I also outlined the various dimensions of decivilizing – individual, group, societal, inter-societal and humanity – and their dynamics.

Elias's work on England further highlights the characteristics of civilizing processes and the way in which he handles specific historical examples. Through demonstrating how Elias accounts for the social development of both England and Germany I made explicit that his theory of civilizing processes is not narrowly based upon the development of one particular society, namely France. The discussion of England also allowed the contrasts with Germany and Elias's comments on that country to be shown more clearly, particularly in terms of continuities and discontinuities in processes of state formation and the resulting patterning of social habitus. This approach not only increases our understanding of how Elias deals with specific historical examples, it also formed a backdrop to similar themes which were touched upon subsequently in relation to Germany.

Elias's discussion of a 'civilizing spurt' revealed certain prob-lems with the way he uses his theory of civilizing processes to explain particular historical examples in his discussion of the development of English society and the relationship between the formation of modern Parliament and the emergence of 'sport', particularly foxhunting. The empirical evidence to which he refers does not fit neatly into his own model. Indeed, the scope of the theory is potentially restricted to the explanation of killing by proxy among the upper classes in foxhunting and to accounting for the rise of clubs in this social circle. Again, this points to areas for further research. However, Elias's useful conceptions of violent social dynamics surface in considering his ideas on the English national 'adaptation crises' and we- and they-images in relation to violence on the intra- and inter-state levels. These insights retain their relevance, despite his apparently rather simple view of the English social habitus and the role of the press in the formation of public opinion.

Elias's reflections on we-identity, nationalization and violence in Germany were outlined in chapter 6. This entailed detailed reference to one of his most important later publications, *The Germans*, in which Elias specifies a culture of violence among the German upper classes and accounts for the lowering of both sensibility thresholds with respect to the observation and perpetration of violence, as well as the level of mutual identification. I argued that Elias possibly over-exaggerated the extent to which physical prowess was significant in the duelling bouts of the student fraternities, although the 'hard' attitude and severe control of emotions within these social circles played an important part in the generation of the ethos shared by paramilitary groups such as the *Freikorps* in the Weimar Republic. I also drew together the longer- and shorter-term social processes highlighted by Elias in the development of Germany. This clarified the group-specific decivilizing processes involving the continuity of a culture of violence among the upper classes and sections of the middle classes, stemming from imperial Germany through to the end of the Weimar Republic and the rise of Hitler.

Many of the ideas and themes discussed earlier were brought together in considering decivilizing processes in Nazi Germany. Again, reference was made to *The Germans* and also to parts of a little-known recently translated essay in which Elias applies his theory of established-outsider relations to understand the position of the Jews in Germany (1994c). Elias argues that the Nazi perpetration of mass murder was in part the result of 'contemporary growth processes' in modern societies. However, I suggested that his perspective does not take into account sufficiently the features of modern twentieth-century societies which would allow greater understanding of these events. Some aspects of the explanation offered by Zygmunt Bauman (1988), which emphasize the discontinuous nature of modern societies, provide a complement to Elias, who tended to emphasize societal continuities. A perspective which appreciates the *balance* between continuities and discontinuities in social processes was advocated in adding to our understanding of the Nazi era. But the theory of decivilizing processes was not seen to be redundant in relation to the fact that the Nazis held a monopoly of violence within the context of a relatively stable economy and relatively dense and long chains of interdependence. Events preceding the Nazi rise to power *do* fit the theory of decivilizing processes and contribute to a more adequate understanding of that time in terms of Elias's work. Needless to say, no theory provides an entirely 'adequate' explanation of these events.

Elias frequently uses terms like 'barbarity' or 'barbarization' when writing about violence in Germany more generally and the Nazi perpetration of genocide in particular. The words 'barbarism' and 'barbarity' are peppered throughout his essay on the subject in *The Germans*,[1] where he describes the mass murder of the Jews as 'a throwback to the barbarism and savagery of earlier ages' (1996: 302) and as 'one of the deepest' regressions to barbarism of the twentieth century (1996: 308). The title of this essay, 'The Breakdown of Civilization', itself merely serves to compound an impression of primarily normative valuations in Elias's use of these terms.

It is important to bring out the ambivalencies surrounding the *experiences* of situations or behaviour and the process of *theorizing* about them. I would not wish to suggest that the terms 'barbarism' and 'barbarity' are inappropriate to describe the actions of certain people in Nazi Germany. Indeed, I see no problem in using these terms in this normative way. But for Elias to use them without further comment merely invites questions as to whether and to what extent he uses the word *civilization* normatively. The importance of these observations lies in the fact that Elias is so careful to develop a more detached concept of civilization: he differentiates civilization as an ideal from that referring to factual processes. For the sake of clarity, the opposite of this notion as an ideal is the normative concept of 'barbarism' or 'barbarization'. To be consistent, therefore, Elias should refer to the opposite of the factual process of civilization with the technical term decivilization.[2] He in fact refers to the Nazi era in terms of 'rebarbarization' (1996: 31, 38) and a 'spurt towards barbarization' (1996: 444n), but he does not comment on his choice of words.

However, while Elias, as a German of Jewish descent, had good reason to be less detached in this respect, he still managed to achieve considerable detachment in his comments on the mass murder of the Jews. As I have argued above, there is a model of decivilizing processes implied in his work which is logically more in keeping with the way he developed his theory of civilizing processes. Elias wrote his essay on the 'breakdown of civilization' in the early 1960s,[3] many years before his belated international recognition which came with the translation into English of *The Civilizing Process*. It seems likely, however, that his views on the subject of the Nazis were formed in reaction to critical responses to his ideas on civilization presented in lectures and seminars since the 1950s. There can be no question that he wrote his synthetic study of civilization as a direct result of living through and witnessing events during the Weimar Republic and the Nazi rise to power. Clearly, Elias provides a relatively detached analysis which is largely devoid of moralistic judgements and comprises a determined effort simply to understand what happened. I have singled out only his use of particular words for criticism because of their implications for Elias's use of the term civilization.

In discussing the development of knowledge in seminars and lectures, Elias often used the metaphor of the next generation seizing a baton and running with it, like athletes in a relay race. But what can the next generation of those who seek to understand and explain social processes take forward and use from Elias's work? The synthetic figurational approach Elias develops offers a useful conceptual framework with which to investigate violent social processes in a non-reductionist fashion, without prioritizing the biological, psychical or economic aspects of human beings. In particular, it brings to the centre of a sociological investigation of violence the role and forceful nature of group fantasies, both those groups hold of themselves and of others with which they become interdependent. Elias clarifies that such relationships can generate an immanent dynamic of their own. This highlights the largely blind, unplanned character of such processes and the fact that they are often beyond the control of those bound up in them. It also brings into focus the central place of fear in social relations in the generation of violence. Because the synthesis to which Elias sought to contribute is equally 'theoretical' and 'empirical', his work on violence and civilization implies a dialectical model, one which is constantly provisional, to be used and revised in the light of further research.

One way in which the theory of decivilizing processes I have sketched – although implied in Elias's work – may be relevant to an understanding of violence in Europe today is in relation to the war in former Yugoslavia. This human catastrophe is a highly pertinent example of a decivilizing process occurring in the context of a disintegration of structural ties. There, a central state monopoly of violence disintegrated and a society fragmented into cellular groups divided by vehement hatred and locked in violent double-bind processes, fighting in the name of deeply held national and religious convictions. The less inclusive we-identities and we-images of the main groups concerned fuelled a compelling dynamic of violence against each other and those defined as outsiders within their own groups.

This particular decivilizing process was, however, quite limited in terms of the potential use of instrumental violence. 'Ethnic Cleansing', the catchword of this war on the doorstep of Europe, bears structural similarities with the mass murder of the Jews in Nazi Germany. However, as far as we know, the murder in Bosnia was not as awesomely efficient, simply because the perpetrators were unable to summon those capacities of modern forms of social organization which were placed at the disposal of the Nazi leaders in the 1940s. Ironically, it is precisely these capacities which could have averted the Bosnian war through the deployment of international forces in the early phases of its development (Mennell 1995a: 17). The member states of the European Union are certainly able to mobilize formidable military force, as many of them did in the Gulf War, but they hesitated to sanction full-scale intervention in Bosnia partly because of their own heritage of 'civilization' which balked at the use of violence as a form of conflict resolution.

The three main criteria of decivilizing presented earlier can serve as a model with which to investigate violent social processes. However, the levels or dimensions of decivilizing processes must be specified when considering particular examples, as well as those decivilizing processes which are longer-term, more encompassing and gain a greater permanence because of the fragmentation of structural links in interdependency chains. Group and societal decivilizing processes can emerge within the broader context of long-term trends of the increasing intra- and inter-state interdependence, which may in turn increase the likelihood of conflicts between specific groups within those nation states involved. Generally then, decivilizing processes can be short term, occurring in the context of long-term structured processes spanning many generations. This formulation sees the idea of continuity as bound up with that of discontinuity, representing a *balance* between both perspectives. The connections of civilizing and decivilizing processes to longer-term or shorter-term social processes can be established with reference to evidence, thereby avoiding terms such as 'modernity' which embody a tendency to reification and may even serve as a means of blame attribution in assigning responsibility for events such as the Holocaust (cf. Van Benthem van den Bergh 1980c). In diagnosing decivilizing processes, empirical evidence is required which would probably span at least three generations (Mennell 1990a: 211); and it is in the context of empirical research where the value of the theory of decivilizing processes can be established. As Elias and Scotson correctly remark, 'in the last resort, the crucial test for the fruitfulness or sterility of a sociological theory is the fruitfulness or sterility of empirical enquiries stimulated by and based on it' (1994: 171).

The twentieth century has highlighted the difficulties encountered by human beings in their attempts to achieve some kind of balance between violence and civilization which they find acceptable or bearable. It is perhaps doubtful that we can share the optimism and plain wishful thinking of Elias's comments at the end of *The Symbol Theory*. He reminds us that, but for a major catastrophe, the potential lifetime of humanity is some four thousand million years, the life expectancy of the sun. He points out that humanity does not know how to curb wars or effectively eliminate violence from human relations: 'We know already *that* human beings are able to live in a more civilized manner with each other, but we do not know *how* to bring it about in our life with each other, or at least only sporadically'. Nevertheless, he concludes: 'It should not be beyond the reach of humanity in the thousands of years ahead of us' (1991b: 147). Fifty-two years earlier, while speculating on the possibility that humans may achieve a better balance between the demands of social life and personal desires, Elias more aptly remarks that we can only say: 'the civilizing process is under way, or, with old Holbach: "la civilisation . . . n'est pas encore terminée"' (1994a: 524). With these words Elias implies the likelihood that conflict and violence will remain for human beings an integral component of their unending and constantly endangered process of civilization.

Notes

Chapter 1 Introduction

1 Elias's father believed Nazi Germany to be a *Rechtsstaat* or 'lawful state', hence his and Elias's mother's refusal to join their son in exile.

2 On the story of the difficulties involved in the publication of *The Civilizing Process* see Mennell (1992: 18).

3 A detailed biography of Elias is provided by Stephen Mennell (1992: 3–26), although this is based upon events related by Elias himself.

4 For responses to Elias's work in various European societies see Goudsblom (1977b).

5 Where possible, I refer to English translations of books and articles throughout, while all quotations from German texts are my own translations. Citations in brackets without the author's name refer to the work of Elias.

6 Notable exceptions include Mennell (1990a: 205–23), Dunning et al. (1988: 242–5), Dunning and Sheard (1979: 288–9) and Bogner (1987: 250).

Chapter 2 Civilization, habitus and civilizing processes

1 Further discussion of the concept of civilization can be found in Bauman (1985: 1–14), Bleicher (1990: 98–9), Febvre (1973: 219–57) and Williams (1967: 273–5). Cf. the pamphlet published by the British Sociological Association (n.d.) in which Elias's use of the term is singled out as an exception to the way in which it is usually employed with all its ethnocentric and racist undertones.

2 My purpose in this context is to draw out the main themes which are

relevant to the central concerns of this book. It is not my intention to provide an exhaustive summary of the themes found in the two volumes of *The Civilizing Process*. For this, I refer the reader to Stephen Mennell's excellent book, *Norbert Elias: An Introduction* (1992, particularly: 27–111). *The Civilizing Process* was originally published in German in 1939 but did not appear in English until 1978 (vol. 1) and 1982 (vol. 2); both are now available as one book (Elias 1994a). It seems that the titles of the two volumes were intentionally changed for the English translation and this has resulted in some confusion surrounding the themes Elias covered in the book. The complete titles of the English translations are: *The Civilizing Process*, vol. 1: *The History of Manners* and vol. 2: *State Formation and Civilization*. An accurate translation of the titles of both volumes reads: 'On the civilizing process: sociogenetic and psychogenetic investigations'; and the subtitles: 'Changes in the behaviour of the secular upper classes of the West', and 'Changes of society: an attempt at a theory of civilization'.

3 *The Society of Individuals*, first published in German in 1987 but not released in English translation until 1991, comprises three essays written between 1939 and 1987. In the first essay in German, 'Die Gesellschaft der Individuen': 15–98, written at the same time as *The Civilizing Process*, the term habitus appears once, but is translated as 'make-up' (p. 40, German p. 65). In the second essay, 'Probleme des Selbstbewußtseins und des Menschenbildes': 99–205, written some time between the 1940s and 1950s, the term does not appear at all. It is in the last essay, 'Wandlungen der Wir–Ich-Balance': 207–316, written in 1987, that the term is developed and elaborated. Here we find not only the concept of 'psychical habitus' and 'social habitus' present in much earlier work, but also the notions of 'national habitus' and 'traditional habitus'. It is here also that we find at last an accurate translation of the word 'habitus', although this is not consistently maintained.

4 Cf. Goudsblom (1984b: 129–47; 1992: 7–8) who differentiates three levels of civilizing processes: the individual level; the socio-cultural level; and the level of humanity as a whole. Cf. the differentiation made by Rehberg (1991: 69–70).

5 For statements on his theory of the sciences – including the nature of social science – and scientific development see Elias (1972: 117–33, 1974: 21–42 and also 1987a, particularly: 3–42).

6 While there is no 'beginning' or a point before which it can be said that a particular group referred to in these manners books was definitely 'uncivilized', Elias argues that the standards of behaviour discussed would seem to a latter-day observer naive, with fewer psychological nuances and complexities. This has led some commentators to suggest that Elias thought medieval people were like children (Lasch 1985: 113; Thomas 1978: 30), but he is quite clearly referring to *aspects* of the behaviour of medieval people which *we* would be likely to call 'childish' because in our society these types of behaviour are more commonly found among children (1994a: 164).

7 Elias uses the term *Fremdzwänge* which literally translated reads 'alien-'

or 'stranger-constraints'. In comparison, the concept of 'social constraints' has a reifying tendency and I therefore prefer the phrase 'constraints by others', despite its relative inelegance.

8 Following the suggestions of Bruno Bettelheim (1982: 53–9), I would prefer the more accurate translation of Freud's categories. Thus, *das Ich*, *das Über-Ich* and *das Es* are rendered in English as the 'I', the 'Over-I' and the 'It'. However, these terms are not particularly pleasing to the ear and therefore I will defer to the established ones in this context.

9 See Elias (1994a: 159) where he cites Luchaire's reference to the wife of a knight who assists her husband in acts of torture, mutilation and destruction, against both men and women. However, this example may well be exceptional.

10 Cf. Maso (1982: 229–300) who argues that medieval literature was so frequently written for polemical political purposes that it is difficult to take it at face value.

11 The power of women in the courts increased generally, especially in relation to younger, landless nobles. This situation formed a principal root of *Minnesang* (Elias 1994a: 323ff).

12 See for example Barraclough (1982: 37), Adams (1978: 1015), Mosse (1978a: 180), Maso (1982: 296–325), Van Krieken (1989: 201–8) and Robinson (1987: 2–3). For defences of Elias see Dunning (1988: 299–307) and Kuzmics (1990: 232–41).

13 Among the many possible sources one could cite, see Huizinga (1955: ch. 1); Rouche (1987: 415–549); Stone (1983: 22–33); Thomas (1984); Beattie (1986); Cockburn (1991); Franke (1991); and Spierenburg (1993). For a contrary view, based on English material, see Macfarlane (1981).

14 Elias later criticized the concept of 'laws' in sociology. See Elias (1987a: 123ff).

15 For references to 'instincts' in vol. 1 of *The Civilizing Process* which seem to support this, while not directly addressing aggression, see Elias (1994a: 113, 114, 156–7).

16 See Elias and Dunning (1986c: 110–16) and cf. Kilminster and Wouters (1995: 110–11). Elias writes, 'babies protect themselves hand and foot' and 'children like to wrestle and box' (1988c: 180), but he also notes that a taboo on violence is instilled from early on through adolescence and is connected to the monopoly of violence by central ruling authorities – more on this in chapter 3.

17 In *The Civilizing Process* Elias uses the term 'lust for attack' (*Angriffslust*), or in more vernacular usage this might be rendered 'blood-lust'. The term 'aggression' does not appear in the original German version. It seems to have become fashionable with the rise of behaviouristic psychology, antedating Elias's discussion.

18 Elias later sketches a theory of sublimation in his book on Mozart (see 1993: 52–61).

19 The term first appeared in Elias and Dunning (1969: 50–85).

20 Elias distinguishes between sports, which are 'played' physically, games which are not physical but are also 'played', and sport-games, like athletics which are not exactly 'played' (Elias and Dunning 1986a: 297n).

Chapter 3 Violence, habitus and state formation

1 I have retained the English translation of this passage except for the word 'drive' (*Trieb*) which appears in the first volume of *The Civilizing Process* as 'instinct' (cf. the original German 1988a: 278).

2 In emphasizing the *claim* to and *legitimacy* of this monopoly Weber qualifies his definition, thereby restricting its scope. Elias, on the other hand, does not mention the role of legitimacy in this context and very rarely distinguishes between the legitimate and illegitimate use of physical force, although the process of functional democratization would, to a certain extent, necessarily entail the legitimacy of its perpetration by state representatives. Elias, unlike Weber, would not conceive of this issue in dichotomous terms: for example, the police are legitimately allowed to use force but frequently use it illegitimately in order to achieve legitimate or illegitimate aims. For Elias, in contrast to Weber, the formation of a monopoly of violence by a central ruling authority need not necessarily entail legitimacy (cf. Blok 1977: 179–89). In this context the meaning of the term legitimacy is unclear: for whom is a monopoly legitimized, by whom and in what manner? Legitimacy in the sense of legality does not obviously entail support or justification for the use of physical power. Weber's use of the term legitimacy seems to be slanted in favour of the holders of a violence monopoly by his reference to the successful upholding of a *claim*, but it also alludes to the compliance of those over whom the monopoly extends. Legitimacy is thus an inherently ambiguous concept.

Alternatively, it is possible to speak of legitimacy in terms of a social *belief*. In this sense, when a relatively stable regime has dominated for a long time, it attains a sense of legitimacy for the ruled (Bogner 1992b: 3). In modern societies, however, this legitimacy becomes increasingly difficult to maintain in the absence of a state's long-term ability to develop a stable monopoly of violence within its territory. Thus, with respect to legitimacy, Van Benthem van den Bergh points out:

> whether a government succeeds in this depends on the coercive power of state institutions and on the balance between positive and negative valuations among the mass of the population or the manner in which the central state monopolies are in fact used, especially in their distribution of costs and benefits. (1980b: 15n. I am grateful to Godfried van Benthem van den Bergh for sending me a copy of the English original of this essay.)

3 Where these do not operate and a ruling establishment threatens and uses violence against its own people in an arbitrary manner, then a regime of terror is the result. See Van Benthem van den Bergh (1980b: 117–31).

4 Elias uses the term mechanism, although the concept is absent in his later work as he rejected its physicalistic connotations. The phrase monopoly process would more adequately reflect his later thinking.

5 The suffix -*ization* denotes process, although this inevitably leads to the creation of awkward neologisms in Elias's work. Cf. Wilbert van Vree who traces the process of what he calls the 'parliamentarization of courtiers' (1994).

6 There are obvious parallels here with the rise of Hitler. Elias admits that this was one of his reasons for embarking upon such a study in a German television programme, *Zeugen des Jahrhunderts* (Witnesses of the Century), an interview with Hans Christian Hof, broadcast by ZDF in two parts on 3 and 24 July 1990. This connection is also made explicit by him in *The Court Society*, where he devotes an appendix to the dynamics of the Nazi state.

7 In the English version, the term 'non-physical violence' appears in this connection (Elias 1994a: 447). This translation gives the impression that Elias thinks physical force is replaced by forms of 'non-physical violence' in economic relations. I argue in the last section of this chapter that Elias's notion of violence is restricted to physical force: the notion of 'non-physical violence' is alien to his work. This apparent contradiction is resolved in referring to the German edition where the term *Gewaltformen* (forms of force) is used, as distinct from *körperlicher Gewalt* (bodily or physical force) (1988a: 320–1). Some of the various meanings of the German word *Gewalt* will also be clarified in the last section of this chapter.

8 Non-Dutch readers are referred to Mennell (1992: 238–41) for a summary of this and the following two articles cited here.

9 In the more developed societies, Van Krieken advocates taking more account of bureaucratic forms of organization (1989: 209–10).

10 The idea of 'directional changes' may imply some kind of teleological necessity. While this notion is alien to Elias's work, in a perfect world it would perhaps be preferable to avoid the use of the term 'direction' simply because of these associations.

11 Cf. Elias (1996: 32), where he discusses four types of constraints to which human beings are exposed.

12 See Elias (1978a) for his theory of game models and the implications for an understanding of unplanned social dynamics (see also chapter 4 below); cf. Bogner (1986: 387–411).

13 Elias would sometimes cite Hegel's phrase 'the cunning of reason' (for example, 1978a: 146; and 1991a: 62), but he does this in order to distance himself from Hegel's metaphysical formulations.

14 Cf. the work of Cas Wouters (1977: 437–53; and 1987: 405–27) who has taken up these ideas in elaborating the balance between what he has called processes of formalization and informalization.

15 Giddens does not specify into which stream Elias's work can be placed, but he suggests Elias's approach is 'largely submerged in a generalized evolutionism' (1984: 241).

16 *The Symbol Theory* (1991b) represents Elias's clearest formulations on the non-reductive interweaving of biological evolution and societal development. See also Elias (1987a: 117–78).

17 For example, if there is more than one meaning given to the term civilization, it would then be unclear as to which concept of civilization

the prefix *de-* might apply in Elias's work. I am grateful to Helmut Kuzmics who suggested this way of expressing the idea to me. See Kuzmics (1988: 518) where he clarifies three main concepts of civilization found in Elias.

18 The English edition, however, was published some forty years later, when the use of the term was highly unfashionable. In this hostile climate, Elias could have admitted the deficiencies of the word and chosen another. He had until the late 1970s in which to make any necessary alterations to the book for the English publication, during which time he would have been well aware of the various changing connotations of the word civilization. But in deciding to go ahead with translation and publication regardless, Elias was either naive, or had something particular to say, and was fully aware of the implications of the term and how it took on a specific meaning in his work.

19 For some reason this introduction appears at the end of the first volume as an appendix.

20 Note that in the English translation this is rendered: 'Civilization is never completed and constantly endangered' (1988c: 177; cf. 1996: 225) – the intentional allusion to the associations of the term civilization which are peculiar to Elias are lost in this translation.

21 There are several words and phrases which are frequently used interchangeably with violence, such as coercion, threat, terror, persuasion, subversion, that which induces misery or alienation, the infringement of 'needs' or self-realization, and so on (see, for example, Galtung 1969, 1988). The concept is also frequently used to describe great force, severity or vehemence of personal feelings, actions or language. Another influential term is that of 'structural violence', developed in the context of so-called 'Peace Research'. This is seen in opposition to 'direct violence' which would refer to the notion introduced above. I do not intend here to go into the broader definitional problems of what does or does not constitute violence; or indeed, whether it is at all possible to speak of violence in a way which includes dimensions other than those mentioned in the definition above. But in the absence of empirical evidence, it is interesting to speculate whether the term violence has increasingly come to be applied to other non-physical phenomena in the course of a civilizing process. As pacification occurs, sensitivity to psychical humiliation, cruelty and tension increases, along with the need to describe such experiences. The word violence may have come to fulfil the role of expressing strong feelings of repugnance or outrage with an appropriately strong word. Other words, such as coercion, torture or cruelty, do not seem stark enough, or are deemed to be less generally applicable. This may have led to the term violence being applied indiscriminately to anything which results in a range of events from brutal death through to loud and aggressive shouting or a feeling of 'alienation'.

22 The argument that Western nation states are to a large extent historically exceptional in this respect is forcefully made by Blok (1977: 175–91).

23 But see Elias (1994a: 138–56) on changes in attitudes in relations

between men and women, which is quite unusual in a book written by a man and published in 1939. See also Elias (1983: 194, 243–4; and 1987d: 287–316), the latter being an essay based on a planned book on the subject, the draft manuscript of which was accidentally destroyed.

24 The nearest he comes to this issue is in the second volume of *The Civilizing Process* (1994a: 508–9).

25 During civilizing processes, however, changes in the self-steering of people are not represented simply as *increases* in self-restraint (cf. Elias 1992a: 147; 1992d: 385–6). One may find extreme forms of self-restraint at earlier phases in civilizing processes existing side by side with the relatively free gratification of pleasures (Elias 1994a: 451; 1992a: 153–4, 157–60, 206–7n), for example among medieval orders of monks within a warrior society. Later phases of these processes are characterized by a tendency towards greater temperance in all aspects (cf. Baumgart and Eichener 1991: 96–7 on phases of restraint in civilizing processes).

26 The fact that Elias's theory is based primarily on European data does not mean that it is *necessarily* Eurocentric (cf. Mennell 1992: 207–8), or even ethnocentric, as some claim (Albrow 1969: 234; Thomas 1978: 30).

27 In his earlier work, Elias concentrates on the intra-state sociogenesis of civilization, whereas later on he also refers to civilizing processes at the global level of 'humanity' (1992d: 383; see also 1987a: 74–118; 1991b: 136–9, 146–7; 1992c: 236; cf. Haferkamp 1987: 545–57).

Chapter 4 Identity, violence and process models

1 The term *configuration*, which appears in Elias's earlier work (for example Elias and Scotson 1994: 8ff, 155ff), is later discarded in favour of the word *figuration*. Stephen Mennell (1992: 251) suggests that the term 'figurational sociology', which is used by Elias and his associates to describe their approach was originally employed by opponents of Elias's approach to describe those who are interested in and use his ideas. But it is more likely that Elias and his followers began to describe their own activities with the term figurational sociology quite independently. Towards the end of his life, Elias attempted unsuccessfully to distance himself from the associations of a 'school' centred around him which this phrase inevitably brings to mind, preferring the term 'process sociology' instead.

2 Elias also discusses 'models of interweaving processes with norms' (1978a: 80–103) which serve to clarify the complexities of social relations and the structure of the social processes formed by human interdependence. For a commentary on the various dimensions to these game models, see Mennell (1992: 258–64).

3 That is, as a political organization whose 'administrative staff successfully upholds the claim to the *monopoly* of the *legitimate* use of physical force in the enforcement of order' (Weber 1978: 54).

4 For a discussion of issues surrounding the concept of national character reworked as 'national culture', see Hofstede (1991).

5 Here the term 'barbarians' obviously refers to the normative opposite

of 'civilization' expressed as an ideal. See my comments in chapter 8.

6 The formulation of the established-outsider dynamic can be found in the original German version of *The Civilizing Process*, although the term does not appear there. During the course of revising the typescript for the English publication, however, Elias decided to include the concept in the English version.

7 There is, however, an untranslated German essay (1990: 291–314) in which Elias deals directly with this theme and I refer to it in this section.

8 Cf. Elias's discussion of USA–USSR relations (1985b: 138ff).

9 One could of course cite exceptions to this, for example, the enduring national friendships between Portugal and England, or Scotland and France.

10 For an exposition of Elias's comments on integration processes and their relevance to a theory of globalization, see Mennell (1990b: 359–71) and Robertson (1992: 211–27).

11 I would prefer the more elegant phrase 'competitive interweaving processes'.

12 Here the term 'integration' does not imply attempts to plan interventions in social processes, or harmonious relations, or the idea that certain processes are heading towards such a future. I use it to refer to relatively autonomous social processes which involve the interdependence of increasing numbers of people.

13 In line with Elias's theory of civilizing processes presented in chapters 2 and 3; together, these three features would be likely to arise in conjunction with the development of a ruling authority's more centralized, stable, continuous and impersonal monopoly of physical force which effectively curbs the perpetration of face-to-face violence within a particular territory. This in turn facilitates an increase in the length and density of interdependency chains (political, commercial, emotional and cognitive bonds) – the development of the division of functions, trade relations, commercial growth and identification with the broader political territory as well as an increased cognitive awareness of having to take more people into account more often. This further increases the likelihood that the scope of inter-group identification becomes more encompassing, including people in different situations, strata or societies. The growing density of interdependency chains increases the need for people to restrain themselves in specific ways: the necessity for planning and rational thinking increases, together with changes in the way people steer their emotions in ways deemed to be socially acceptable. Greater efficiency and precision is required, for example in organizing meetings, delivering goods or travelling from one place to another. These processes in turn facilitate the consolidation of the monopoly of violence function through taxation measures and a strengthening of norms surrounding the control of violent actions in public.

14 The following appears at the beginning of *The Civilizing Process* – a book written in exile – and seems to have been missed by some readers: 'Dedicated to the memory of my parents, Hermann Elias, d. Breslau, Sophie Elias, d. Auschwitz 1941 (?)'. This certainly reveals some aware-

ness of the fragility of modern civilization, contrary to the interpretation of Coser (1978: 566).

15 Relatively little attention has been given to developing a theory of decivilizing processes. Some writers, such as Dunning and Sheard 1979: 288–9), Dunning et al. (1988: 242–5), Goudsblom (1989c: 84) and Wouters (1990a: 38), have referred to the possibility of such a theory implied in Elias's work, and Elias himself mentions the idea (1986a: 46; 1988d: 183). Only the sociologist Stephen Mennell (1992; 1992: 227ff) and the anthropologist Mart Bax (1993) have taken up the issue in any depth, each with a respective emphasis on the theory and empirical documentation of decivilizing processes.

16 Indeed, he states much later in a footnote in *Quest for Excitement* that 'feudalization' represents an opposite trend to a 'civilizing *spurt*' (1986b: 297n).

17 For a detailed summary of the issues involved, see Mennell (1989, 1992: 241–6). See also Wouters (1977 and 1987).

18 Eric Dunning and his colleagues (1988: 242–5) hypothesize that a decivilizing upsurge in violence may be occurring in Britain in the latter part of the twentieth century. They claim that this may be the result of functional democratization in the civilizing process producing consequences which are generally civilizing in their early stages, but which later are decivilizing and promote disruptive conflict. In a similar vein, Mennell suggests that the link between socio-structural and civilizing controls on behaviour may be 'curvilinear'; that beyond a certain point in social development, the process generates 'pockets of metropolitan anonymity within which the external constraints on impulses (from the sexual to the violent), and in time also the effectiveness of pressures towards self-constraint, are diminished' (Mennell 1990a: 211–12).

Chapter 5 Social habitus and civilizing processes in England

1 Cf. Otto Hintze's argument (1975: 180–215) which evidently influenced that of Elias.

2 See also Hill (1974) and Moore (1969), who put forward what are now considered to be contentious interpretations of this period. For a comparison with a more traditional historical approach, see for example Russell (1990). Elias, for his part, was still relying on an interpretation of English history derived from the 1940s, particularly the work of Plumb (1950).

3 Elias also says that 'feudalization' is an example of a spurt in the opposite direction (1986c: 297n).

4 An exception to this was the occasional duel, although this form of conflict is of course highly controlled. For a historical account of duelling in European societies see Kiernan (1988).

5 These articles were written as lectures given at a German Hochschule and were presented on 23 April 1959 and 7 October 1960 respectively. I refer here to the published pamphlets. I am grateful to Cas Wouters for supplying me with copies of them. The term habitus does not appear in

these articles, but in his discussion Elias refers to codes of behaviour and ways of expressing feelings, which I assume to mean the same thing as social habitus.

6 On the differences between the emergence of public opinion in England, France and Germany, see Habermas (1992: 57–79).

7 Of course, a similar phenomenon occurred during the Falklands War.

8 I do not intend to address all of Elias's publications on sport. Most of these are written in collaboration with Eric Dunning. See the essays in Elias and Dunning (1986a) in which only two of them, plus the introduction, are written solely by Elias, while four of the remaining eight are written with Eric Dunning or by Dunning and his Leicester colleagues. The first of Elias's essays, 'The Genesis of Sport as a Sociological Problem' (1986b: 126–49) covers the etymological developments of 'sport' and other associated words, but is largely concerned with comparing differing levels of violence in Ancient Greek combat-games in particular with the comparatively low levels of violence in modern sports more generally. As this chapter focuses primarily on England, I shall deal here mainly with material relating to that country, which is found in the 'Introduction' (1986a: 19–62) and 'An Essay on Sport and Violence' (1986c: 150–74).

9 Elias describes one Englishman's reaction to the more overt expressions of competitive vigour exhibited by other countries in the Olympic Games. When he was President of the Olympic Association, the Marquis of Exeter – himself an Olympic Hurdles Gold Medallist in 1928 – commented that one should not align prestige with sporting success in international events and that one nation is no better than another (Elias 1961: 21).

10 This may not seem to be strictly true in the case of sports such as boxing. However, if its development over many generations is taken into account, it is possible to see that what we call 'boxing' today previously involved far higher levels of violence, but these earlier forms could hardly be called a 'sport' in the modern sense. See Sheard (1992).

11 This echoes passages in *The Civilizing Process* where the transformation or displacement of pleasure is discussed. Elias draws this connection himself (1986c: 298n; see 1994a: 166).

Chapter 6 Nationalism and decivilizing processes in Germany

1 The reader is reminded that *The Germans* was published in 1989 as *Studien über die Deutschen*, although it contains essays written over a span of time stretching from the early 1960s. The project was the initiative of Michael Schröter who edited the book.

2 This inter-group tension was expressed in the tension between the use of the concepts *Zivilisation* and *Kultur* discussed in chapter 2; it surfaced as a dichotomy among academic historians between those who emphasized 'political history' as opposed to 'cultural history' (Elias 1996: 129ff). Cf. Ringer (1969: 87–90).

3 This English article corresponds to Elias (1996: 171–203). However, the

version printed in *The Germans* includes footnotes and sections which have been rearranged or added by the editor and, more importantly, new notes written by Elias for the publication of the book.

4 Although there was no 'Germany' before 1870, Elias argues that there was a group of people who shared a 'German' self-image, whether Prussian, Hanoverian, Bavarian, or whatever.

5 Elias adopts this term from the work of Cas Wouters. See Wouters (1977: 437–53; 1986: 1–18; and 1987: 405–27).

6 The rules of most German student fraternities even today specifically bar women from membership.

7 Elias suggests that the works of Nietzsche contain a formulation of some implicit articles of faith inherent in the *satisfaktionsfähige Gesellschaften* (1996: 115).

8 As an example of the appropriation and then coarsening of these models Elias cites the promotion of the idea that every 'Aryan' must be able to identify a specified number of 'Aryan' ancestors, just as the aristocracy had justified their position through 'blood lineage'.

9 While I am aware of the limitations of validity in presenting my personal account of the following events, I think it is helpful to introduce it in this context because my experiences would seem to counter some points made by Elias. The meeting lasted a whole Saturday and was attended by approximately 100 men ranging in age from about 19 to 75. It was held in the back rooms of a pub in Stiepel, Bochum, on 12 December 1992. Eight duels were fought during the course of the day.

10 Some of these items were optional, such as the leather protection for the upper body or the earpieces: whether they were worn or not depended on the conditions of the duel agreed upon by the combatants beforehand.

11 As I mentioned at the beginning of this chapter, I shall comment on Elias's use of terms like 'barbarizing' in chapter 8.

12 Many different Freikorps were formed; see Waite (1970: 33).

13 The bylaws of the Organization Consul reflected an extreme national identification of groups such as the Freikorps; they are quoted in Waite (1970: 214).

14 For example, Franz Seldte, founder of the *Stahlhelm* (Steel Helmet), the main fighting league, had this to say on behalf of the German front-line veterans of the First World War: 'We must fight to get the men into power who will depend on us front soldiers for support – men who will call upon us to smash once and for all these damned revolutionary rats and choke them by sticking their heads into their own shit' (quoted in Jones 1987: 110). For an interesting psychoanalytical perspective on the fantasies and images of Freikorps members, particularly those involving women and 'communists', see Theweleit (1987).

15 After they were disbanded in the summer of 1920 many Freikorps members carried on their association in secret clubs or under the guise of some kind of social, economic or sporting organization. Trucking companies, bicycle-renting agencies, road gangs, private detective bureaus and travelling circuses were some of the many businesses set up for this purpose. The most popular, however, were the *Arbeitsgemeinschaften* (labour camps). See Waite (1970: 189).

16 On street fighting in this period see Merkyl (1975) and Rosenhaft (1983). On the membership of the SA of the NSDAP, see Fischer (1978: 131–59; 1982: 651–70).

17 In fact, Jünger did not want anything to do with Nazism. His vision of an international warrior elite found Nazi racism crude and Nazi 'mass thinking' philistine. Jünger went into 'internal exile' by joining the army.

Chapter 7 Genocide and decivilizing processes in Germany

1 Cf. Elias's comments in *The Court Society* (1983, Appendix II: 276–83) where he discusses the tensions inherent in the social dynamics of the absolutist court of Louis XIV and draws structural comparisons between the dynamics of this social configuration and that of the Nazi state.

2 As Alan Sica remarks, 'If 13th century throat-slitters had to go into therapeutic absolving sessions with their priests, we do not know of it, but we do know of the mental disturbances endemic to SS personnel during and after the Third Reich' (1984: 64). Cf. Lifton (1986).

3 I find this surprising in view of the fact that Bauman was one of the first sociologists unconnected with the Leicester University Sociology Department, where Elias taught for several years, to publicly acknowledge the innovatory importance of Elias's work on civilization. See Bauman (1979: 117–25).

4 Cf. Elias (1987a: 81), where he points out that the practical problem of how to control the controllers of violence monopolies remains unsolved.

5 Bauman refers to Hannah Arendt (1976: 106) with whom he agrees on this assumption

6 As we have seen, imperial Germany was a modern, recently formed state with a warrior ethos. Even imperial German Good Society can be partly characterized as decivilizing, as it included the spread of a warrior ethos which involved the slave-like obedience from 'the weak' and the 'lower orders'.

7 On the rise of Nazism through democracy and mass movements see Arendt (1973: 305–40); Mosse (1978b); and cf. Talmon (1986).

Chapter 8 Elias on violence, civilization and decivilization

1 The terms 'barbarism', 'barbarity' and 'barbaric' appear throughout the essay, for example: 302, 303 (twice), 308 (twice), 309, 315 (twice), 330, 345, 346, 355, 359, 381 and 402 (Elias 1996).

2 In his article on decivilizing in the former Yugoslavia Mart Bax also uses the term 'barbarization' (Bax 1993; see also Bax 1995).

3 Michael Schröter's editorial note (Elias 1996: 301) points out that it was written (in English) during or before 1961–2. Elias's original inspiration to write the piece apparently came from the trial of Adolf Eichmann.

References

Adams, R. M. (1978) 'Western Man and His Manners', *Times Literary Supplement*, 15 September: 1015.

Adler, A. (1958) *The Individual Psychology of Alfred Adler: A Systematic Presentation in Selections from his Writings*. Edited and annotated by Ansbacher, H. L. and Ansbacher, R. R. London, George Allen & Unwin.

Albrow, M. C. (1969) 'Review of *Über den Prozeß der Zivilisation*', *Jewish Journal of Sociology*, 11: 227–36.

Arendt, H. (1973) [1951] *Origins of Totalitarianism*. London, André Deutsch.

—— (1976) [1963] *Eichmann in Jerusalem: A Report on the Banality of Evil*. New York, Penguin.

Argyle, M. (1976) 'Personality and Social Behaviour', in Harré, R. (ed.) *Personality*. Oxford, Basil Blackwell: 145–88.

Armstrong, J. A. (1982) *Nations Before Nationalism*. Chapel Hill, University of North Carolina Press.

Arnason, J. (1987) 'Figurational Sociology as a Counter-Paradigm', *Theory, Culture & Society*, 4: 429–56.

Barraclough, G. (1982) 'Clockwork History', *The New York Review*, 21 October: 36–8.

Bauman, Z. (1979) 'The Phenomenon of Norbert Elias', *Sociology*, 13: 117–25.

—— (1985) 'On the Origin of Civilization: A Historical Note', *Theory, Culture & Society*, 2: 1–14.

—— (1988) *Modernity and the Holocaust*. Cambridge, Polity Press.

Baumgart, R. and Eichener, V. (1991) *Norbert Elias: Zur Einführung*. Hamburg, Junius.

Bax, M. (1993) 'Medjugorjes kleine oorlog: barbarisering in een bosnische bevaartplaats', *Amsterdams Sociologisch Tijdschrift*, 20: 3–25.

—— (1995) *Medjugorje: Religion, Politics and Violence in Rural Bosnia*. Amsterdam, Vrij Universiteit Press.

198   *References*

Beattie, J. M. (1986) *Crime and Courts in England, 1660–1800*. Oxford, Clarendon Press.

Bennholdt-Thomsen, V. (1985) 'Zivilisation, moderner Staat und Gewalt: Eine feministische Kritik an Norbert Elias' Zivilisationstheorie', *Beiträge zur feministischen Theorie und Praxis*, 8: 23–35.

Benthem van den Bergh, G. van (1971) *The Structure of Development: An Invitation to the Sociology of Norbert Elias*, Occasional Paper no. 13. The Hague, Institute of Social Studies.

—— (1980a) *On the Dynamics of Development of Contemporary States: An Approach to Comparative Politics*, Occasional Paper no. 84. The Hague, Institute of Social Studies.

—— (1980b) 'On the Development of the Monopoly of Violence of the State' (in Dutch), *Symposium*, 2: 117–31.

—— (1980c) 'De schuldenvraag als oriëntatiemiddel', in his *De staat van geweld en andere essays*. Amsterdam, Meulenhoff.

—— (1990) *The Taming of the Great Powers*. Aldershot, Gower.

Berghahn, V. R. (1962) *Modern Germany: Society, Economy and Politics in the Twentieth Century*. Cambridge, Cambridge University Press.

Bessel, R. (1984) *Political Violence and the Rise of Nazism: The Storm Troopers in Eastern Germany, 1925–1934*. New Haven and London, Yale University Press.

Bettelheim, B. (1979) [1952] 'Violence: A Neglected Mode of Behaviour', in Bettelheim, B. *Surviving and Other Essays*. London, Thames & Hudson: 185–200.

—— (1982) *Freud and Man's Soul*. London, Fontana.

Bleicher, J. (1990) 'Struggling with *Kultur*', *Theory, Culture & Society*, 7: 97–106.

Blok, A. (1977) '*Selbsthilfe* and the Monopoly of Violence', in Gleichmann, P. R. et al. (eds) *Human Figurations: Essays for Norbert Elias*. Amsterdam, Amsterdams Sociologisch Tijdschrift: 179–89.

Blumer, H. (1969) *Symbolic Interactionism: Perspective and Method*. Englewood Cliffs, Prentice-Hall.

Bogner, A. (1986) 'The Structure of Social Processes: A Commentary on the Sociology of Norbert Elias', *Sociology*, 20: 387–411.

—— (1987) 'Elias and the Frankfurt School', *Theory, Culture & Society*, 4: 249–85.

—— (1988) 'Review of Elias and Dunning, *Quest for Excitement*', *Sociological Review*, 36: 209–12.

—— (1992a) 'The Theory of the Civilizing Process – An Ideographic Theory of Modernization?', *Theory, Culture & Society*, 9: 23–53.

—— (1992b) 'Ethnicity and the Monopolization of "Legitimate" Violence', paper presented at the 7th EIDOS conference in Bielefeld, May.

Bossert, H. T. and Storck, W. F. (eds) (1912) *Das Mittelalterliche Hausbuch*. Leipzig, E. A. Seemann.

Bourdieu, P. (1990) [1980] *The Logic of Practice*. Translated by Richard Nice. Cambridge, Polity Press.

Braudel, F. (1980) 'The History of Civilizations: The Past Explains the Present', in Braudel, F. *On History*. London, Weidenfeld & Nicolson.

British Sociological Association (n.d.) *Anti-Racist Language: Guidance for Good Practice*. London, BSA.

Buck-Morss, S. (1978) 'Review of *The Civilization* [sic] *Process'*, *Telos*, 37: 181–98.

Bullough, V. L. (1979) 'Review of *The History of Manners'*, *American Historical Review*, 84, April: 444.

Burkitt, I. (1991) *Social Selves: Theories of the Social Formation of Personality*, *Current Sociology Monograph*, 7.

Burns, T. (1979) 'Review of *The History of Manners'*, *British Journal of Sociology*, 30: 373–5.

Chalk, F. and Jonassohn, K. (1990) *The History and Sociology of Genocide*. New Haven, Yale University Press.

Chartier, R. (1988) 'Social Figuration and Habitus: Reading Elias', in Chartier, R. *Cultural History: Between Practices and Representations*. Cambridge, Polity Press: 71–94.

Cockburn, J. (1991) 'Patterns of Violence in English Society: Homicide in Kent, 1560–1985', *Past and Present*, 130: 70–176.

Copley, A. R. H. (1980) 'Review of *The History of Manners'*, *History*, 65: 86–7.

Coser, L. (1978) 'The Bridling of Affect and the Refinement of Manners', *Contemporary Sociology*, 7: 563–66.

Davidoff, L. (1973) *The Best Circles: Society, Etiquette and the Season*. London, Croom Helm.

Dawidowicz, L. S. (1987) [1975] *The War Against the Jews, 1933–45*. Harmondsworth, Pelican Books.

De Swaan, A. (1995) 'Widening Circles of Identification: Emotional Concerns in Sociogenetic Perspective', *Theory, Culture & Society*, 12: 25–39.

Dicks, H. V. (1972) *Licensed Mass Murder: A Socio-psychological Study of some SS Killers*. Brighton, Sussex University Press.

Duerr, H. P. (1988) *Nacktheit und Scham: Der Mythos vom Zivilisationsprozeß*. Frankfurt a.M., Suhrkamp.

Dunning, E. (1986) 'Social Bonding and Violence in Sport', in Elias, N. and Dunning, E. *Quest for Excitement: Sport and Leisure in the Civilizing Process*. Oxford, Basil Blackwell: 224–44.

—— (1987) 'Comments on Elias' "Scenes from the Life of a Knight"', *Theory, Culture & Society*, 4: 366–71.

—— (1988) 'Reply to R. J. Robinson's, "The Civilizing Process Revisited: Some Remarks on Elias's Social History"', *Sociology*, 23: 299–307.

—— (1992) 'Figurational Sociology and the Sociology of Sport: Some Concluding Remarks', in Dunning, E. and Rojek, C. (eds) *Sport and Leisure in the Civilizing Process: Critique and Counter Critique*. London, Macmillan: 221–84.

Dunning, E., Murphy, P., Newburn, T. and Waddington, I. (1987) 'Violent Disorders in Twentieth-century Britain', in Gaskell, G. and Benewick, R. (eds) *The Crowd in Contemporary Britain*. London, Sage: 19–75.

Dunning, E., Murphy, P. and Williams, J. (1988) *The Roots of Football Hooliganism: An Historical and Sociological Study*. London, Routledge.

Dunning, E. and Rojek, C. (eds) (1992) *Sport and Leisure in the Civilizing*

Process: Critique and Counter Critique. London, Macmillan.

Dunning, E. and Sheard, K. (1979) *Barbarians, Gentlemen and Players*. Oxford, Martin Robertson.

Durkheim, E. (1984) *The Division of Labour in Society*. London, Macmillan.

Elias, N. (1950) 'Studies in the Genesis of the Naval Profession', *British Journal of Sociology*, 1: 291–309.

—— (1960) *Die öffentliche Meinung in England*. Berlin and Zürich, Dr. Max Gehlen.

—— (1961) *Nationale Eigentümlichkeiten der englischen öffentlichen Meinung*. Berlin and Zürich, Dr. Max Gehlen.

—— (1969) 'Sociology and Psychiatry', in Foulkes, S. H. and Steward Prince, G. (eds) *Psychiatry in a Changing Society*. London, Tavistock: 117–44.

—— (1972) 'Theory of Science and History of Science: Comments on a Recent Discussion', *Economy and Society*, 1: 117–33.

—— (1974) 'The Sciences: Towards a Theory', in Whitley, R. (ed.) *Social Processes of Scientific Development*. London, Routledge & Kegan Paul: 21–42.

—— (1978a) [1970] *What Is Sociology?* London, Hutchinson.

—— (1978b) 'On Transformations of Aggressiveness', *Theory and Society*, 5: 227–53.

—— (1980) 'Zivilisation und Gewalt: Über das Staatsmonopol der körperlichen Gewalt und seine Durchbrechungen', in Matthes, J. (ed.) *Lebenswelt und soziale Probleme: Verhandlungen des 20. deutschen Soziologentages zu Bremen, 1980*. Frankfurt a.M., Campus: 98–122.

—— (1982) 'Scientific Establishments', in Elias, N., Martins, H. and Whitley, R. (eds) *Scientific Establishments and Hierarchies: Sociology of the Sciences Volume VI*. Dortrecht, Holland, D. Reidel: 3–69.

—— (1983) [1969] *The Court Society*. Translated by Edmund Jephcott. Oxford, Basil Blackwell.

—— (1985a) *The Loneliness of the Dying*. Oxford, Basil Blackwell.

—— (1985b) *Humana conditio: Beobachtungen zur Entwicklung der Menschheit am 40. Jahrestag eines Kriegsendes (8. Mai 1985)*. Frankfurt a.M., Suhrkamp.

—— (1986a) 'Introduction', in Elias, N. and Dunning, E. *Quest for Excitement: Sport and Leisure in the Civilizing Process*. Oxford, Basil Blackwell: 19–62.

—— (1986b) 'The Genesis of Sport as a Sociological Problem', in Elias, N. and Dunning, E. *Quest for Excitement: Sport and Leisure in the Civilizing Process*. Oxford, Basil Blackwell: 126–49.

—— (1986c) 'An Essay on Sport and Violence', in Elias, N. and Dunning, E. *Quest for Excitement: Sport and Leisure in the Civilizing Process*. Oxford, Basil Blackwell: 150–74.

—— (1987a) *Involvement and Detachment*. Oxford, Basil Blackwell.

—— (1987b) *Die Gesellschaft der Individuen*. Edited by Michael Schröter. Frankfurt a.M., Suhrkamp.

—— (1987c) 'The Retreat of Sociologists into the Present', *Theory, Culture & Society*, 4: 223–47.

—— (1987d) 'The Changing Balance of Power between the Sexes – A Process Sociological Study: The Example of the Ancient Roman State', *Theory, Culture & Society*, 4: 287–316.

—— (1987e) 'On Human Beings and their Emotions: A Process-Sociological Essay', *Theory, Culture & Society*, 4: 339–61.

—— (1988a) [1939] *Über den Prozeß der Zivilisation: Soziogenetische und psychogenetische Untersuchungen*, vol. 1: *Wandlungen des Verhaltens in den weltlichen Oberschichten des Abendlandes*. Frankfurt a.M., Suhrkamp.

—— (1988b) [1939] *Über den Prozeß der Zivilisation: Soziogenetische und psychogenetische Untersuchungen*, vol. 2: *Wandlungen der Gesellschaft: Entwurf zu einer Theorie der Zivilisation*. Frankfurt a.M., Suhrkamp.

—— (1988c) 'Violence and Civilization: On the State Monopoly of Physical Violence and its Infringements', in Keane, J. (ed.) *Civil Society and the State: New European Perspectives*. London, Verso: 177–98.

—— (1988d) 'Wir sind die späten Barbaren', *Der Spiegel*, no. 21 (vol. 42), 23 May: 183–90.

—— (1988e) 'Was ich unter Zivilisation verstehe', *Die Zeit*, no. 25, 17 June: 37–8.

—— (1990) 'Weitere Facetten der Etablierten-Außenseiter-Beziehung: Das Maycomb-Modell', in Elias, N. and Scotson, J. *Etablierte und Außenseiter*. Frankfurt a.M., Suhrkamp: 291–314.

—— (1991a) [1987] *The Society of Individuals*. Edited by Michael Schröter and translated by Edmund Jephcott. Oxford, Basil Blackwell.

—— (1991b) *The Symbol Theory*. Edited with an introduction by Richard Kilminster. London, Sage.

—— (1992a) [1984] *Time: An Essay*. Translated in part from the German by Edmund Jephcott. Oxford, Basil Blackwell.

—— (1992b) [1986] 'Figuration', in Schäfers, B. (ed.) *Grundbegriffe der Soziologie*, 3rd edn. Opladen, Leske & Budrich: 88–91.

—— (1992c) [1986] 'Prozesse, soziale', in Schäfers, B. (ed.) *Grundbegriffe der Soziologie*, 3rd edn. Opladen, Leske & Budrich: 234–41.

—— (1992d) [1986] 'Zivilisation', in Schäfers, B. (ed.) *Grundbegriffe der Soziologie*, 3rd edn. Opladen, Leske & Budrich: 382–87.

—— (1993) [1991] *Mozart: Portrait of a Genius*. Edited by Michael Schröter and translated by Edmund Jephcott. Cambridge, Polity Press.

—— (1994a) [1939] *The Civilizing Process*. Translated by Edmund Jephcott. Oxford, Basil Blackwell.

—— (1994b) [1976] 'Introduction: A Theoretical Essay on Established and Outsider Relations', in *The Established and the Outsiders*. London, Sage.

—— (1994c) 'Notes on a Lifetime', in Elias, N. *Reflections on a Life*. Cambridge, Polity Press: 81–154.

—— (1996) [1989] *The Germans: Power Struggles and the Development of Habitus in the Nineteenth and Twentieth Centuries*. Edited by Michael Schröter, translated by Eric Dunning and Stephen Mennell. Cambridge, Polity Press.

Elias, N. and Dunning, E. (1969) 'The Quest for Excitement in Leisure', *Leisure & Society*, 2: 50–85.

—— (1986a) *Quest for Excitement: Sport and Leisure in the Civilizing Process*. Oxford, Basil Blackwell.

—— (1986b) 'Folk Football in Medieval and Early Modern Europe', in Elias, N. and Dunning, E. *Quest for Excitement*. Oxford, Basil Blackwell: 175–90.

202   *References*

—— (1986c) 'Leisure in the Spare-time Spectrum', in Elias, N. and Dunning, E. *Quest for Excitement*. Oxford, Basil Blackwell: 91–125.

Elias, N. and Scotson, J. L. (1994) [1965] *The Established and the Outsiders: A Sociological Enquiry into Community Problems*. London, Sage.

Febvre, L. (1973) '*Civilization*: Evolution of a Word and a Group of Ideas', in Burke, P. (ed.) *A New Kind of History*. London, Routledge & Kegan Paul: 219–57.

Feldman, G. D. (1992) *Army, Industry and Labor in Germany 1914–1918*. Oxford and Providence, Berg.

Fischer, C. (1978) 'The Occupational Background of the SA's Rank and File Membership during the Depression Years, 1920 to mid-1934', in Stachura, P. D. (ed.) *The Shaping of the Nazi State*. London, Croom Helm: 131–59.

—— (1982) 'The SA of the NSDAP: Social Background and Ideology of the Rank and File in the Early 1930s', *Journal of Contemporary History*, 17: 651–70.

Flap, H. D. and Kuiper, Y. (1981/2) 'Figurationssoziologie als Forschungsprogramm', *Kölner Zeitschrift für Soziologie und Sozialpsychologie*, 33: 257–72.

Fletcher, J. (1993) 'Violence and Civilization in the Work of Norbert Elias'. Unpublished PhD thesis, University of Cambridge.

Fontaine, S. (1978) 'The Civilizing Process Revisited: Interview with Norbert Elias', *Theory and Society*, 5: 243–53.

Franke, H. (1991) 'Geweldscriminaliteit in Nederland: Een historisch-sociologisch analyse' ('Criminal Violence in the Netherlands: An Historical-sociological Analysis'), in Franke, H., Wilterdink, N. and Brinkgreve, C. (eds) *Alledaags en Ongewoon Geweld (Everyday and Unusual Violence)*. Amsterdam, Amsterdams Sociologisch Tijdschrift/Wolters-Noordhoof: 13–45.

Freud, S. (1982) [1930] *Civilization and its Discontents*. London, Hogarth.

Frevert, U. (1991) *Ehrenmänner: Das Duell in der bürgerlichen Gesellschaft*. Munich, C. H. Beck.

Fulbrook, M. (1992) *A Concise History of Germany*. Cambridge, Cambridge University Press.

Galtung, J. (1969) 'Violence, Peace and Peace Research', *Journal of Peace Research*, 3: 167–91.

—— (1988) *Transarmament and the Cold War: Peace Research and the Peace Movement*. Copenhagen, Christien Ejlers.

Garland, D. (1990) *Punishment in Modern Society*. Oxford, Clarendon Press.

Giddens, A. (1984) *The Constitution of Society: Outline of a Theory of Structuration*. Cambridge, Polity Press.

—— (1985) *The Nation-State and Violence: Volume Two of a Contemporary Critique of Historical Materialism*. Cambridge, Polity Press.

—— (1992) 'Review of N. Elias, *The Society of Individuals*', *American Journal of Sociology*, 98: 388–9.

Gleichmann, P. R., Goudsblom, J. and Korte, H. (eds) (1977) *Human Figurations: Essays for Norbert Elias*. Amsterdam, Amsterdams Sociologisch Tijdschrift.

—— (eds) (1979) *Materialien zu Norbert Elias' Zivilisationstheorie*. Frankfurt a.M., Suhrkamp.

—— (eds) (1984) *Macht und Zivilisation: Materialien zu Norbert Elias' Zivilisationstheorie* 2. Frankfurt a.M., Suhrkamp.

Goudsblom, J. (1977a) *Sociology in the Balance*. Oxford, Basil Blackwell.

—— (1977b) 'Responses to Norbert Elias's Work in England, Germany, the Netherlands and France', in Gleichmann, P. R. et al. (eds) *Human Figurations*: 37–97.

—— (1984a) 'Die Erforschung von Zivilisationsprozessen', in Gleichmann, P. R. et al. (eds) *Macht und Zivilisation: Materialien zu Norbert Elias' Zivilisationstheorie* 2. Frankfurt a.M., Suhrkamp: 83–104.

—— (1984b) 'De civilisatietheorie in het geding' ('Civilization Theory under Discussion'), *Sociologische Gids*, (XXXI): 138–63.

—— (1987) 'The Sociology of Norbert Elias: Its Resonance and Significance', *Theory, Culture & Society*, 4: 323–37.

—— (1989a) 'Human History and Long-Term Social Processes: Towards a Synthesis of Chronology and "Phaseology"', in Goudsblom, J. et al. (1989): 11–26.

—— (1989b) 'Ecological Regimes and the Rise of Organised Religion', in Goudsblom, J. et al. (1989): 63–78.

—— (1989c) 'The Formation of Military Agrarian Regimes', in Goudsblom, J. et al. (1989): 79–92.

—— (1992) *Fire and Civilization*. London, Allan Lane.

—— (1995) 'De civilisatietheorie: kritiek en perspectief', *Amsterdams Sociologisch Tijdschrift*, 2: 262–82.

Goudsblom, J., Jones, E. L. and Mennell, S. (1989) *Human History and Social Process*. Exeter, University of Exeter Press.

Habermas, J. (1992) [1962] *The Structural Transformation of the Public Sphere: An Enquiry into a Category of Bourgeois Society*. Translated by Thomas Burger with the assistance of Fredrick Lawrence. Cambridge, Polity Press.

Haferkamp, H. (1987) 'From Intra-State to Inter-State Civilizing Processes?', *Theory, Culture & Society*, 4: 545–57.

Hargreaves, J. (1992) 'Sex, Gender and the Body in Sport and Leisure: Has There Been a Civilizing Process?', in Dunning, E. and Rojek, C. (eds) *Sport and Leisure in the Civilizing Process: Critique and Counter Critique*. London, Macmillan: 161–82.

Harte, N. B. (1979) 'Review of *The History of Manners*', *Economic History Review*, 32: 2.

Hiden, J. (1977) *Germany and Europe, 1919–1939*. London, Longman.

Hill, C. (1974) [1961] *The Century of Revolution, 1603–1714*. London, Cardinal.

Hintze, O. (1975) 'Military Organization and the Organization of the State', in Gilbert, F. (ed.) *The Historical Essays of Otto Hintze*. New York and Oxford, Oxford University Press: 180–215.

Hobsbawm, E. J. (1990) *Nations and Nationalism Since 1780: Programme, Myth, Reality*. Cambridge, Cambridge University Press.

Hofstede, G. (1991) *Cultures and Organizations: Software of the Mind*. London, McGraw-Hill.

Horkheimer, M. and Adorno, T. W. (1979) *Dialectic of Enlightenment*. Translated by John Cumming. London, Verso/New Left Review Editions.

Horne, J. and Jary, D. (1987) 'The Figurational Sociology of Sport and Leisure of Elias and Dunning: An Exposition and Critique', *Sociological Review Monograph*, 33: 86–112.

Huizinga, J. (1955) *The Waning of the Middle Ages*. London, Pelican.

Hunt, A. (1988) 'Left Behind', *The Listener*, 12 February: 29–30.

Jagers, R. (1987) 'Geweld in tribale samenlevingen', *Sociologische Gids*, 29: 210–24.

Jones, N. H. (1987) *Hitler's Heralds: The Story of the Freikorps, 1918–1923*. London, John Murray.

Kalberg, S. (1992) 'The German *Sonderweg* De-mystified: A Sociological Biography of a Nation', *Theory, Culture & Society*, 9: 111–24.

Keane, J. (ed.) (1988) *Civil Society and the State: New European Perspectives*. London, Verso.

Kiernan, V. G. (1988) *The Duel in European History: Honour and the Reign of Aristocracy*. Oxford, Oxford University Press.

Kilminster, R. (1988) 'Review of *State Formation and Civilization*', *Sociology*, 17: 399–402.

—— (1991) 'Evaluating Elias', *Theory, Culture & Society*, 8: 165–76.

Kilminster, R. and Wouters, C. (1995) 'From Philosophy to Sociology: Elias and the Neo-Kantians (A response to Benjo Maso)', *Theory, Culture & Society*, 12: 81–120.

Kocka, J. (1984) *Facing Total War: German Society 1914–1918*. Translated by B. Weinberger. Oxford and Providence, Berg.

Kohn, H. (1976) [1962] *The Age of Nationalism*. Westport, Conn., Greenwood Press.

Korte, H. (ed.) (1990) *Gesellschaftliche Prozesse und individuelle Praxis: Bochumer Vorlesungen zu Norbert Elias' Zivilisationstheorie*. Frankfurt a.M., Suhrkamp.

Kranendonk, W. H. (1990) *Society as Process: A Bibliography of Figurational Sociology in the Netherlands (up to 1989): Sociogenetic and Psychogenetic Studies*. Universiteit van Amsterdam, Sociologisch Instituut.

Krarup, K. (1979) 'On the Sociological Significance of Norbert Elias's Sociogenetic Modelling Approach to Societal Transformations', *Acta Sociologica*, 22: 161–73.

Krieken, R. van (1989) 'Violence, Self-Discipline and Modernity: Beyond the "Civilizing Process"', *The Sociological Review*, 37: 193–218.

—— (1990) 'The Organization of the Soul: Elias and Foucault on Discipline and the Self', *Archives for European Sociology*, 31: 353–71.

Kruithof, B. (1980) 'De deugdzame natie', *Symposium*, 2: 22–37.

Kuzmics, H. (1987) 'Civilization, State and Bourgeois Society: The Theoretical Contribution of Norbert Elias', *Theory, Culture & Society*, 4: 515–31.

—— (1988) 'The Civilizing Process', in Keane, J. (ed.) *Civil Society and the State: New European Perspectives*. London, Verso: 149–76.

—— (1989) *Der Preis der Zivilisation: Die Zwänge der Moderne im theoretischen Vergleich*. Frankfurt a.M., Campus.

—— (1990) 'Das "Moderne Selbst" und der langfristige Prozeß der Zivilisation', in Korte, H. (ed.) *Gesellschaftliche Prozesse und individuelle Praxis: Bochumer Vorlesungen zu Norbert Elias' Zivilisationstheorie*. Frankfurt a.M., Suhrkamp: 232–41.

—— (1991) 'Embarrassment and Civilization: On some Similarities and Differences in the Work of Goffman and Elias', *Theory, Culture & Society*, 8: 1–30.

Kuzmics, H. and Mörth, I. (eds) (1991) *Der unendliche Prozeß der Zivilisation*. Frankfurt a.M., Campus.

Lasch, C. (1985) 'Historical Sociology and the Myth of Maturity: Norbert Elias's "Very Simple Formula" ', *Theory and Society*, 14: 705–20.

Leach, E. (1986) 'Violence', *London Review of Books*, 23 October: 13–14.

Lee, H. (1974) *To Kill a Mocking Bird*. London, Pan Books.

Lenhardt, C. (1979) 'Civilization and its Contents', *Canadian Journal of Political and Social Theory*, 3: 119–30.

Lifton, R. J. (1986) *The Nazi Doctors: A Study in the Psychology of Evil*. London, Macmillan.

Loewenberg, P. (1971) 'The Psycho-Historical Origins of the Nazi Youth Cohort', *American Historical Review*, 76: 1457–1502.

Macfarlane, A. (1981) *The Justice and the Mare's Ale: Law and Disorder in Seventeenth-Century England*. Oxford, Basil Blackwell.

MacRae, D. G. (1978) 'The Bourgeois Revolution', *New Statesman*, 30 June: 844–5.

Manvell, R. (1969) *SS and Gestapo: Rule by Terror*. New York, Ballantine Books.

Marcuse, H. (1969) *Eros and Civilization*. London, Sphere.

Maso, B. (1982) 'Riddereer en Riddermoed – ontwikkelingen van de aanvalslust in de late middleeuwen', *Sociologische Gids*, 29: 296–325.

Mennell, S. (1989) 'Short-Term Interests and Long-Term Processes: The Case of Civilization and Decivilization', in Goudsblom, J. et al. *Human History and Social Process*. Exeter, Exeter University Press: 93–127.

—— (1990a) 'Decivilizing Processes: Theoretical Significance and Some Lines of Research', *International Sociology*, 5: 205–23.

—— (1990b) 'The Globalization of Human Society as a Very Long-Term Social Process: Elias's Theory', *Theory, Culture & Society*, 7: 359–71.

—— (1992) *Norbert Elias: An Introduction*. Oxford, Basil Blackwell.

—— (1995a) *Civilization and Decivilization, Civil Society and Violence*. Inaugural Lecture, University College Dublin.

—— (1995b) 'The Formation of We-Images: A Process Theory', in Calhoun, C. (ed.) *Social Theory and the Politics of Identity*. Oxford, Basil Blackwell: 175–97.

Merkyl, P. H. (1975) *Political Violence under the Swastika: 581 Early Nazis*. Princeton, NJ, Princeton University Press.

Mitscherlich, A. and Mitscherlich, M. (1975) *The Inability to Mourn: Principles of Collective Behaviour*. New York, Grove Press.

Mitzman, A. (1987) 'The Civilizing Offensive: Mentalities, High Culture and Individual Psyches', *Journal of Social History*, 20: 663–87.

Moore, B. (1969) *The Social Origins of Dictatorship and Democracy: Lord and Peasant in the Making of the Modern World*. Harmondsworth, Penguin.

Mosse, G. L. (1978a) 'Review of *The History of Manners*', *New German Critique*, 15: 178–83.

—— (1978b) *Nazism: A Historical and Comparative Analysis of National Socialism*. An interview with Michael A. Ledeen. New Brunswick, NJ, Transaction Books.

Murphy, P., Williams, J. and Dunning, E. (1990) *Football on Trial: Spectator Violence and Development in the Football World*. London, Routledge.

Nicholls, A. (1979) [1968] *Weimar and the Rise of Hitler*. London, Macmillan.

Pearson, G. (1983) *Hooligan: A History of Respectable Fears*. London, Macmillan.

Peuckert, R. (1992) 'Gewalt', in Schäfers, B. *Grundbegriffe der Soziologie, 3rd edn*. Opladen, Leske & Budrich: 114–17.

Plumb, J. H. (1950) *England in the Eighteenth Century*. Harmondsworth, Penguin.

Rasing, W. (1982) 'Over conflictregulierung bij de nomadische Inuit', *Sociologische Gids*, 29: 225–42.

Rehberg, K.-S. (1991) 'Prozeß-Theorie als "Unendliche Geschichte": Zur Soziologischen Kulturtheorie von Norbert Elias', in Kuzmics, H. and Mörth, I. (eds) *Der Unendliche Prozeß der Zivilisation*. Frankfurt a.M., Campus: 59–78.

Ringer, F. (1969) *The Decline of the German Mandarins: The German Academic Community, 1890–1933*. Cambridge, MA, Harvard University Press.

Robertson, R. (1992) '"Civilization" and the Civilizing Process: Elias, Globalization and Analytic Synthesis', *Theory, Culture & Society*, 9: 211–27.

Robinson, R. J. (1987) '"The Civilizing Process" Revisited: Some Remarks on Elias's Social History', *Sociology*, 21: 1–17.

Rouche, M. (1987) 'The Early Middle Ages in the West', in Veyne, P. (ed.) *A History of Private Life*. Cambridge, MA, Harvard University Press: 415–549.

Rosenhaft, E. (1983) *Beating the Fascists? The German Communists and Political Violence, 1929–1933*. Cambridge, Cambridge University Press.

Rule, J. B. (1988) *Theories of Civil Violence*. Berkeley, University of California Press.

Russell, C. (1990) *The Causes of the English Civil War: The Ford Lectures Delivered in the University of Oxford 1987–1988*. Oxford, Clarendon Press.

Salomon, E. von (1931) *The Outlaws*. London, Jonathan Cape.

Sampson, S. F. (1984) 'The Formation of European Nation States, the Elaboration of Functional Interdependence Networks and the Genesis of Modern Self-Control', *Contemporary Sociology*, 13: 22–7.

Schäfers, B. (1992) *Grundbegriffe der Soziologie, 3rd edn*. Opladen, Leske & Budrich.

Scheff, T. J. and Retzinger, S. M. (1991) *Emotions and Violence: Shame and Rage in Destructive Conflicts*. Lexington, MA, Lexington Books.

Schröter, M. (1990) 'Scham im Zivilisationsprozeß: Zur Diskussion mit Hans Peter Deurr', in Korte, H. (ed.) *Gesellschaftliche Prozesse und individuelle Praxis*. Frankfurt a.M., Suhrkamp: 42–84.

Seibt, G. (1990) 'Zyklus von Erniedrigung und Überhebung: Norbert Elias' Studien über die Deutschen', *Merkur: Deutsche Zeitschrift für Europäisches Denken*, 44: 330–4.

Seigel, J. (1979) 'Review of *The History of Manners*', *Journal of Modern History*, 51: 123–6.

Sheard, K. (1992) *Boxing in the Civilizing Process*. PhD thesis, Anglia Polytechnic University.

Sica, A. (1984) 'Sociogenesis versus Psychogenesis: The Unique Sociology of Norbert Elias', *Mid-American Review of Sociology*, 9: 49–78.

Smith, A. D. (1978) 'Review of *The History of Manners* and *The Court Society*', *The Sociological Review*, 32: 367–89.

Spierenburg, P. (1993) 'Lange termijn trends in doodslag' ('Long-term trends in Homicide'), *Amsterdams Sociologisch Tijdschrift*, 20: 66–106.

Steinberg, M. S. (1977) *Sabers and Brownshirts: The German Students' Path to National Socialism, 1918–1935*. Chicago and London, University of Chicago Press.

Stokvis, R. (1992) 'Sports and Civilization: Is Violence the Central Problem?', in Dunning, E. and Rojek, C. (eds) *Sport and Leisure in the Civilizing Process: Critique and Counter Critique*. London, Macmillan: 121–36.

Stolk, B. van and Wouters, C. (1983) *Vrouwen in tweestrijd. Tussen thuis en tehuis: relatieproblemen in de verzorgingsstaat, opgetekend in een crisiscentrum (Women Torn Two Ways: Relationship Problems within the Welfare State)*. Deventer, Van Loghum Slaterus.

—— (1987) 'Power Changes and Self-Respect: A Comparison of Two Cases of Established-Outsider Relations', *Theory, Culture & Society*, 4: 477–88.

Stone, L. (1983) 'Interpersonal Violence in English Society, 1300–1980', *Past and Present*, 101: 22–33.

—— (1986) [1984] *An Open Elite? England 1540–1880*. Oxford, Oxford University Press.

Talmon, J. L. (1986) [1952] *The Origins of Totalitarian Democracy: Political Theory and Practice during the French Revolution and Beyond*. Harmondsworth, Penguin.

Tester, K. (1989) 'The Pleasure of the Rich is the Labour of the Poor: Some Remarks on Elias' "An Essay on Sport and Violence"', *Journal of Historical Sociology*, 2: 161–72.

Theweleit, K. (1987) [1977] *Male Fantasies*, vol. 1. Cambridge, Polity Press.

Thomas, K. (1978) 'The Rise of the Fork', *The New York Review*, 9 March: 30.

—— (1984) *Man and the Natural World: Changing Attitudes in England, 1500–1800*. Harmondsworth, Pelican.

Tiger, L. (1969) *Men in Groups*. London, Nelson.

Velzen, T. van (1982) 'The Djuka Civilization', *The Netherlands Journal of Sociology*, 20: 85–97.

Vree, W. van (1994) *Nederland als vergaderland: opkonist en verbreiding van een vergaderregime*. Groningen, Wolters-Noordhoff.

Waite, R. G. L. (1970) *Vanguard of Nazism: The Free Corps Movement in Postwar Germany, 1918–1923*. Cambridge, MA, Harvard University Press.

Weber, M. (1930) *The Protestant Ethic and the Spirit of Capitalism*. Translated by T. Parsons. London, George Allen & Unwin.

—— (1978) *Economy and Society: An Outline of Interpretive Sociology*, vol. 1, Berkeley, University of California Press.

Wehowsky, A. (1978) 'Making Ourselves More Flexible Than We Are – Reflections on Norbert Elias', *New German Critique*, 15: 65–80.

Williams, J., Dunning, E. G. and Murphy, P. (1984) *Hooligans Abroad: The Behaviour and Control of English Fans in Continental Europe*. London, Routledge & Kegan Paul.

208   *References*

Williams R. (1967) 'Culture and Civilization', in *The Encyclopedia of Philosophy*. New York, Macmillan: 273–5.
—— (1989) 'Violence', in *Keywords: A Vocabulary of Culture and Society*. London, Fontana: 329–31.
Wilterdink, N. (1984) 'Die Zivilisationstheorie im Kreuzfeuer der Diskussion. Ein Bericht vom Kongress über Zivilisationsprozesse in Amsterdam', in Gleichmann, P. R. et al. (eds) *Macht und Zivilisation: Materialien zu Norbert Elias' Zivilisationstheorie 2*. Frankfurt a.M., Suhrkamp: 280–304.
—— (1993) *Ongelijkheid en interdependentie: ontwikkelingen in welstandsverhoudingen*. Groningen, Wolters-Noordhoff.
Wouters, C. (1977) 'Informalization and the Civilizing Process', in Gleichmann, P. R. et al. (eds) *Human Figurations: Essays for Norbert Elias*. Amsterdam, Amsterdams Sociologisch Tijdschrift: 437–53.
—— (1986) 'Formalization and Informalization: Changing Tension and Balances in Civilizing Processes', *Theory, Culture & Society*, 3: 1–19.
—— (1987) 'Developments in the Behavioural Codes between the Sexes: The Formalization of Informalization in the Netherlands, 1930–85', *Theory, Culture & Society*, 4: 405–27.
—— (1990a) *Van minnen en sterven: Informalizering van omgangsvormen rond seks en dood*. Amsterdam, Bert Bakker.
——(1990b) 'Social Stratification and Informalization in Global Perspective', *Theory, Culture & Society*, 7: 69–90.
—— (1992) 'On Status Competition and Emotion Management: The Study of Emotions as a New Field', *Theory, Culture & Society*, 9: 229–52.
—— (1994) 'Duerr und Elias. Scham und Gewalt in Zivilisationsprozessen', *Zeitschrift für Sexualforschung*, 3: 203–16.
—— (1995) 'De lustbalance van liefde en sex: ontwikkelingen sinds de seksuele revolutie', *Amsterdams Sociologisch Tijdschrift*, 2: 368–401.

Index